BUSINESS STRATEGIES FOR MAGAZINE PUBLISHING

Business Strategies for Magazine Publishing explores tactics for creating financially sustainable publications in the 21st century. Mary Hogarth, media specialist, Senior Fellow (HEA) and Lecturer in Journalism at Bournemouth University, analyses the historical development of the magazine industry, as well as current and future challenges for publishers, to illustrate different approaches to revenue generation and the maintenance of magazine brands.

The book examines the wide-ranging impact of digital technology on how magazine content is consumed, revealing the dramatic consequences for advertising, distribution and marketing strategies. Traditional business models are evaluated alongside new online approaches and readers will be introduced to the Magazine Publishing Strategic Quadrant, a model created by the author as an alternative to the Business Canvas Model. In addition, in-depth interviews with high-profile industry figureheads and magazine editors, such as Jessica Strawser of *Writer's Digest* and former *Good Housekeeping* Editorial Director Lindsay Nicholson, offer readers an insight into how to produce and monetise online content. These interviews appear alongside exercises and action plans that give readers the opportunity to put what they've learned into practice.

With real-world advice and practical activities and resources throughout the book, journalism students and young professionals will find this an essential guide to successfully building a career in the modern magazine industry.

Mary Hogarth is an experienced educator, media specialist and writer, who previously led Features Journalism at Southampton Solent University, before joining Bournemouth University. Mary also runs a consultancy practice, themagazineexpert Ltd, specialising in advising on new title launches, audience engagement, editorial development and developing sustainable magazine business strategies.

Steve Hill is Joint Course Leader of the MA Multimedia Journalism at Westminster University in London. He has worked in technology and business journalism for over 20 years and has written for the *Independent, Sunday Express, New Statesman, New Media Age* and *Web Designer* magazine, among many other print and online publications. He has also appeared as a pundit on the BBC News Channel, Sky News, ITN and numerous radio outlets and has written books about technology.

BUSINESS STRATEGIES FOR MAGAZINE PUBLISHING

How to Survive in the Digital Age

Mary Hogarth

Routledge
Taylor & Francis Group
LONDON AND NEW YORK

First published 2018
by Routledge
2 Park Square, Milton Park, Abingdon, Oxon OX14 4RN

and by Routledge
711 Third Avenue, New York, NY 10017

Routledge is an imprint of the Taylor & Francis Group, an informa business

© 2018 Mary Hogarth

Monetising Online Content © Steve Hill

The right of Mary Hogarth and Steve Hill to be identified as author of this work has been asserted by them in accordance with sections 77 and 78 of the Copyright, Designs and Patents Act 1988.

All rights reserved. No part of this book may be reprinted or reproduced or utilised in any form or by any electronic, mechanical, or other means, now known or hereafter invented, including photocopying and recording, or in any information storage or retrieval system, without permission in writing from the publishers.

Trademark notice: Product or corporate names may be trademarks or registered trademarks, and are used only for identification and explanation without intent to infringe.

British Library Cataloguing-in-Publication Data
A catalogue record for this book is available from the British Library

Library of Congress Cataloging-in-Publication Data
A catalog record has been requested for this book

ISBN: 978-1-138-20576-5 (hbk)
ISBN: 978-1-138-20577-2 (pbk)
ISBN: 978-1-315-46457-2 (ebk)

Typeset in Bembo
by Sunrise Setting Ltd, Brixham, UK

CONTENTS

List of figures vii
List of tables viii
List of contributors: industry perspectives ix
Foreword xiii
Acknowledgements xv

Introduction 1

1 Lessons from the past 5

2 The value of market research 21

3 Audience engagement 36

4 A successful business model 57

5 Market sectors that pay – and those that don't ... 76

6 See your readers as stakeholders 89

7 The 360-degree approach to content 102

8 Monetising online content 117
 Steve Hill

| 9 An insight into advertising | 134 |
| 10 A sustainable future? | 150 |

The last word with Alice Freeman   *160*
A to Z of industry resources   *162*
Index   *170*

FIGURES

1.1	*Vogue* centenary cover	17
2.1	*Celebrating Poundbury* covers collage	30
2.2	*Sublime* cover	33
3.1	Magzter newsstand fees	40
3.2	*Good Housekeeping* cover	43
3.3	*Writer's Digest* print cover	48
3.4	*Writer's Digest* iPad image	49
3.5	*BBC History Magazine* cover	54
4.1	The Magazine Publishing Strategic Quadrant (author's own model)	60
4.2	*List for Life*'s timeline	63
4.3	*Country Living* cover	66
5.1	*Home Handbook* cover	82
5.2	*Food and Travel* cover	86
6.1	Membership model (author's own model)	90
6.2	*The Mint* cover	92
6.3	Balancing the scales of advertising and editorial	96
6.4	*The Lady* cover	98
7.1	Components of a successful brand model	103
7.2	The 360-degree feature package model	106
7.3	*The Lawyer* media pack	109
7.4	*The Lawyer* cover	113
9.1	A native advertising model – from concept to platform	137
9.2	An advertising sales pipeline	142
9.3	*Empire* cover	146
10.1	A survey of magazine revenue streams	152

TABLES

2.1	Author's interpretation of ABC audience demographics	22
2.2	Suggested rationales and aims of research	24
3.1	Pros and cons of digital editions	39
3.2	Comparison of three writing titles	50
4.1	Primary areas of focus	59
4.2	Comparison of brand extensions across three sectors	69
7.1	B2B vs consumer	108
8.1	Magazines achieving high sales	126

CONTRIBUTORS: INDUSTRY PERSPECTIVES

Below are the biographies of all those who have taken time out of their busy lives to contribute their perspectives. They have carefully answered my in-depth questionnaires, responding with a wealth of knowledge and experience.

Rob Attar is Editor of *BBC History Magazine*. After studying history at Bristol and then magazine journalism at Cardiff, he joined the *BBC History Magazine* team as Editorial Assistant in 2004. From then on he has held a variety of posts at the title, from Editorial Assistant to Deputy Editor, before taking over from Dave Musgrove as Editor of the magazine in 2012.

Rob has been nominated for several industry awards, and won Editor of the Year in the special interest category of the 2015 BSME awards. He lives in Bristol with his wife and newborn twins.

Ranj Begley is the managing director of Readly UK, the ground-breaking, all-you-can-read magazine service, which has won a series of awards around Europe, including the PPA's prestigious App of the Year.

Ranj built this start-up from the bottom up to its current position where it now deals with all the leading UK publishers, and its rapidly growing consumer footprint already covers 50 territories worldwide. In addition to her UK responsibilities, she is now leading Readly's expansion into new markets around the world.

Prior to founding Readly UK, Ranj held several senior management positions in marketing and business development roles in publishing and fulfilment companies including Dovetail, Highbury House, CDS Global and UBM plc.

David Bostock is an independent media consultant, trainer and lecturer. He started his career in print media, working as an editor and publishing director at Emap (now known as Bauer Media) across a wide range of sectors, including men, music, film, parenting and women's lifestyle. In 2001, he moved into online publishing and launched the Bliss website, which quickly became one of the UK's leading youth websites. More recently, he has led some of the most successful multi-platform digital content brands, including empireonline.com, which is the UK's biggest movie website.

In addition, he was responsible for the business development of parenting brand motherandbaby.co.uk and legendary music brand kerrang.com, leading the team to deliver record traffic levels and increased profitability. As a publisher, he has launched and led profitable magazine, email, tablet edition, eBook, premium rate text and paid app services.

Ben Budworth, Publisher and CEO of *The Lady*, held numerous varied roles – from traded options market making to helicopter piloting and 12 years in commercial radio – before taking over the reins of his great grandfather's magazine.

He recently bought Bylaugh Hall in Norfolk with his partner Helen Robinson, Managing Director of *The Lady*. After restoring what was once the third largest estate in Norfolk they plan to convert it into a training centre for household staff, from bodyguards and chauffeurs to domestic service staff. When complete the centre will be integrated into *The Lady*'s recruitment division.

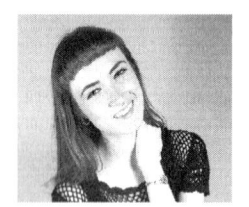

Alice Freeman (The last word) is a magazine journalist, photographer and two-time Magazine Academy award-winner. After graduating from Southampton Solent University with a First Class Honours in magazine journalism in 2016, Alice is now a writer for *IKEA Family Magazine*, which is produced by content agency August Media.

Contributors: industry perspectives **xi**

Steve Newbold is a divisional managing director at Centaur Media Plc for the media and events businesses. He directly oversees the marketing and creative, legal, engineering, financial, business travel, meetings and HR portfolios.

Prior to joining Centaur Media in 2015 Steve held managing director roles at WGSN, i2i Events, Emap Communications (now Ascential), Emap Consumer Media and Hearst. He has experience of running multimedia, international businesses in key sectors across both B2B and consumer markets.

Gregor Rankin has over 35 years in publishing, the last 20 as publisher of *Food and Travel* magazine. His career began in 1981 in ad sales at Myddleton Publishing. He then moved to Haymarket Publishing where he was ad manager of MIMS Ireland, MIMS UK before being posted to New York to help launch *Monthly Prescribing Reference* (MIMS' equivalent) in the US. Gregor returned as Ad Manager of *Autocar*, then Group Ad Manager of *Autocar* and *What Car?*

He joined Redwood Publishing (BBC Magazines) in 1988 to launch a string of magazines – *M&S Magazine, BBC Holidays, BBC Good Food, BBC Vegetarian, BBC Gourmet Good Food*, the BBC Sports series, launch work on *BBC Gardeners World* and *BBC Top Gear*.

In 1993 he was head-hunted by Waterlow Information Services (Wilmington Group) as Publishing Director of the legal, music and financial sectors to help the company to a float on the stock market. Gregor formed Fox Publishing in 1996 with Angela Dukes to launch *Food and Travel* magazine in 1997; the company went on to publish several consumer and contract titles including *Eurosport, GMTV, Cresta Holidays, Tesco* and *Perfect Home*. In 2004 unrecovered debt forced its closure. Rankin and Dukes bought back *Food and Travel* magazine and have since built the brand into the world's leading gastronomic travel title with seven international editions and various spin-offs.

Laura Santamaria is a consultant, researcher and lecturer. She has extensive experience in brand strategy, innovation and cultural trends, having worked with clients in the corporate and third sector for over 15 years.

She has a PhD in Design Innovation and her research interests focus on the relationship between sustainability, symbolic consumption and the diffusion of radical innovation. Laura is also a lecturer at Loughborough University London, and Visiting Fellow at the School of Business, Law and Communications, Southampton Solent University.

Alexandra Shulman, CBE was the editor of British *Vogue* for 25 years from 1992–2016. During this time, she was granted the Order of the British Empire in the 2005 New Year's honours for services to the magazine industry; and has been awarded several accolades including BSME Editor of the Year.

In 2010 she was awarded an honorary degree by The University of Creative Arts for her contribution to the creative arts and in 2013 was included in BBC Radio 4's *Women's Hour* list of the 100 Most Powerful Women in the UK. In 2016 Alexandra was named PPA Editor of the Year in the magazine's centenary year. In addition to her work with *Vogue*, Alexandra has written two novels, *Can We Still Be Friends* (2012) and *The Parrots* (2015), as well as a memoir, *Inside Vogue: A Diary of My 100th Year* (2016).

Terri White is Editor-in-Chief of Bauer Media's flagship film and entertainment brand, *Empire*, and is an award-winning editor with 16 years' experience working for publishing companies on both sides of the Atlantic. She joined Bauer from *Time Out New York* where she worked as Editor-in-Chief, overseeing the brand's editorial direction and content across all platforms.

Previously, Terri was Editor of men's freemium title *ShortList* and *Buzz*, the magazine distributed with *The Sun*. She has also written for *Q*, *Red*, *Elle*, *The Pool*, *Grazia* and *The Observer Magazine*. She was named one of Folio's Top Women in US Media, 2015, and has won BSME's Men's Magazine of the Year and PPA's New Editor of the Year.

FOREWORD

I came away from a recent industry event wondering whether I'd turned left instead of right at the entrance and gone to the wrong talk by mistake. There was a great deal of discussion about algorithms, native app strategies and influencer ecosystems, and even more about event management and long-term marketing strategies. But where was the talk about magazines? Or maybe I really had gone to the pharmaceuticals company event after all.

So much background noise. So many distractions. So easy to lose sight of what underpins the whole shebang.

Our industry has changed rapidly and profoundly over the last decade or so, and in ways I suspect no one – and I really do believe *no one* – could have foreseen. What's more, the pace of change isn't going to slow down any time soon. I'm already bracing myself for the next communications breakthrough that will leave us wondering how on earth to transform our businesses and reskill our teams all over again and still have some money left in the bank.

But the one thing that hasn't changed is what drives everything we do, and that's quality, targeted content, delivered in the most appropriate way to its audience. This is where our value as an industry lies, and you can have as many strategies for apps and algorithms and influencer ecosystems as you like but if they don't have great content at their core then you're simply wasting your time.

It's great content that makes me optimistic for the future.

Let's give a big hand to fake news here, because it's led to a renewed appreciation of the sources we *can* trust. We want to know the provenance of the content we read, the trustworthiness of the writers and the independence of the source. Enough of the queasy morality of social media pundits who don't always come clean about why they're suddenly raving about this lipstick or that business. We want sources that are accountable to their audiences.

We also want sources that are authorities in their field, whether that's international relations or cake baking. It's all very well being able to access a seemingly infinite amount of material on every platform, but our waking hours remain stubbornly finite, so the things we do manage to make time for have simply got to be better and more relevant than the rest.

There's a growing groundswell of voices prepared to accept that, when it comes to quality, you get what you pay for. Yes, I do mean *pay*. And, of course, that includes advertisers, who stand only to gain from their association with credible and compelling content.

Our core skill will always be in creating authentic and immersive experiences for our audiences. And hey – whatever the magazine business strategy, how much better and more fun can a starting point be?

Gill Hudson is the former multi-award-winning editor of a wide range of consumer titles, including *Radio Times*, *Maxim*, *New Woman* and *Reader's Digest*. She is now an editorial consultant and represents the magazine industry on the Complaints Committee of the Independent Press Standards Organisation.

ACKNOWLEDGEMENTS

I would like to thank everyone who has contributed to this book, all of whom are extremely busy people, who kindly made time to talk to me about their knowledge and experiences.

My industry experience and more latterly my work as a consultant has taught me many valuable lessons. But the most important one of all is not to take things at face value or follow the trend because 'everyone else is doing so' – always do your homework, something my mentor and friend John Jenkins always insisted upon.

A big 'thank you' to my colleagues on the BAMMJ team at Bournemouth University, who have supported my ongoing research. Also to Southampton Solent University for their generous research grant in those early days.

Finally, my grateful thanks to all my friends and family who never fail in their friendship and support – particularly Wendy Kearns for her invaluable insights and my long-time friend/former colleague Steve Hill.

INTRODUCTION

Having worked in industry and as a practising media specialist for many years I have seen numerous publishing models – some good, some bad and, of course, the truly ugly. While many are anxious to move with the times, with an eye firmly fixed on the future, it is crucial to first consider what can be learned from those early publishing models.

Such models should be adapted, but not abandoned just because they are old-fashioned. Why? Because lessons from the past are extremely valuable as they offer an insight into what worked well and those strategies that resulted in a downturn. History also allows the observer to pinpoint the timeline where things began to change – either heading towards a crash or improving.

The past also offers an understanding of how society, trends and other key influences such as a new editor or change in layout/content may have impacted on a magazine. Two such titles come to mind – *NME* and *Company*.

NME aka *The New Musical Express* was a solid title until it experienced a sharp downturn in circulation in the mid 2000s, which resulted in its adoption of the freemium model. What went wrong? Factors such as having a string of editors in quick succession resulting in a loss of strong leadership and a clear editorial voice are likely to have impacted on circulation. This in turn is likely to have affected *NME*'s brand identity thus further contributing to the magazine's challenges. Readers voted with their feet – or wallets to be more precise – making *NME* unsustainable for the newsstands.

Company, along with many lifestyle titles in the sector, experienced a fall in circulation in the late 2000s. Thus action was taken with a radical relaunch in 2012 to engage its existing audience while enticing younger readers with a blog-style layout. Sadly the relaunch failed to turn the decline around. *Company* lost the core of its readership and was forced to go digital as a result of falling sales making the print edition unsustainable on the newsstands. The last print edition to go on sale was the October 2014 issue.

Trends and life cycles

In *How to Start a Magazine*, Kobak argues that every publication has its own life cycle from infancy to living death where publishers are unable to face the reality that the title is no longer valued by readers, let alone sustainable (Kobak, 2002). While in some cases this may be true, particularly with regard to lifestyle or specialist magazines, there are many exceptions to the rule. *The Lady*, *Good Housekeeping* and *Vogue* immediately spring to mind, but also satirical publications such as *Private Eye* and *The Oldie*, while not forgetting business titles such as *The Economist*, which has adapted to the digital age ensuring it is not only sustainable, but thriving.

As I write this there are numerous trends emerging on the newsstands. One particular fascination is the emergence of cycling magazines. Currently, according to BRAD, there are 11 print national cycling titles, some weekly, a few monthlies plus an annual guide to the Tour De France. By contrast there are some 26 digital editions, not to mention blogs and websites – a reflection of the nation's growing interest in the sport. Yes, London 2012 and Bradley Wiggins certainly played a part in developing this trend as the majority of cycle magazines are road-focused, in other words mostly about racing bikes. But there are other factors too, such as the emphasis on sustainable transport with the government investing £62 million to make cycling easier and improve cycle–rail integration.

As an avid cyclist, I am keen to watch this trend evolve. Will it cater for everyday riders like myself, who use their bikes to commute in the week and may want a moderate off-road adventure on the weekends? Hopefully in the long term, but currently not so. At the time of writing there is a clear divide – road or mountain bike. Certainly the number of road bike magazines is rapidly expanding to the point of becoming unsustainable for some of those titles. Again, this will be interesting to watch in the long term.

Another surprising aspect of this trend is that unlike *Women's Running*, *She Kicks* or *Women's Football*, there aren't currently any cycling titles specifically aimed at women. The only one – *Women's Cycling* magazine, a bi-monthly title published by Wild Bunch Media, launched in March 2013, aimed at beginners and regular cyclists – sadly lasted just nine issues, proving it to be unsustainable as a print edition. Why was that? Surely a lack of female riders is not the problem. Therefore, it must be down to poor marketing, consumer habits, poor timing or the title not sufficiently appealing to its audience. I will be exploring this more in Chapter 5 on 'Market sectors that pay'.

The question now is how many more cycling magazines will evolve from this trend and out of those which ones will prove to be in it for the long haul?

Print vs social media

A few years ago many were saying 'print is dying' and digital is the way to go. Mainstream and independent publishers made major investments in their online products, many without a clear revenue strategy. The result has been a lack of significant return on that investment, not to mention the poor sales in digital editions.

As for print copies, these are making a comeback and many editors agree that it is here to stay for the foreseeable future. Why is that? Is it because most audiences still enjoy the physical feel of a magazine? Or perhaps they don't want to be on their screens 24/7. The truth is many publishing houses aren't sure why their digital products aren't working as well as they thought. But did they ask the audience first or consider how their readers actually consume the magazine? Probably not, as mostly in the majority of editorial offices it's a rush to keep up with the Joneses. That mentality of 'we have to mirror our rivals at any cost and produce superior content' is the primary instinct here.

Anyone who has been in publishing will recall similar experiences. I am always amazed at how editors seem obsessive about having a presence on every social media platform whether it's relevant or not. For example, at a preliminary meeting with a potential client the question of social media coverage came up. It seemed they hadn't given much thought to their social media strategy, instead setting up pages on numerous platforms. Nothing wrong with that at first glance, you might think, given that brand identity must prevail.

But when this modus operandi stretches resources and fails to achieve the necessary subscriptions, likes, followers, etc., then it's time to review. My first question was why are you on Instagram when you rarely post and have so few followers? Wouldn't it be better to focus on those platforms that are working for you? This was a revelation as common sense began to dawn.

The moral of the story? Editors and publishers must be wary of jumping on bandwagons too quickly. Any investment made must demand good returns. Sometimes it is better to take a step back, think about your audience – their habits and preferences – and most importantly see what is working and discard what is not. Every publication is different as are the readers; therefore caution, combined with in-depth analysis, is crucial if a magazine is to survive and thrive.

Always ensure you know what your reader wants – and needs. Consider how and where the audience will be likely to read the title. How they will use the editorial content is an important factor too. Never assume, always ask and keep asking.

Using this text

Throughout the book there will be examples from a variety of sources, including my own experiences as well as input from publishing entrepreneurs, editors and other industry professionals. Use this book as a resource. Read it cover to cover or just dip into those parts that are relevant. It has been set out in sequence to guide you through the high and lows of publishing, steering you towards success and sustainability for the long term.

Resources include case studies as well as advice from industry experts who will contribute their experiences to help you along the way. At the end of each chapter you will find *industry perspectives* – an insight from a relevant publisher or editor sharing their thoughts – plus *action plans* designed to help you take your magazine forward in terms of your audience, content, online and business strategies. Tempting as it might be, do not skip these tools as they are tried and trusted methods to help your publication not only survive, but thrive.

Online tools

Although this book contains everything you need to know about magazine business strategies, www.themagazineexpert.com has been set up as an online, interactive tool. As well as regular blog posts and newsletters, there will be opportunities to engage and share knowledge, in addition to a variety of other useful resources. There will also be blogs from a variety of contributors looking at current magazine trends, the future of publishing and other related issues. The emphasis is on building a community resource. I hope you will join me online and share your experiences too.

Last, embrace innovation and keep moving forward. The focus should always be on taking measured actions rather than reacting without a clear rationale or strategy. As magazine editors and publishers we are all guardians of something very special, which needs to be preserved.

Bibliography

BRAD. 2016. Number of Cycling Magazines. BRAD Insight. http://tool.bradinsight.com/brad/Browse/Digital accessed 21 September 2016.

Government Press Release. 2013. Minister Announces Record £62 Million Investment in Cycling. https://www.gov.uk/government/news/minister-announces-record-62-million-investment-in-cycling accessed 20 September 2016.

Kobak, J. 2002. The Life Cycle of a Magazine. *How to Start a Magazine*. New York: M Evans & Company (p. 26).

Sutton, M. 2014. *Women's Cycling* Magazine to Close. Bike Biz. www.bikebiz.com/news/read/women-s-cycling-magazine-to-close/017025 accessed 20 September 2016.

1
LESSONS FROM THE PAST

As I start to write this book Time Inc has just announced its *InStyle* UK magazine will shortly become a digital-only publication, relaunching it as digital first early in 2017. Not really that surprising. Why? Because it is a classic case of market correction – currently there are too many lifestyle titles on the newsstands, plus essentially this is a fashion/shopping title so it makes sense that it would be stronger as an interactive digital title.

As yet another publication ceases its print edition, other publishers and entrepreneurs understand that market corrections are a part of the cycle of magazines. How do you avoid it happening to your title? Well, I am a great believer in learning from history, which is why I have chosen to start this chapter from an historical perspective. There are valuable lessons to be found in our publishing history, ones that just might help magazines become sustainable and profitable again.

Those early pioneers

Great publishers have always had something of a pioneer spirit. In those early days magazines were produced and published by men – even if aimed at a female audience, starting with *The Ladies Mercury* in 1693, the first women's magazine published by John Dunton. Its USP was simple: *to answer all questions relating to love*. As well as having entertainment value it sought to engage readers from the very first issue by seeking their contributions. Sadly – despite being ahead of its time in some respects – *The Ladies Mercury* lasted just four issues. Failure might be attributed to many aspects, from low literacy rates and the fact that readers were not yet ready for this style of content, to the challenge of effective distribution being difficult during that era.

Only those involved are likely to have known the real reason for its failure, but as observers of publishing history we could make an educated guess. Perhaps a male publisher and editor did not sufficiently understand what their readership actually wanted. Though more often than not magazine failure is about poor timing – right product but wrong time.

Some 40 years later in 1731 Edward Cave published and edited *The Gentleman's Magazine*. Deemed one of the most successful literary magazines of all time, it was to become a sustainable title for more than 200 years. Cave had something of a turbulent childhood that included a brush with the law after being accused of stealing a rooster. Yet that entrepreneurial spirit was there from an early age – a valuable skill in any publisher. While away at school in Rugby he was caught selling lessons to his classmates. Ironically, some 300 years later many tutors profit from writing then selling their courses online. Cave also had many jobs – from tax collector to apprentice printer and journey printer – thus gaining valuable life skills along the way.

As history demonstrates, successful publishers are often mavericks with a strong persona. Of those from the 21st century, Felix Dennis comes to mind, as does founder of *The Huffington Post*, Arianna Huffington. Both Huffington and Dennis shared similar traits to Cave – the pioneer of the monthly magazine. They were forward thinking with an acute sense of timing and took big risks. Cave, despite being described by 'The Society of 18th Century Gentleman' as not having "a keen wit or remarkable intelligence", was a clever publisher and sufficiently forward-thinking to practice that well-known mantra KISS (keep it simple stupid). His business model was basic – publish interesting articles that people want to read in order to build a good circulation. This formula worked then and continued to be successful for many years, although there is some dispute as to when circulation ceased. Some claim it was in the 1870s, others that the final issue went to press in 1907, while a few suggest it was 1914.

Now more than 300 years later the KISS principle is being replaced by an over complicated approach with a myriad of platforms and in some cases a one-size-fits-all approach. Today newsstands are saturated with magazines on every subject, including numerous women's lifestyle publications, along with a few titles for male counterparts.

In this chapter we are going to be looking at how long-established business models such as those of *Vogue*, *The Lady* and *Private Eye* have not only survived, but have thrived and evolved in today's digital age.

Cashing in on fashion and culture

Classed as the most iconic magazine of all time, *Vogue* is celebrated today as much for longevity as its editorial and syndication strategy. As well as the UK and America, Condé Nast International publishes worldwide editions including Australia, China, Russia, Turkey and France, with each publication reflecting the culture of the country as well as *Vogue*'s brand identity. As much can be learned from examining the magazine's history as can be gained from evaluating its current business strategies. Not only is it sustainable; it is thriving despite today's tough economic climate.

Vogue started out as a small New York society magazine founded by Arthur Baldwin Turnure in 1892. While its target audience was New York's aristocracy, the editorial pillars were aimed at a male readership focusing on style, sports and social affairs. Key aspects of its success were already evident – it had a clearly defined audience and was written by those who were from that society. Hence they understood and knew what their readers wanted.

It was not until 1909, when the title was bought by Condé Montrose Nast, that focus shifted to fashion, targeting female readers, but the name stayed the same. Then in 1916, *British Vogue* evolved as a result of First World War shipping restrictions making it impossible to ship the magazine from the States to Europe. Initially the title was mostly a reproduction of the US version until Elspeth Champcommunal was appointed the first editor-in-chief of *British Vogue*. Champcommunal was forward-thinking; she believed that editorial boundaries needed expanding to include health, beauty, sport, travel and opinion pieces.

Sadly, it was a case of right content, wrong era, as it seemed this was not what readers wanted, and when the circulation dropped Nast replaced Champcommunal with Dorothy Todd in 1922. Todd favoured a literary approach to content. However, this shift in focus to literature didn't fit with the US's vision and in 1926 Todd was replaced by Alison Settle, who essentially set the tone for what *Vogue* was to become.

Settle, it seems, had that essential ingredient – awareness of what the readers wanted and needed. She understood her audience, and thus was able to grow the readership – setting down the blueprint for what the publication *Vogue* would become. Her editorship lasted nine years before she handed the reins to her deputy Audrey Withers, Editor-in-Chief for 1940–60. Two more editors followed before *Vogue*'s most iconic Editor-in-Chief, Anna Wintour, took the helm in 1985 and she remains editor-in-chief of American *Vogue*.

Fast forward to 2016, when having just celebrated its centenary, *Vogue* is thriving with a readership of more than 1.1 million. At the time of writing this chapter I had recently interviewed *Vogue*'s UK current Editor-in-Chief, Alexandra Shulman, for *InPublishing* magazine (Hogarth, 2016). Alexandra was about to mark her 25th anniversary in the role and my brief was to find out how the title had evolved, particularly with meeting the challenges of this digital age, and more importantly what excited her most about *Vogue*'s future.

Alexandra took over the helm in 1992 from Liz Tilberis, who had edited the title from 1987 to 1992 before moving to New York herself to edit *Harper's Bazaar*. Liz had previously taken over from her predecessor Anna Wintour who, at the time, had gone to New York to edit *House & Garden* before returning to *Vogue* to take over the American edition. Liz had worked at *Vogue* for more than 20 years, after securing an internship at the magazine in 1967. Under Tilberis the title won numerous awards and the circulation rose.

During the interview for *InPublishing* I learned that Alexandra doesn't believe that print is dead; unlike some editors she has a strong grasp on the boundaries between print and digital editions. In other words, both have a place. During the conversation we both agreed that you must consider not only how but also where the magazine will be consumed by readers. Yet when Alexandra first took over she admitted it was a learning curve. "There were certain things I didn't understand. For instance the way fashion shoots are put together," she revealed, adding that she also had to find out if "what was being done was done because that is the way it has to be or because it had always been done that way".

But Alexandra was willing to challenge existing structures in order to build a stronger title – an essential trait in any editor. One of her first changes was to give the magazine a wider editorial vision, to "take a broader approach to fashion and bring more writing to the title".

So why is *Vogue* so successful? Perhaps it's because those who have been in charge understand the fundamentals of publishing. Know your audience, understand what it is they want and ensure editorial pillars keep evolving in the right direction. Today that direction focuses on strategic partnerships, relationships with up and coming designers as well as the big fashion houses plus some canny brand extensions. These include a festival, four supplements a year, Vogue video and recently Vogue Salons' Night Out. Despite being the 'Fashion Bible', content is eclectic, engaging and still built on solid journalistic values.

For this pioneering editor-in-chief the great joy of *Vogue* is that it does have quite a wide remit. "Although fashion is very much its kind of spine, you are able to hang other things off it. Whether that's business, film or social observation, you can deal with a lot of different subject matter, which I like."

It is that flexibility across the brand combined with a willingness to adapt and the magazine's strong foundations that have not only ensured its survival, but have seen *Vogue* continue to grow on a worldwide basis when other publications have floundered.

The Lady – a magazine for all?

Another equally iconic magazine and staple of British history is *The Lady*, which – having begun in the Victorian era – is Britain's longest running weekly women's magazine. Much can be learned from this household name, which has stood the test of time and, despite recent challenges, continues to evolve. Yet today, while *The Lady* is surviving, it has yet to thrive once again. The foundations are strong – it is after all a trusted brand with a rich history, an excellent reputation and a stoic set of readers. But there is much to evaluate and question as we examine what lessons can be taken from the title's past and present strategies.

Founded by the Mitford sisters' grandfather, Thomas Gibson Bowles, *The Lady* was originally set to be a journal for gentlewomen. The first issue was published in 1885, yet the title did not have an official editor until 1894 when Bowles appointed his children's governess Rita Shell, whose stint lasted 31 years – until 1925. Evidence shows that it was a successful title under Rita's editorship, one that made money. Bowles – who had also founded *Vanity Fair* in 1868 but sold it for £20,000 to finance his parliamentary career – according to the memoirs of former editor Rachel Johnson (2010), kept *The Lady* as "it was a nice little earner".

That success continued. In the 1930s Thomas's son George took over as publisher. His greatest achievement was keeping the magazine profitable throughout the Depression and the Second World War, which was no mean feat given the economic uncertainty that existed throughout those challenging times. How did he do it and what lessons can today's publishers draw from it?

Bowles' great grandson Ben Budworth – who took over the reins as publisher and CEO from his Uncle Tom in 2008 – says *The Lady* had always been sustainable. But, he admits, there have been a few dips, citing 1890–1900 plus the pre-Second World War Depression. During this period family members dug deep and a number of shares changed hands with the Mitfords to support the magazine, which he says was "realistically broke".

> My grandfather had to effectively sell the collection of buildings – this building, 38–40 Bedford Street and 26–27 Maiden Lane – on the proviso that he could buy them back. We might call it a mortgage today, but my uncle insists this wasn't a mortgage – just a private sale with an option to buy back. My uncle remembers my grandfather (his father) paying off the last instalment to get back the building.

It is in such times where unforeseen events such as wartime or a recession take a toll that refinancing is necessary in order to sustain a magazine or publishing business. However, *The Lady*'s latest crisis was more about the evolution of society into the digital age with copy sales slashed and page advertising yields at an all-time low. A crisis familiar to many publishers, some of which have survived but others haven't. Thus, drastic action was needed and under Ben's stewardship *The Lady* succumbed to some radical changes, including new staff and the controversial appointment of Rachel Johnson as Editor in 2009. This was mainly to breathe new life into the title and build up its dwindling circulation, which had dropped to 23,000 at its lowest point in December 2008.

But, as every CEO should be, Ben Budworth was prepared to fight for the title. Why? Because he believed in the magazine's relevance in today's society.

With a brief to modernise its style, Ben's first job was to undertake a radical assessment of staff and resources. Ben explains,

> The first point was the management that my uncle had allowed to flourish beneath him who were ill equipped to manage, had had no training and had only looked inwards. In some instances that had been 30–35 years and it had suited my uncle to not encourage any contact with the outside world.

He adds that a cult had developed whereby there was an element of divide and rule: *the answer is no, now what's the question?*

It is clear that the situation occurred following classic management errors such as allowing stagnation, not anticipating future developments and poor communication at all levels, all of which resulted in the magazine accumulating losses of £20,000 a week.

> The editorial team never spoke to the advertising department, who in turn didn't understand what page yield was and certainly would never have

countenanced pro-active calling or contact potential advertisers. So the first thing I had to dismantle was that management.

Ben found that each department had grown into a mini-fiefdom which had to be taken apart. He explains,

> It wasn't a question of talent rising to the top but identifying the talent that had been trampled to within an inch of its life. The priority was keeping that talent and allowing them to flourish whilst getting rid of those who had done nothing but feather their own nest for the past 30 years.

Following an in-depth assessment Ben had the grim task of making staff redundant.

> Morally it wasn't terribly difficult to sit here and say goodbye to 75% of the people I did say goodbye to. There were 25% who I found it incredibly hard to say goodbye to. It wasn't their fault that they couldn't communicate, had had no training or that their will to learn, engage and develop had been trampled out of them, but sometimes you have to clear the baby out with the bathwater. There was nothing I could do with the staff that had to go.

Those that stayed formed the bare bones of a re-developed magazine. "I had to sort out the sales department and the editorial," he continued, adding that the editorial needed to make a noise, while the sales department needed to be run and reorganised by a credible sales director, who understood page yields.

> Naively I thought – bearing in mind that at that time we had a very low base again, 28,000 to 29,000 – it would be relatively easy to develop the circulation to 40,000 or 50,000. I hadn't appreciated how we were in a declining market. Fortunately, there were so many savings to be made with the magazine that we have turned a £20,000 a week loss into a modest profit.

Hence Budworth's decision to appoint a high-profile figure as editor with good connections, someone who could attract the media's attention.

When appointing Rachel Johnson as Editor he gave her two key priorities. The first was to raise the magazine's profile and the second was to increase circulation. She delivered on both points. Shortly after her appointment a TV documentary followed, recording Johnson's first few months in the role; this gave the title a massive publicity boost. One of her first tasks was to give *The Lady* a wider appeal. New writers were brought in and the magazine received something of a facelift. Circulation did indeed rise and by July to September 2010 it achieved a regular circulation of just over 30,000, as cited in *The Guardian*.

After Johnson's departure in 2012 the then Assistant Editor, Matt Warren, took over. He was the first male editor in over 100 years. He took on a huge challenge because, despite the high-profile publicity following the documentary and Johnson's appointment, *The Lady*'s circulation, according to a breakdown of magazine sales in *Press Gazette*, was low – 27,977, down 4% on the previous year.

So why did Warren relish this challenge, which he cited as the most bizarre offer of his career?

> Most journalists at some point in their career like the idea of running the show, so when the opportunity [arose] to edit a magazine with as long a history – and as big a profile as *The Lady* – it was too good an offer to pass up.

Warren explains, revealing he had watched the infamous documentary, *The Lady and The Revamp*.

> The magazine did seem like it had been an anachronistic artifact before Rachel Johnson took over. Although it seemed like an unlikely place to go, it did pose an interesting, colourful challenge and at the same time I could see it had a strong future ahead of it and I wanted to be a part of it.

Unlike previous editors, his approach was to view the magazine as a publication for people – rather than targeting a primarily female audience.

> *The Lady* wasn't really a women's magazine in the popular sense. It was called *The Lady* and was largely read by women, but then a lot of women's magazines are a bit patronizing in that way. They are about the same old thing – seemingly assuming that women are only interested in diets and fashion. I thought *The Lady*, first and foremost, should be a publication for 'people' rather than one for 'men' or 'women'. I wanted it to appeal to an interested audience who were looking for something else that didn't speak to their gender, but their interests.

His biggest challenge, he admits, was to change the public's view of a magazine from a different era that had lost its way and persuade them it was a title worth reading: "That unlike most other magazines it had something for everyone in it. That *The Lady* wasn't just something from the past, it had a future too." Unfortunately, as Warren concedes, the public's view was compounded by the fact that the magazine is called *The Lady*. "If you were starting a magazine today it's probably the last name you would choose. It's one of those words in English that really is seen as terribly anachronistic."

Yet despite discussions about a potential rebrand of the name, this was not really an option.

> *The Lady*'s name is also its strongest suit – a title that everyone knew and that linked it to this long, distinguished history that went back over a 100 years. To surrender that would be to lose something really important. Its heritage and

link with the past, the sense that people trusted it irrespective of whether people thought it was something worth picking up or not. So the trick was to balance the magazine's heritage with a vision for the future.

In those golden days of publishing *The Lady* didn't have to sell itself nor did it have to compete with such a saturated market on the newsstands. "At the time, the classified adverts for domestic help and nannies sold *The Lady*," Warren concedes. "Now that's no longer the case as selling classifieds is much more of a struggle so you have to sell a magazine on the content."

Taking into consideration the staggering post-millennial costs of distribution combined with falling circulation alongside a somewhat saturated market, the question is can *The Lady* thrive once more? And if so, how?

Warren feels the key is tapping into its heritage and reputation as a trusted brand of journalism.

> There is this idea in this 'post-truth' age that expertise is something to be frowned upon. But people still want to hear from those who can be trusted. *The Lady* can sell into that niche, especially at a time when good journalism is diminishing and being replaced by click bait stuff. It could cash in on the idea that it still has high-quality writers doing things in a high-quality way, that it is a brand that can be trusted, that doesn't hack phones and kowtow to celebrities.

The Lady has, says Matt, an opportunity to cash in on the fact that many people have lost faith in mainstream media. "And of course the whole Victoriana, steam punk, hipster thing as well, there is a whole range of possible audiences *The Lady* could appeal to – the key is embracing as many of those as possible."

It is an astute observation, so where would he start?

> First and foremost, the magazine's standard has to be kept high and you have got to ask what is this magazine and who is it for? You have to have an idea of who you want reading it – these are the people who need it. The magazine has a brand and you have to remain loyal to that, but at the same time you have to consider, given that foundation stone, who might be interested in it, what type of person they are and what do they want? And are other magazines already doing it? You can't sell something unless you know what it is. Keep that in mind and the quality high and then let people know that it's out there and how it's different.

He also cites the need to secure as much press coverage for *The Lady* as possible.

> The one thing we had no problem with was getting publicity. The wider media seemed to cast the magazine as this batty old thing but they did like to write about it. To get coverage, you have to play up to the pantomime, but also get across that it is now a serious enterprise as well.

Today the magazine is considerably more stable now than it was eight years ago and is currently in profit. However, Ben admits there are still debts to repay.

> We have an awful lot of people to pay back. Many of our debts are soft family debts and that's not to say we will continue to make that sort of money if we stand still. If we solely had a magazine I would have closed it yesterday. The magazine continues to thrive on the basis of its reputation of being the gatekeeper for recruitment advertising. We have lost the guesthouses, hotels and holiday home adverts. A lot of *The Lady*'s small, classified advertisers have gone online.

However, Ben understands where the magazine's future clearly lies – as a specialist in domestic recruitment with the editorial developing a strong voice.

> As far as recruitment advertising is concerned we are regarded as the must destination for that sort of advertising – where reputable staff look, and reputable employers advertise. Were my great grandfather to look at it he would say you are trying to pander to too many diverse groups and yet you are serving none of them properly. I think he would instantly introduce an element of backbone into *The Lady*, something that hasn't been in the magazine for 70–80 years.

Ben is a formidable leader who has a strong vision for *The Lady*'s future and is not afraid to take chances. What would his great grandfather do?

> He would give *The Lady* an editorial purpose. I don't think at the moment we have that. I think the magazine benefits from a number of diverse groups whose purpose it suits for them to subscribe, read or advertise in *The Lady*. But to take the average of that demographic and try to produce editorial for it is wholly wrong.

Throughout its history *The Lady* has survived numerous challenges and no doubt will continue to do so. Looking at it from an analytical perspective I feel it needs strong leadership in the form of another iconic editor – one who has a strong sense of identity but can also blend with the magazine's heritage.

Why political satire endures

Nearly in its sixth decade, *Private Eye* continues to thrive with perhaps one of the simplest models in publishing – low production costs and strong focus on subscription sales. Co-founded in 1961 by Richard Ingrams, and his former school friends Christopher Booker, Paul Foot, Willie Rushton and Peter Usborne, it was developed at a time when publishing was more viable than today – despite the digital revolution. Since then the magazine has provoked something of a cult following, building a base of loyal readers who support it through good times and bad.

Launched with a start-up fund of just £300 provided by Andrew Osmond, friend of Peter Usborne, costs had to be kept low. As well as providing the seed money, *Private Eye*'s name also came from Osmond. At the time a relatively new printing technique, off-set litho, enabled the publishing quintet to bypass the need for the traditional and expensive hot metal techniques used by newspapers and magazines. Subsequently production costs were more affordable.

On Friday 25th October 1961, priced at sixpence, the first issue of *Private Eye* was distributed in coffee shops around South Kensington. Initially edited by Booker and designed by Rushton, who drew the cartoons, the *Eye*'s ethos was: a magazine that refused to take sides – having a go at anyone regardless of rank or political ideology. It has never changed. "In the beginning if we had an aim it was to provide an alternative to *Punch*, which was then like the Bank of England," Richard Ingrams told Sue MacGregor when discussing the launch on BBC Radio 4's *The Reunion* (2016).

Ingrams took over as editor from Booker in 1963 and continued until 1986 when Ian Hislop took the reins. With articulate content that is a combination of satire and investigative journalism, *Private Eye* has unsurprisingly received numerous libel writs following its reports on scandals revolving around the rich and powerful.

Those writs appear to have further encouraged reader loyalty. Currently with a print circulation of 250,204, with 140,661 coming from subscription sales and a readership of 880,000 according to the publication's BRAD (from 1 January to 1 June 2016) it is phenomenally successful. Since 2002 its circulation has risen by 30% at a time when other titles have experienced substantial falls in theirs. *Private Eye*'s substantial subscription achievement is also a fantastic feat, further reinforcing the success of its business model.

The emphasis, according to *Private Eye*'s managing director, Sheila Molnar, "is and always has been very much on keeping the business model simple with focus on three factors, newstrade, subscriptions and advertising". As the evidence shows, it works.

Molnar attributes the *Eye*'s success to old-fashioned journalism values and having a wide age span.

> It has and always will seek to question the official version of events. It is the unique content and loyalty of our readers that has made *Private Eye* successful. Word of mouth is also a factor – it is as crucial today as it was in the 1970s.

However, Molnar insists that only having a print edition also helps circulation. Evidence reinforces this despite many publishers maintaining print is in decline and citing digital as the answer.

To further support her point Molnar recalls a reader writing in and telling the story of when he left the magazine on his coffee table where it was read by his son and then the son's friend.

> Had it have been a digital edition on the iPad this just wouldn't happen. Digital copies are usually just read by one person, whereas printed magazines can be passed on and on – giving a readership of three to four times that of the circulation.

It is this factor – to be able to hand *Private Eye* on to the next generation of readers – that Molnar believes is fundamental to the title's long-term sustainability. "It is why our audiences' age range spans from 13 to 90."

Thus unlike many magazines *Private Eye* doesn't have a digital issue and its website is used as a signpost for the magazine. The system works because, unlike some publications, the *Eye* has been careful not to give away content. This is part of a deliberate strategy, as Molnar explains: "We will not be giving away content for free. Our aim is maintain our position as the number one best-selling news and current affairs magazine." Clearly that strategy has paid dividends. There is something rather charming and authentic about *Eye* as a printed edition. It would, I feel, be virtually impossible to replicate *Private Eye*'s persona in a digital format.

Although the magazine has always been sustainable, it was during the 1970s that copy sales began to take off and the profit margin grew. "In the first half of 1966 sales were 39,868 and by 1972 they were around 98,047. This in part was due to some notable innovations during this period," Molnar recalls. These innovations included the introduction of Pseuds Corner, the Crossword, Nooks and Corners In the Courts and In the City. But investigative journalism plus a series of high-profile libel cases also played a part.

Yet, despite its popularity, having had to pay out extensive libel damages has at times impacted on the magazine's cash-flow. As rumour has it, at one point *Private Eye* came so close to going under the team agreed not to be paid for a few issues. Molnar cites the lowest point as 1989 when the Yorkshire Ripper's wife Sonia Sutcliffe was awarded record damages of £600,000. "Had we not have won on appeal reducing libel damages to £60,000 the magazine would have gone under."

As MD, Molnar is extremely effective. Why? Because she has a strong vision and by her own admission "the right team on board". Her strategy of keeping the business team small and ensuring all departments work closely together no doubt plays a key part in the magazine's continued success. Having a high-profile editor in Ian Hislop also adds weight to the magazine. However, it is good communication between all departments that is a key factor here. It means decisions can be made quickly, and that can have a huge impact on the business. Clearly this, together with a simple business model, is why the *Eye* is thriving when others are not.

Summary

In this chapter we have focused on three iconic publications – two of which have marked their centenary. From each one valuable lessons can be drawn; perhaps the most important one is that all three titles focus on the printed issue – a strategy which has not only worked in the past but continues to do so. While digital publishing certainly has a place, print is not dead nor will it be, I suspect, in the foreseeable future.

So what other lessons can we draw from looking from the history of publishing? The next and perhaps most fundamental lesson should be timing. One of the earliest examples of poor timing is perhaps John Dunton and his pioneering title, *The Ladies Mercury*, published in 1693. It was the first women's magazine with love as its editorial focus and a strategy to engage and seek contributions from readers.

Yet after just four issues it failed. Why? I suspect timing was a key issue. Low literacy among women likely played a part, thus limiting the audience. It is also probable that love was not perceived as a key issue in marriage. This was after all a time when well-to-do families sought to preserve their wealth lines through marriage. Education in women was also not a priority. In fact it wasn't, until the latter part of the century when women began to become interested in education. Abrams (2014) refers to this as the impact of the 18th-century Enlightenment encouraging women towards literacy and thus intellectual evolution. Had the magazine been published 100 years later, its chance of success may have been considerably higher. After all, many of today's lifestyle titles feature love as a key editorial pillar.

This brings me to the next lesson – understanding your audience. *Vogue*, *The Lady* and *Private Eye* all have an army of loyal readers – albeit some larger than others. This is because the editors understand not only their readers but also their needs and aspirations and as a result are able to produce editorial which provides. These editors are bold, hold strong journalistic values and are not afraid to follow their instincts as opposed to focusing on what is popular on the newsstands.

Last, all three editors know the value of their content and realise that giving it away rarely works. Thus they have learned to adapt the concept 'less is more' in response to the digital age. Not only that, but *Vogue*, *The Lady* and *Private Eye* all use the Internet to their advantage – as a signposting tool to raise their publication's profile.

Moving on from the past, subsequent chapters will look at strategies that have worked and those that have not while evaluating potential ideas that have yet to be tried and tested.

INDUSTRY PERSPECTIVES

Alexandra Shulman, *Vogue*'s Editor-in-Chief, firmly believes print isn't dead (Figure 1.1). Despite having successfully steered the iconic title through the digital maze, Alexandra remains firmly in favour of the printed issue.

Here she shares her experiences, revealing the key to managing change and achieving a successful editorship.

The printed magazine has changed so much since I began editing Vogue *in 1992. Back then the role was very much about dealing with the big fashion houses, having close relationships with them and knowing everything that was going on. There wasn't anything like the number of brands there are now, nor did the publication have such a high output.*

Taking over such a high-profile worldwide magazine renowned for its verve and longevity was both exciting and a little scary. Building sustainability for the long term was key. To do this I realised we need to extend the editorial and take a slightly broader approach to fashion in Vogue *so I not only changed the amount of high*

FIGURE 1.1 *Vogue* centenary cover, courtesy of *Vogue*

street and middle market clothes that were featured in the magazine, but also bought in more writing.

Today editorial teams have to produce much, much more than a magazine. When I came to Vogue *there were 12 issues a year – that was the job. Now in addition to those 12 issues there are four supplements, a website,* Vogue *videos, events and a festival to manage. That said, the pace is vibrant and no two days are the same.*

Like most publications the digital landscape has impacted the title and we now work across all the platforms. Getting the balance right is always tough but it's crucial to remember that each medium is unique and therefore we have a very separate approach for digital and print. We understood early on that there needs to be unity so both teams now work closely together – cross platform signposting and a continuation of content is a core part of our strategy. My print journalists write for online, and online journalists can take the baton on from a story published first in print.

Although digital is still a relatively small part of our revenue stream, our website is the biggest part of it and profits are growing steadily. A magazine must have strong revenue streams to ensure growth and sustainability; therefore income comes from our whole social media programme rather than one stream.

In publishing there is no one-size-fits-all model, in terms of either its digital or social media engagement. Each magazine has its own blueprint, particularly from a growth perspective. For Vogue social media allows people to engage with the notion of the title. More people across the world can access a part of Vogue than at any time in its 100-year history and that's good for its future – more people are interested in the idea of it. That's the holy grail, the aspect everyone has got to work out – how do you use your social media to actually drive people to buy magazines?

As an editor I believe caution is essential with regard to free content. The more you put out that allows people to access an element of Vogue for free – whether that's something like Apple News, putting pieces online or our Instagram feed – you are actually diverting readers away from buying that magazine because you need time to read it. And if you can fulfil a little bit of desire through these other things then it's much harder to say to people 'hang on, it's the magazine you've got to get'. Free content would all be very well if it brought in sufficient revenue, but all publishers know there is a gap. Mind the gap . . .

Do digital editions work? Sometimes, but it's about looking at your magazine model and how it is consumed. For Vogue print production is very much part of its USP as the magazine is a treat – it's very tactile so I'm not sure that a digital app is ever going to be the best way to see Vogue. My opinion is that at the moment the idea of a tablet app has to be viewed as a niche product; it's for people who for one reason or another want to read the magazine in that way.

Apps do have a place. For example, digital magazines are great for those who frequently travel. There are a lot of women who fly around the world the whole time so they buy all their magazines on their iPad, they put the tablet in their bag and it's job done for the aeroplane.

I also think that the iPad is possibly a transitory thing. Everybody is now saying that this business has moved to mobile (we have a mobile version as well), but it's hard to really see that this is going to be the way that people are really going to choose to read the magazine. They will read other Vogue content, but my feeling is that what I produce as a monthly magazine is best viewed the way it is – in print.

Digital apps are best used for other things. Four years ago everyone was saying 'in two years' time everyone is going to be reading magazines on the iPad'; well I never thought they were and they still aren't.

Looking to the future is a must for any editor. For Vogue, brand extensions will play a big part. It's a question of looking at what can you do best with your published magazine – the print edition – and what can you do best in other ways. Also what new things can you do with different extensions – whether they are digital, live events or education? What can you do – and how can you use the magazine to be the core of that? For me that is really interesting.

There are big conversations happening in the fashion business. People are looking at different methods of showing clothes as well as changing the timings of fashion shows. There is a big debate now about whether events should be closer to the time of when the clothes go actually into the stores and that kind of thing. It's a very interesting discussion if you publish a fashion magazine and will impact on the kind of publication that we can produce so I am excited about being part of that conversation.

Continuing to evolve is crucial for any successful business – be it publishing or fashion. Therefore my advice to those future editors would be to immerse yourself in experience – read a lot and look at a lot. Know what's going on out there. Not so that you can do the same thing but so that you are literate in the world. Don't be tunnel-visioned or think that there is only one way to do things. Try to work at lots of different places, get experience and meet a lot of people.

People are the key in the end. I've always got my jobs through getting on well with people. Working with a team and starting at the bottom is important – it's where you learn the biggest lessons.

YOUR INITIAL ACTION PLAN

1. Draw up a list of your two strongest competitor titles that have a long history.
2. Undertake in-depth research of each title – from evolution to the present day, noting the pits and troughs.
3. Evaluate those strategies that have worked best and identify where dips in circulation have occurred. For example, did the title have a succession of editors during that period?
4. Now identify four essential lessons to take from your research.

Bibliography

Abrams, L. 2014. *The Making of Modern Woman: Europe 1789–1918*. London: Routledge.
BBC Radio 4, Broadcast 4 September 2016. The Launch of Private Eye. *The Reunion*. www.bbc.co.uk/programmes/b07sxhx9?ns_mchannel=social& accessed 28 October 2016.
Greenslade, R. 2010. Judge the Lady, and Its Editor, by the Figures. *The Guardian*. www.theguardian.com/media/greenslade/2010/oct/07/rachel-johnson-magazines accessed 26 October 2016.

Hogarth, M. 2016. Alexandra Shulman Interview. *InPublishing*. Sept/Oct 2016 edition.
Hughes, K. 2008. Zeal and Softness: Women's Magazines Down the Ages. *The Guardian*. www.theguardian.com/books/2008/dec/20/women-pressandpublishing accessed 29 September 2016.
Johnson, R. 2010. *A Diary of the Lady*. London: Penguin Books Ltd.
Macqueen, A. 2011. The Eye at 50 Blog. *Private Eye*. www.private-eye.co.uk/blog/?p=371 accessed 28 October 2016.
Millar, R. 2016. Vogue 100: A Complete History of British Vogue Editors-in-Chief. The Culture Trip. https://theculturetrip.com/europe/united-kingdom/articles/vogue-100-a-complete-history-of-british-vogue-editors-in-chief/ accessed 25 October 2016.
Mollison, A. 1999. Obituary: Liz Tilberis. *The Independent*. www.independent.co.uk/arts-entertainment/obituary-liz-tilberis-1088961.html accessed 25 October 2016.
Pentelow, O. 2017. Vogue Editors through the Years. www.vogue.co.uk/gallery/past-british-vogue-editors-history accessed 19 January 2017.
Ponsford, D. 2012. Full Breakdown of Magazine Sales for First Half of 2012. *Press Gazette*. www.pressgazette.co.uk/full-breakdown-of-magazine-sales-for-first-half-of-2012 accessed 26 October 2016.
The Gentleman's Magazine. The Society of 18th Century Gentlemen. Ballindalloch Press. www.ballindalloch-press.com/society/gentsmag.html accessed 29 September 2016 (page no longer available).

2
THE VALUE OF MARKET RESEARCH

Whether you have an established publication, are new to the market or are working on developing a new concept, market research is a crucial development tool. But before you rush to act or engage a consultant like me, remember preparation is the key to success. The question is where do you start?

First, it's essential to identify your primary aim – what do you want to achieve? This should be followed by developing a set of key objectives for research: those old journalist basics – *who*, *what*, *where*, *when*, *why* and *how* – which will be discussed later in the chapter.

Second, as nearly every action will cost money in terms of an investment of time and cash, each one must be scrutinised to ascertain its potential ROI (return on investment).

Last, any research undertaken must be justifiable. Without fully understanding why the market research needs to be done you are unlikely to reap the full benefit. Only once you have identified all the above points can you take it further. If done correctly the data collected will be extremely valuable. It will help your publication or concept develop in the right direction and meet the audience's and other stakeholders' needs. Otherwise it could prove to be a costly waste of your time and money.

In this chapter I will explain how to identify and understand your research target group (be it your audience or advertisers), develop key objectives, decide which type of research is best suited to your needs and evaluate the data collected. Remember, while collecting data is useful, research alone will not produce an ROI unless it is carefully evaluated and results in action points.

Always keep in mind that the point of such a study is ultimately to make your output stronger, more sustainable and profitable. Market research objectives should:

- Aim to find out what your audience likes
- Identify points they are not keen on
- Ascertain what else they want from the publication/brand extensions.

Know your target audience

It is crucial that you know who your audience – and potential readers – are, and have at least a basic demographic profile. Having that basic profile will enable you to not only decide on those questions that need to be asked, but also determine where to find your target groups. The latter is essential if you are researching a new magazine concept or have decided to branch out with the aim of extending your existing audience.

A basic audience demographic of your core target should reflect a mini profile, including key age groups, the ratio of male/female readers and the likely ABC classification (or social classification, as it is still referred to by some publishers). The ABC system was developed more than 50 years ago and is outlined in Table 2.1 – my table is an adaptation of the original model. It not only demonstrates how the classification is determined by the Chief Income Earner (CIE), but also includes other key factors that should be considered – because today's ABCs are not that easy to pigeon hole.

Many people are not as clearly defined as they were 30 or 40 years ago when it was, to some extent, based on the former class system that still existed to some extent. Now

TABLE 2.1 Author's interpretation of ABC audience demographics

Social group	CIE's occupation	Wealth status	Disposable income	Education level
A	Higher managerial, entrepreneur, professional, business owner	Independent income, multiple wealth streams	Extremely high	Likely postgraduate
B	Intermediate-management, small business owner, academic and professional	Salaried position likely to have at least another income stream	High	Graduate, postgraduate including doctorate
C1	Supervisory, administration, junior management, freelance, early career starter and HE student	Salary likely to be in line with national average – unless HE student	Above average	Undergraduate degree or FE qualification
C2	Skilled manual worker	Salaried or hourly paid	Average	May have vocational qualification
D	Semi-skilled manual worker/retail	Hourly paid or on zero hours contract	Low	Basic level
E	State pensioner, casual and lowest grade worker, unemployed	Basic living allowance	Little or none	Basic, but could vary

the ABC system not only includes earnings but also reflects education levels, because the more educated the reader, the more discerning they are likely to be. There are groups on the cusp of a social grade where while their current earnings are low, education levels are high or evolving from HE pursuits. Such groups might include postgraduate and undergraduate students, freelancers and those starting a business. And of course, there will be an exception to every rule . . .

Table 2.1 is a model I have used when researching new magazine concepts for clients. While taking into account less clear-cut factors such as wealth, disposable income and education level, it also facilitates flexibility between the groups, including HE students and those starting out on a career pathway – both are factors that may take people into a higher social grouping as they progress.

Once you have established a basic demographic profile, you are more like to successfully develop questions that will harvest rich data. However, first there are three questions you need to focus on:

- How many respondents will be sufficient to provide reliable data?
- Where will I find my target group of potential respondents?
- What incentive can I secure to ensure participation?

How many respondents do you need to achieve reliable, informative data? This depends on the rationale. For example, if targeting existing readers to ascertain their views on content, brand extensions, etc. then the target reach should be around 20–30%. For those researching a new concept, the more responses the better. Aim for 500+, although realistically a response rate of between 100 and 200 may be more achievable and should provide sufficient data to test and develop the idea. With new start-ups you will also need to determine where your target groups are mostly likely to reside. This can be done by focusing on your magazine's genre. If launching a specialist title such as one on writing, then the first targets will be social media writing groups and members of national writing groups or circles. The same goes for spiritual groups, sports or B2B.

Social media is a great place to start if seeking out new potential audiences. Editors and publishers wanting to extend their audience reach should target current readers plus their friends and family first, and then move to wider circles. Do factor in that people are often bombarded with all kinds of surveys; offering an incentive, preferably provided by a sponsor, is likely to achieve a higher response rate. Conducive prizes could include a meal for two, health, beauty or food products, a holiday or perhaps even a free subscription to your magazine or tickets to an event.

Aims and objectives

Good research must be carefully organised with a structured approach. As previously mentioned, every research project must have a definitive aim that is clear from the outset. So, before clicking on survey tools, clearly define the aim of the study and desired outcomes first. Know what are you trying to achieve and why. Only then can you ensure an ROI is achieved.

Typically, the rationale will most likely be one of the five points outlined in Table 2.2. Setting clear objectives to define how to achieve those aims is the next step. But what should those objectives be and how should they be developed?

Every publication has its unique blueprint. While publishers may be tackling similar challenges to their rivals, there will be variations due to differentials between titles. Therefore, the approach to research must be unique to that magazine or newspaper. Thus, using the old-school journalism tools – identifying *who*, *what*, *where*, *why* and *how* (outlined below) along with suggested action points for each – will help.

- **WHO:** be clear about who the research target is.
  Action: develop a clear target demographic then seek responses by targeting only those specific groups.
- **WHAT:** decide which research tools will work best – a survey or focus group?
  Action: set up the appropriate research method.
- **WHERE:** where will you find survey respondents or participants for a focus group?
  Action: these can be found using a variety of sources such as an existing database, social media groups and, where relevant, through strategic partners.
- **WHY:** be clear on the primary motivation for the research – are you planning a new concept or do you want to boost circulation and raise the profile?
  Action: design your survey or focus group questions from research aims, while focusing on the desired outcome(s).
- **HOW:** how can you achieve sufficient responses/participation to result in rich data capture? How can people be encouraged to participate?
  Action: encourage participation by coming up with an incentive such as a prize draw or special offer for all respondents.

TABLE 2.2 Suggested rationales and aims of research

Reason for research	*Subsequent aim*
New product – either concept or brand extension	Market testing to ascertain sustainability
Poor newsstand sales or drop in consumption across print, digital or online users	Identify and address key issues in terms of content, platform or circulation
Advertisers complaining of poor response rates	Find evidence – in terms of readers – as to which factors make adverts successful
A spike in a rival title's circulation following a relaunch or new brand extension	Identify content readers prefer and how their interest may have changed
A desire to raise the publication's profile and set higher circulation targets	To increase product reach

These key action points will ensure that the best method of research is chosen – be it a survey or focus group – and that the questions are carefully developed with the desired outcomes in mind. The study will therefore be more likely to harvest rich data that will inform future developments and strategies.

Surveys vs focus groups

Which is more beneficial, a focus group or a survey? This is a question I am often asked as a magazine consultant. There is no right answer. It depends on what you as an editor or publisher are trying to ascertain, but sometimes using both methods will yield valuable results.

First, let's consider the value of a survey or quantitative research as it is otherwise known. When circulation declines, often readers' priorities have shifted or new trends have evolved and a magazine might not be serving its readership as well as it could.

Although the final solution will often come from a complete audit, including a comparison of the magazine's content with that of its closest competitors, a carefully constructed survey will provide a viewpoint from the readers' perspective. This is as true today as it was during my time as deputy editor on *Writer's Forum* magazine; we undertook reader surveys approximately once a year. Then our focus was adapting the content to the changing needs of our audience as we were on the crest of a digital revolution. This was in the era when the Internet and the new iMacs were just evolving, so our readers' needs were constantly changing.

It was an exciting time, especially for writers who were moving away from their trusted typewriters towards computers. Novels, articles or short stories could now be not only written but also edited with ease if readers had a computer or one of the early laptops. Wider Internet access, initially through dial-up, meant query letters (or pitches as they are now known) and synopses were now starting to be emailed rather than posted.

As the leading writing magazine at that time, our role was evolving too; hence audience research was essential to get the content model right so we opted for reader surveys. These were printed in the magazine and a basic adaptation was uploaded to our fledgling website. The response rate was much higher than expected, although the majority were sent in via the post.

How did we get such a high response rate? I suspect that the incentive of a respondent's prize draw that offered some quality prizes helped. But it is also likely that the community aspect – writers feeling they had a stake in the magazine – played a part too. So never underestimate the community aspect of your publication.

The survey proved to be a rich source of data. Results were two-fold. Not only were we able to adapt the content to include a section on technology and an annual web guide booklet to inform our readers, but these additions to our editorial pillars enabled the magazine to expand its advertisers thus increasing advertising revenue. In addition, some of the data was also used to boost the magazine's media kit and further inform advertisers of our audience's changing needs.

However, I should also mention that qualitative forms of research also played a part. We regularly met our readers at national writers' conferences and events, which provided a great opportunity to chat informally with our audience. This is also beneficial to readers, who like to feel important – particularly with specialist publications – and feel they contribute to the magazine in some way, and rightly so. Publishers who understand this are more likely to achieve longevity, such as *Private Eye* and *The Lady* as discussed in the previous chapter, which brings me to focus groups.

When it comes to qualitative research, how do you determine if a focus group might be more beneficial than a survey? It mostly depends on the type of magazine and the nature of your research.

Focus groups facilitate a discussion out of which new ideas can emerge. For example, during the very early stages of the launch of *Vegetarian Living*, a focus group discussion resulted in the magazine widening its initial target audience to include meat reducers as opposed to focusing solely on vegetarians and vegans. Long term this informed decision is perhaps one of the key reasons that the magazine has become a staple in the newsstands.

Today's trend of healthy eating means that many people are conscious of not eating too much meat and thus are seeking inspiration for their meals from vegetarian sources. Would the team have come to the decision without feedback from the focus group? Maybe, but the focus group certainly highlighted the opportunity.

Qualitative research methods or focus groups work well too for those seeking views of either a sample group or a specific type of reader, as they are likely to produce more definitive results than a survey. This is also the case for local magazines closely linked with their community who are looking to get feedback on a new design or change in editorial strategy. The case study on the Dorset magazine *Celebrating Poundbury* demonstrates the positive impact such qualitative research can have not only on the publication but also on the focus group. As with a survey, this type of research gives those readers a voice.

While research data is invaluable to aid growth and development there may be some aspects that appear to have bias or an agenda. Hence careful evaluation of the data is crucial.

Questions and responses

Whether you have opted for qualitative or quantitative research, carefully compiled questions are a must. Many companies using surveys to collect data keep the length to a minimum. Old-style questionnaires of 30+ questions are unlikely to achieve many responses or harvest reliable data as participants may be short on time and therefore not willing to answer too many questions, particularly if the questions require an in-depth response.

When undertaking such research for clients, I prefer to keep surveys to around 10 to 12 questions and include an incentive for participants to complete it, such as a prize or free gift. The survey must be easy for the participant to access and complete.

There are many online survey tools available, making it easy to distribute. The easier it is for a reader to access the survey, the more likely they will be to complete it. This sounds obvious, but it is surprising how often this is overlooked.

Online surveys also make results easier to filter as the data can be presented in a variety of formats such as charts and percentages. Any raw data captured from unstructured questions can also be extracted.

When compiling surveys, experience has taught me that it is best to develop the majority as multiple choice questions. That said, it is always useful to include a couple of unstructured questions whereby the respondent answers from his or her own perspective. This is useful if the purpose of the survey is to develop a new magazine or change the focus of your editorial. Often the results will surprise you, and in some cases bring new ideas or perspectives into the mix. For example, an audience survey for *Writer's Forum* revealed that our readers also had children who wanted a platform for their output. Thus, we developed the *Writer's Forum* Young Writers' Competition, which led to sponsorship from Collins who supplied dictionaries for the runner-up prizes.

Questions must be carefully developed. Consider the key outcomes of the research; these will help identify the questions that need to be asked. Do think about the impact each question might have on the respondent. Phrase awkward questions sympathetically – particularly those that are age and income-related – and steer clear of any that may cause offence as you want as many responses as possible.

A client recently commissioned me to research the potential for a new economic magazine. After an initial analysis confirmed there was a clear gap in the market for a new concept in this genre, a more in-depth approach could be taken in terms of testing to concept with potential readers. First, the client and I determined the basic audience demographic; then, after some discussion we decided a survey to test potential interest in the proposed magazine would work best in the first instance. To develop the survey I used a combination of multiple choice questions and a few unstructured ones, with the latter focusing on potential editorial interests and brand extensions in the form of events.

The key objectives in order of priority were to:

1. Ascertain whether this new concept could succeed
2. Confirm our initial demographic overview of the audience's age ranges, male/female ratios, interest, etc.
3. Decide upon a definitive platform (digital or print), by asking how potential readers would prefer to consume the magazine
4. Identify a clear price point – how much would readers be prepared to pay for the magazine?
5. Ascertain the potential for achieving a high rate of subscriptions
6. Data capture of email addresses of those interested in the magazine.

Once the survey had been developed a good distribution strategy was needed. As with most new concepts it is always best to target a pre-determined demographic, but where do you find potential respondents? In this instance we opted for social media. My client set up a Facebook group and Twitter account then targeted potential readers by identifying suitable groups and pages on which to post, as well as tweeting a link and publishing it on LinkedIn. In addition, the client also distributed the survey link via his extensive email contacts. This strategy ensured the survey achieved a useful number of respondents – nearly 200 respondents. The data gathered revealed that:

- Nearly 70% were interested in the concept, while a further 27% stated they 'may be' interested in reading it.
- Those wanting to consume the magazine online amounted to 72%, while 48% were interested in digital and print editions.
- On average, 68% spent around £15 on economic and financial magazines per month.
- The price point most would be willing to pay was identified by 67% as £4.99.
- Around 17% said they would consider taking out a monthly subscription with 69% stating they would maybe consider it.

The survey results also confirmed our estimated age range and showed an approximate 70/30 split in the ratio of male/female readers. Overall it provided sufficient evidence to show a potential market in the publication's business plan that was subsequently developed to secure funding. These results were also used to develop the initial media kit.

Adhering to data protection codes

When capturing personal contact data such as email and postal addresses, always get the individual's consent to be contacted for marketing purposes. Cited as the foundation of good research, the Market Research Society (MRS) has set out a 10-point Code of Conduct for all its members. It covers all aspects of market research from inception and design to execution and use, as well as the necessary legal requirements.

The 10 Principles of the MRS Code of Conduct are (2014, p. 3):

1. Researchers shall ensure that participation in their activities is based on voluntary informed consent.
2. Researchers shall be straightforward and honest in all their professional and business relationships.
3. Researchers shall be transparent as to the subject and purpose of data collection.
4. Researchers shall respect the confidentiality of information collected in their professional activities.
5. Researchers shall respect the rights and well-being of all individuals.
6. Researchers shall ensure that participants are not harmed or adversely affected by their professional activities.

7. Researchers shall balance the needs of individuals, clients, and their professional activities.
8. Researchers shall exercise independent professional judgement in the design, conduct and reporting of their professional activities.
9. Researchers shall ensure that their professional activities are conducted by persons with appropriate training, qualifications and experience.
10. Researchers shall protect the reputation and integrity of the profession.

It is advisable to adhere to all 10 points of the MRS code; failure to do so may impact on your reputation or that of your publication and attract negative publicity.

CASE STUDY: *CELEBRATING POUNDBURY*

Miriam Phillips, owner of Bright Daisy Publishing, got in touch for advice on developing her new magazine, *Celebrating Poundbury* (Figure 2.1), which she had launched in 2015 as a high-end, local title.

The magazine serves Prince Charles's urban initiative Poundbury, a thriving community adjacent to Dorchester, the county town of Dorset, which began in 1993 with the aim of creating a 'walkable community'. Today it has a population of more than 2,000 people plus 185 businesses. Further growth is projected as the development continues to grow.

Community, combined with an artisan feel, is a key focus of this town. Following some initial fact-finding and discussions with Miriam, it became clear that for *Celebrating Poundbury* to thrive it needed to become an integral part of the town's society. Already endorsed by The Duchy of Cornwall (renowned for its reputation for excellence) and praised by HRH The Prince of Wales during his visits, *Celebrating Poundbury* had overcome some defining start-up hurdles. However, the magazine needed to achieve its key objective to become the focus point of its community in order to achieve success and long-term sustainability.

Initially launched as a free publication, Miriam was keen to take it to a paid-for title which would balance productions costs with the need to match her readers' expectations of discerning content and a high-quality finish production. Thus, it was crucial to gain the readers' perspective on how well the title served the community and ascertain where, if at all, improvements needed to be made.

Thus, audience research was one of the first steps towards this objective, but which method would be more effective – a survey or focus group? Taking into account the fact that *Celebrating Poundbury* is essentially a community magazine, I advised that qualitative feedback in the form of a focus group was more likely to provide the best sources of rich and reliable data. Of course, an opportunity for discussion is another positive aspect of focus groups.

With a date set and a local café appointed as a suitable venue, it was agreed that I would act as the facilitator. Choosing the right venue is crucial as participants need to feel comfortable and the surroundings must be conducive

FIGURE 2.1 *Celebrating Poundbury* covers collage, courtesy of Bright Daisy Publishing

to facilitating a hearty discussion. Those invited were chosen to represent the core readership – a selection of key figures in the community, which included both residents and business owners, all aged between 25 and late 50s.

The outcome of the focus group was positive. All participants were delighted to be involved and welcomed the opportunity to give their feedback on *Celebrating Poundbury*.

Results were as follows:

- Overall, while most participants valued the website/newsletter they very much wanted to keep the printed edition.
- The group were happy to pay for the magazine as they thought it was reflective of a more exclusive feel.
- A majority felt that the cover price was comparative to the magazine's quality in terms of content as well as production.
- A need for more editorial coverage and expanding the area to include other parts of Dorset was highlighted by participants.

While the outcome of the research was incredibly positive – demonstrating that this group valued and supported their magazine – as with all research, there was a danger of bias creeping in. Therefore, I suggested it would be useful for Miriam to do a follow-up survey to obtain quantitative data to get a more collective view.

Miriam said the market research gave her crucial information that was effective for editorial planning and also gave her insights into the readers' passions. "The market research undertook really helped us drive the editorial focus. Also with such a small team it was far more beneficial for a third party to carry these out without bias to get the best results."

I am delighted to report that the research helped *Celebrating Poundbury* to become more established and serve the needs of its readership. It is not only achieving strong local newsstand sales, but also evolving to become sustainable in the long term with plans for brand extensions.

Summary

As stated in this chapter, the key to any successful data is to identify the primary rationale for research. Choose the right methodology for the task then set clear objectives. This will improve your chances of harvesting useful data that could significantly impact on your magazine.

Rob Attar, Editor of *BBC History Magazine*, admits the team do a fair amount of audience research. However, defining a clear demographic, other than a common interest in history, is difficult because the magazine has a broad readership. "It is hard to pin down a BBC reader just by any kind of personality aspect."

As well as commissioning professional studies, Rob also gets a lot of feedback from his readers at the brand's events. "We go to events, and meet readers as well as commissioning reader surveys every couple of years," he explains, adding that the surveys are done professionally by an outside company.

> Mostly the results have shown us how the readerships are changing, highlighting their consumption habits and the fact some are moving to digital. It also shows us what aspects of history people find the most interesting and that is useful in terms of content planning and that kind of thing.

However, he warns that there is always a risk of you being led by research.

> Sometimes you have to lead your audience – you don't want the magazine to be edited by a committee of a 100,000 people. Also, if you are only serving your existing audience all the time you are never going to grow your readership.

But remember, as well as surveys and focus groups there are other opportunities to reach out and get to know your readers. Take every opportunity. Always listen to feedback, analyse research data and look at the sales figures to identify causes of spikes and slumps in circulation. Only then can you make a balanced decision, be it on changes to editorial content, extending brand reach or a relaunch.

INDUSTRY PERSPECTIVES

Dr Laura Santamaria, co-founder and Editor-in-Chief of *Sublime* (Figure 2.2) – a magazine dedicated to making sustainability accessible and aspirational through design and entrepreneurship – shares her expertise.

While Laura agrees audience research is necessary as it is good to know your readers' interests, she warns against taking the data too seriously and being blinded by passion.

In opposition to a consumer magazine driven by the needs of the advertisers, we see our publication as a positive brand that promotes social and environmental sustainability as a lifestyle – this is a new, uncharted territory of magazine genre. The challenge for any new publication is to create and bring to the table topics that might be of interest but have had no space in public debate, setting trends and inviting readers to discover new thinking, aspirations and lifestyles.

It is always good and necessary to know your readers' interests. Some publications gather data through extensive questionnaires to ascertain their readers' changing needs and develop content. However, while questionnaires can be useful they rarely produce illuminating insights. The problem of taking realistic data too seriously is that, as a publisher, you can be misled because realistic data always shows the now, and rarely anticipates emergent interests and trends.

FIGURE 2.2 *Sublime* cover, courtesy of *Sublime*

At Sublime *we know the value of data but we are not driven by it. A lot of our research is based on design thinking and cultural insights – i.e. rather than conventional marketing and market research methods.*

In addition, we use methods derived from the innovation field, such as trend forecasting and future scenarios, as the magazine seeks to build a lifestyle proposition on the way we live today but also propose a lifestyle for the future. The aim is to inspire readers to opt for intelligent lifestyle choices, help them transition from lifestyles of overconsumption to lifestyles of well-being and sustainability, and inspire our readers to discover a new way of looking at our world.

> *The most successful research project we have undertaken is experimenting with cover design and shelf positioning. Investigating these two aspects of how potential readers perceived and understood (at gut level) our publication had a great impact on our brand positioning, target market and editorial strategy. This was done by using ethnography and informal interviewing at point of sale, in addition to feedback we were getting (voluntarily) from new readers and subscribers.*
>
> *Having recently been awarded a doctorate has obviously enhanced my approach in terms of research. There are a lot of skills and capacities that are developed by going through rigorous PhD studies – a better understanding of the different methodologies and how they can complement each other to obtain stronger insights has been a real advantage. Another one is a new appreciation of how knowledge can be generated by integrating theory and practice.*
>
> *A better understanding of theory also helped us identify how our product development process differed from that of other publishers, and we could articulate better our approach and back it up with what we had already applied, perhaps intuitively in practice.*
>
> *Of course, research methods also depend on the objectives of your project. For example, developing a new publication is very different from developing brand extensions. A new publication requires first and foremost the development of the brand and value proposition. Once the brand is established, extensions build on the brand's strength and reputation to extend the brand experience and maximise revenue streams.*
>
> *Therefore, as the aims and objectives are different in each case, the research methodologies may differ greatly. However, we have found that analysing cultural trends and identifying emergent expressions or lifestyle changes in what people consider aspirational and valuable has proven relevant and effective for both.*
>
> *The most challenging research we embarked upon was that prior to formulating the brand and value proposition for* Sublime. *This research took various shapes and forms, and lasted for about three years. Since we were creating a new genre rather than entering a set category in the market, developing the magazine concept and deciding when it was the right time to launch required a lot of good data to make informed decisions. But at the same time, it required us to take the 'data story' with a pinch of salt, and take a leap of faith to materialise our vision.*
>
> *The most important lesson I have learned is that to be truly innovative you need to be open to innovative research methods – i.e. to come up with creative ideas you can't build on what traditional market research tells you . . . Henry Ford said: "If I'd asked people what they wanted, they would have said 'a faster horse'". However, you also need to be realistic about how long it would take people to understand and adopt something that is new to them. In that, creating stories around the product that truly resonate with people and creating concrete value for them is the key to success.*
>
> *My advice to publishers considering commissioning research? Keep your mind open. Be creative and use a combination of methods to map and understand your market. Data collection is great, but good, deep cultural analysis is the most valuable part.*

> *Get the best cultural analyst you can afford to work with your brand strategist. Dispel assumptions. Don't be blinded by your passion, and focus on understanding what value you are creating for the user and how to deliver it through memorable brand experiences.*

YOUR RESEARCH ACTION PLAN

Identify key information you need to obtain about your audience. Remember to set clear objectives at the start, opt for the most suitable method then plan your questions carefully – whether it's for a focus group or survey.

Your structure should follow a logical sequence. There are five key stages:

1. **IDENTIFY:** identify your research targets.
2. **PLAN:** decide which methodology will best deliver the data you need.
3. **EXECUTE:** develop questions, set a clear response timeframe then either circulate your survey to achieve maximum responses or set up a focus group.
4. **EVALUATE:** when all the responses are in, carefully analyse the data.
5. **REFLECT:** go through the whole process looking for any weaknesses or problems that occurred. Could this study be stronger? If so, how?

References

Duchy of Cornwall. Poundbury. http://duchyofcornwall.org/poundbury.html accessed 27 February 2017.

MRS Code of Conduct. 2014. www.mrs.org.uk/standards/code_of_conduct accessed 20 February 2017.

3
AUDIENCE ENGAGEMENT

In previous chapters we explored lessons in sustainability from historic and iconic publications, some of which are still going strong today, and we also looked at the benefits of audience research. Yet sustainability and audiences are interdependent and, as every publisher knows, readerships are continually evolving along with the title. So how do you cultivate a sustainable audience with maximum engagement? One option is to expand your magazine's editorial focus. Yet while this may result in a few more casual readers, it is more likely to lose that loyal core readership who support the title in terms of revenue.

To build a sustainable audience it is imperative to maximise brand reach and this might mean going global. In this chapter the focus will be on extending brand reach with a range of strategies – from geographical expansion to distribution via apps and subscriptions – as well as deepening audience engagement with brand extensions.

As well as evaluating distribution strategies, three iconic brands, *Good Housekeeping*, *Radio Times* and the US title *Writers' Digest* will be scrutinised in terms of audience engagement and brand reach.

Worldwide engagement

Most publishers ensure their magazines are distributed overseas. Not only is this expensive, but it only accounts for a small percentage of their overall circulation. So why bother when the ROI may not cover expenditure? Aside from the fact that both editors and publishers have an intense desire to see their title in as many outlets as possible, it is also about maximising brand reach. Ensuring every potential reader – especially ex-pats – can buy a copy of the magazine. This will always be a good investment and plays a major role in the distribution strategy of both independent publishers and media organisations such as Time Inc, Hearst or Immediate Media.

Specialist titles, some lifestyle magazines and B2Bs export to overseas retailers in English speaking markets. One example of successful overseas sales comes from my time as deputy editor on *Writer's Forum* magazine, when our overseas sales made up about 30% of the overall circulation, which included our overseas subscribers.

Despite being a small, independent publication *Writer's Forum* proved popular, particularly with American readers. This was partly due to our publisher, who – in the early 2000s – would lecture at various conferences around the world, including the renowned Santa Barbara Writers Conference in California: a strategy that boosted the title's reputation and brand reach.

Another *Writer's Forum* strategy was distributing copies to specific overseas areas where our advertisers ran writing events, retreats and courses throughout the year. Another tactic was using back issues as a promotional tool. Working in partnership with those trusted advertisers who ran these events, we would supply back issues free of charge for their events or courses. Frequently, one of the *WF* team would also be speaking at the event – resulting in a boost in subscriptions, particularly if participants were ex-pats.

While some of the above-mentioned strategies employed were effective, it is important to remember that distribution costs – be it digital or print – are expensive and therefore should be carefully costed before any commitment is made. As in the UK, worldwide magazines are distributed to retailers on a sale or return basis. This basically means 'risk free', as publishers take back those unsold copies – retail outlets only pay for those copies sold.

So, is it worth expanding to overseas markets? Distribution expert Keiron Jefferies, assistant circulation manager at Warners Group Publications Plc, says "yes". However, he is quick to point out that the focus should be on the commercial benefits such as sales or advertising first. "Other benefits – brand awareness, subscriptions/digital sales – tend to be a secondary consideration when initially establishing an export sale."

Keiron feels that overseas expansion should be undertaken cautiously.

> While it is cheaper to sell copies overseas than in the UK due to the lower cost to get into retail, there needs to be a clear ROI. Therefore, taking into account the number of copies required, together with the comparatively long period to knowing your sales on an issue-by-issue basis, it is always better to start smaller.

He suggests publishers first identify actual opportunities (such as market size) and then respond accordingly once the sales data is known.

> Export can (initially) be a real burden on cash flow, better to be patient and then react accordingly to closed data. Equally don't be put off – export done correctly can be a real added string to your bow and can open some exciting and lucrative opportunities.

So how much is overseas distribution likely to cost? According to Keiron this depends on the type of deal that your distributor has as some deal in sterling, others in local currencies (certainly for the US/Canada/Australia). There are benefits to both, he explains:

> Dealing in sterling will give a more consistent, simple rate, but dealing in local currencies allows you or your distributor to potentially make the most of exchange rate fluctuations – although these can also go against you. Also, sales efficiencies (the number of copies you sell out of the supply) tend to be lower overseas.

> As far as the breakdown of the cost is concerned it will depend on which combination of options you take but generally you would expect to have a slightly lower remit (cut) of the cover price, either Sterling or overseas currency compared to the UK. Which option works best for you will probably be impacted on by number of copies, weight of the supply, the specific country, the cover price and ultimately the sale and sales efficiency – the number of copies you sell from the supply sent.

Gregor Rankin, publisher and owner of Green Pea Publishing, has extensive experience of overseas distribution. His company publishes consumer and contract titles including *Food and Travel* magazine, which is now published under licence as well as directly owned editions, in Germany, Mexico, Turkey, Arabia, Portugal and Italy, and the original UK edition. He advises having a large brandy and an equally large budget before thinking about what you are trying to achieve through a global distribution.

"Is your rationale based on ego or is it to support another product – in which case your publishing venture is really a marketing exercise," says Gregor, adding that it is more profitable and targeted to produce local-language editions either via a licence agreement or, if you have the local language, resource and patience, have your own offices.

> There is a hybrid where you pay a local publisher to tailor your content for the local market but you still own the title – and risk. Licensing passes much of the risk to the local publisher, along with most of the upside if it does well.

His title, *Food and Travel*, now has seven international editions: UK, Germany, Italy, Turkey, Arabia, Mexico and recently a Portuguese edition – all published locally. However, the German edition, he explains, is owned directly and that was not a planned position. "The licensee tried to steal the title at the end of the contract."

According to Gregor, the cost of overseas distribution usually has a lower margin on the cover price.

> Typically 5–7%, the sting is that you don't control the local selling price as your cover price is stickered over. For example, in the UK *Food and Travel*'s cover price is £4.40, in the US it is $10.95. While they are sold on a sale and return basis there is a very long tail of returns – up to 160 days.

As demonstrated, there are many pros as well as cons. My advice would be to treat it like any other expansion – set a clear objective and do your research to see if it's achievable before investing in overseas distribution. That said, don't forget about digital opportunities.

Going global with digital

Digital magazines have facilitated a higher audience engagement by enabling titles to extend their reach both geographically and demographically, in some cases without going through a distribution chain. Done well this can be a good method of developing a worldwide audience, which is perhaps why many see this as an ideal strategy for expanding into a global market. Hence some publishers have been quick to jump on the digital bandwagon before going through due diligence by thoroughly researching the potential impact or costs involved.

However, caution is advised because publishing a digital version for the majority is a big investment. Therefore, a realistic, in-depth analysis of costs, timeframes, workflow and potential sales/circulation needs to be undertaken.

As discussed in the previous chapter, it is imperative to first ascertain through research how your audience consumes content and if they are more likely to engage with a digital edition than a print edition. As with most strategies, there are pros and cons – as documented in Table 3.1.

In my capacity as a magazine consultant I am often surprised how clients assume digital is a must without undertaking any research. One such example was when

TABLE 3.1 Pros and cons of digital editions

Pros	*Cons*
No printing costs so it can be relatively inexpensive to create if done in-house.	Creating interactive content for digital magazines such as video and podcasts can be time consuming, expensive and increase workflow of the team.
A wide range of layout and interactive options can make content richer and more visually appealing – creating a seamless flow on a tablet or smartphone.	Distribution costs can be prohibitively high if selling through a digital newsstand.
Low cost distribution for customer publishing and membership subscription models as the magazine can be distributed directly to registered users. It is also a good solution for universities that produce student-led magazines.	May impact negatively on cash-flow as achieving target circulation with digital products is at present difficult. It takes time and investment.
Enables educational institutions such as universities to use existing resources to create student-led publications on a low budget.	Audience consumption may not be aligned as readers may prefer the print edition.
Digital edition can be sold directly from a website; therefore there are no direct third-party distribution charges involved.	Poor quality digital magazines will damage a brand's reputation and as a result could decrease engagement.

researching production options for a new start-up. My client had been very definite on the need to produce a digital magazine to launch on the newsstands, having assumed that because there were no printing or wholesale distribution costs that it would be relatively cheap to do.

However, my research corroborated my initial apprehension – financially it wasn't viable at this stage as his fledgling business had yet to become established. Why? Because cash-flow is tight, particularly with new start-ups, and digital distribution can be extremely expensive (as demonstrated below), leaving the publisher with very little of the cover price.

Digital newsstands offer a range of packages, enabling titles to automatically adapt to viewing on tablet, mobile, laptop or desktop screen. Some charge a tiered monthly fee plus transaction charges to Apple, Android, etc. then a 50/50 revenue share of the remaining cover price. The overview of a digital newsstand case study uses Magzter to demonstrate services offered together with the costings involved.

CASE STUDY: AN OVERVIEW OF A DIGITAL NEWSSTAND

Digital newsstand Magzter is well established and publishes well-known titles such as *FHM*, *The Economist* and *TimeOut*, and therefore has been chosen as an example to demonstrate potential costings.

Costs for distribution are comparable with its competitors and are documented in the Publisher Presentation which can be downloaded from its website. Magzter does not charge a set monthly fee for setting up or uploading each issue, but transaction fees along with revenue share will take a big slice of the cover price. Magzter's business terms are as shown in Figure 3.1.

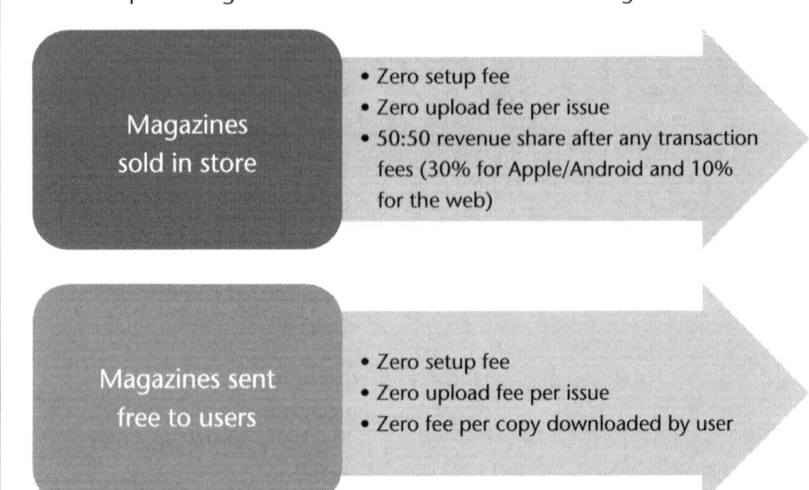

Magazines sold in store
- Zero setup fee
- Zero upload fee per issue
- 50:50 revenue share after any transaction fees (30% for Apple/Android and 10% for the web)

Magazines sent free to users
- Zero setup fee
- Zero upload fee per issue
- Zero fee per copy downloaded by user

FIGURE 3.1 Magzter newsstand fees

While digital publishing can be an excellent tool for expanding your audience to include international readers, caution is advised. If you can produce the edition in-house at a relatively low cost and sell it via the website directly to your audience, then it is worthwhile. Or, for those membership-only or part of a customer publishing titles, it may be a worthwhile risk, but ensure that all the necessary resources – such as staff, content and time – are in place first. However, with on-sale magazines you must undertake the relevant risk assessment through research and costings – only when a reasonable ROI can be predicted backed up by data is it worth the investment.

Subscriptions increase brand loyalty

While subscribers don't increase brand reach to a great degree in terms of newsstand publications, in the long term they are a valuable commodity. The subscription model encourages reader loyalty, helps cash-flow and cuts distribution costs to some extent. By selling direct to the readers, publishers get to keep more of the cover price, thus avoiding the chain of distributors, wholesalers and retailers – all of whom take a percentage of the on-sale charge.

That said, it must be acknowledged that most subscriptions tend to be sold at a loss in the first year because the cost for acquiring a subscriber may be as much as 8–10% of the subscription price, particularly when factoring in marketing and incentive costs. For overseas subscriptions those costs are substantially higher due to rising air/freight charges.

While subscriptions are at an all-time low in the lifestyle market, in some sectors a partial or subscription-only model can work well, particularly for new start-ups. Those sectors tend to be B2B or specialist whether it's financial, writing, sport or hobbies. Readers will pay for quality titles that give them specialist knowledge, but expect value for money.

However, today the term subscriber is fast becoming outdated and is gradually being replaced with membership-style packages. Such packages are now being tiered by a few savvy publishers. For example, this method might offer three packages such as gold, silver or bronze with the gold package featuring the most benefits and the bronze offering a more affordable, basic alternative.

This is a clever tactic which works by:

- **Offering a perceived value:** membership suggests added value in terms of benefits offered as opposed to a simple subscription model.
- **Tiered system:** this increases the range of options and can infer exclusivity with the top package.
- **Affordability:** the lowest tier may appeal to those readers on a budget or who are less inclined to commit themselves long term.
- **Defines the reader as a member:** this reinforces the idea that the reader is part of a club and therefore more invested in the magazine.

Certainly, a tiered membership package is more appealing than a subscription and therefore is likely to be a bigger incentive to sign up. Why? Because in today's climate choice is a big factor as is a fact that readers expect far more in terms of content, incentives and benefits.

From a publisher's perspective, the question is how can subscription become a more profitable option that will facilitate cash-flow and contribute towards increasing sustainability? While there is no simple, quick-fix answer a few initiatives are likely to go a long way towards those goals. These include forming strategic partnerships to offer more benefits, focusing on achieving a higher retention of subscribers – perhaps by rewarding long-term subscribers and ensuring the magazine is a quality product with relevant, intelligent content.

But perhaps the biggest problem is how to build a decent subscription base – one that not only increases audience reach but also is not defined by geographic boundaries. The right brand extensions such as events can help. But, remember, every magazine is different so it is not a case of one size fits all. Do your research, analyse facts and figures, but ultimately you must decide which model will best suit your audience.

Good Housekeeping – a worldwide success story

- **Established:** 1922
- **Cover price:** £4.30
- **Audience demographic:** 72% ABC1, female aged 35+
- **Brand extensions include:** digital edition, website, Good Housekeeping Institute, cookery books and events

First launched in the States in 1885 by William Randolf Hearst, *Good Housekeeping* (Figure 3.2), one of the first examples of international publishing, was a phenomenal success from the start. By 1900 it had opened the pioneering Good Housekeeping Institute – its first brand extension and an innovation in consumer product testing. No doubt this led to the magazine achieving a circulation of 300,000 by 1911, when it was bought by the Hearst Corporation. In March 1922, shortly after the First World War, the magazine's reach became international when Hearst created a British edition reflecting similar editorial values.

Often launches are as much about timing as the magazine's content, and in the UK times were changing radically for women following the war, both socially and economically. By then many were unable to afford domestic staff. Consequently, the middle-classes had limited experience and were lacking skills in housekeeping – work previously undertaken by servants. At the same time household appliances were fast emerging.

Thus, these economic and social factors presented an opportunity for a quality magazine aimed at middle-class women thirsty for knowledge of domestic matters. Therefore, it is not surprising that the UK launch issue – which had a print run of 150,000 – sold out, and by the June issue *Good Housekeeping* was making a profit. Two years later in 1924, *Good Housekeeping* would launch the Good Housekeeping Institute. With facilities, such as a modern kitchen, bathroom, launch and research laboratory as well as an office and a terrace for photography, the Institute went on to

FIGURE 3.2 *Good Housekeeping* cover, courtesy of *Good Housekeeping*

become the rubber stamp of quality for household goods – covert approval for manufacturers of today's appliances.

Now approaching its centenary in the UK, *Good Housekeeping* has retained its reputation for trusted reviews and high-quality content.

At the time of writing this book, the magazine currently has a combined average, ABC-certified circulation of 454,697, taken from *Good Housekeeping*'s ABC certificate (July–December 2016) published on BRAD Insight. This includes around 192,064 print subscribers and 6,361 digital copy sales. The media pack states a readership of around 1.5 million, mostly females aged 25–54 of whom 72% are ABC1 and have a median age of 35.

Clearly its brand reach is extensive with standalone products, books, services and standalone magazines designed to expand its audience reach – all of which have been built on a reputation of trust and quality.

Today, despite a general downturn in lifestyle titles, *Good Housekeeping*'s circulation is experiencing a growth cycle with figures not far off its 2006 peak of 475,000. ABC figures (*Good Housekeeping*, 2017b) reveal there have been a few pits and troughs circulation-wise over the past 17 years, which culminated in a slump in 2014 when it dipped below 400,000.

Over the years, editorial pillars have expanded to widen audience engagement. These include beauty, consumer advice, fashion, food, health, homes, gardens and real-life. There is also a section on money, although, in my opinion, this could be expanded as their target reader – my age group – are taking a more active role in securing their financial futures. The articles are informative, educational and relevant.

Clearly content has evolved with the times, aligns with brand values and, most importantly, is reader-orientated. Hearst states the brand "gives the user the key tools to make better choices about every aspect of her life" and depicts the *Good Housekeeping* reader as: "confident, informed, discerning, organised and up-to-date".

So how has the brand achieved a global audience and achieved sustainability in such a precarious climate for lifestyle titles? *Good Housekeeping*'s award-winning Editorial Director Lindsay Nicholson (from 1999 to 2017) says it's the Good Housekeeping Institute that makes the brand such a formidable rival to similar titles.

> What I think sets us apart from most other magazines is that we have a bricks and mortar proposition, we carry out our own research and have done for 93 years. I think it is that bizarrely, although there is a whole universe of infinite knowledge available on our smart phones now. There is also a lot of fake news so actual, accredited information, checkable verifiable facts are in increasingly short supply – therefore, the market conditions as they are favour us.

So how did this phenomenal testing lab – whose seal of approval is sought by some of the biggest names in household items – evolve? Lindsay tells how fate played a part. When the magazine launched in the UK in 1922 the editor, James McPeake, had to sail back and forth on the Queen Mary to New York so he could show William Randolf Hearst the page proofs. On one such voyage he was taken ill with appendicitis and died on board. His replacement was Alice Maud Head, who despite never having edited a magazine before took the reins and promptly established the Good Housekeeping Institute.

Clearly Alice understood what her readers wanted and needed. Today the Institute continues to build on its success. Lindsay feels this is because the Institute's core DNA is still about empowering women as it did in the 1920s.

> Women were having to run their own households in the 1920s as the servant class did not want to go back into living in people's homes and only having every other Sunday afternoon off. In the beginning, *Good Housekeeping* was based on women having to run their own homes when they had never done it before. This is what I have wanted to do for slightly different reasons, because women are in the same situation today. More are working outside of the home than ever before, but they still want their homes to be comfortable, welcoming places, to put food on the table and need to manage their finances. What I am most proud of is the evolution of that first principle. It is very important to understand what the thread of DNA that runs through it is and to interpret it for the current day.

It is perhaps not surprising that when asked which has been her most successful audience engagement strategies Lindsay cites product testing.

> In terms of audience engagement, I suppose the most radical thing I have done is test everything. We tested vibrators, on the grounds of beg forgiveness rather than ask permission. I didn't tell any of my bosses in the UK or US that I was doing that. The first they knew of our test was when it popped up on the website in the US.

Lindsay admits her counterparts in the US were very shocked, particularly as the US edition has a slightly different brand identity.

> But in terms of saying 'actually, because what we are not about is making cupcakes and polishing the candelabra – we are about real life, making good decisions and vibrators come into that' it went a long way to demonstrate what we are about now. Because today's woman has to juggle everything … including her sex life.

While other brand extensions have played a key part in increasing audience engagement, Lindsay reveals it has been the *Good Housekeeping* cookery books that have proved the most influential.

> There is barely a celebrity chef that has been interviewed who hasn't said that at some point part of their food education has come from the *Good Housekeeping* cookery books, so I would say in terms of brand influence that is the most important. But in terms of revenue opportunities and future proofing our accreditation schemes – the commercial partnerships in the GH Institute – is a whole business that on its own makes more than most other magazines make even without the print edition.

Worldwide the title currently researches around 5 million readers including in the US where the circulation is 4.25 million as well as Russia, Uzbekistan, South Africa and the Philippines. Rather than using the traditional syndication model, Hearst has set up the Global Nexus of *Good Housekeeping* so all the content produced in the UK and US all goes into a big pot; all of the editions can take from it what they want.

"We have just had a very successful collaboration with US *Good Housekeeping* who did a fashion shoot with Prince Harry's girlfriend Meghan Markle," says Lindsay. "We picked that up and ran it in the last issue (June 2017) and generated a generous amount of PR. Again, slightly surprising for what image people might have of our magazine."

Unsurprisingly – and thankfully – Lindsay is not among those saying print is dead.

> Anyone who says print is dead well, they forgot to tell us. Last ABC figures: *Good Housekeeping*'s circulation was up 10%. While I would be surprised if we were up 10% every year for the next five years, I would expect it to increase. I am heading for 500,000.

And I suspect *Good Housekeeping* will achieve that goal. This magazine is one of the few lifestyle titles that understands what its readers want and produces relevant, quality content. Yes, I'm a big fan and often cite its contents to my students when talking about writing for your audience.

However, as this book goes to press, it was announced in the October 2017 issue of *Good Housekeeping* that the executive editor, Michelle Hather, has taken over the reins from Lindsay. A sad loss for the magazine as I feel Lindsay is a hard act to follow, but of course I wish Michelle every success in her new role.

Innovation sustains the *Radio Times*

- **Established:** 1923
- **Cover price:** £2.50
- **Audience demographic:** 66% ABC1, 44% AB with 50/50 gender split
- **Brand extensions include:** digital edition, website, Radio Times Festival, Radio Times Discover TV

Once a household name, it seems the *Radio Times* – or *RT* as it is affectionately known – like many other titles has suffered a dramatic circulation drop over the past 20 years. In 1997 its total average circulation was 1,400,270, but at the time of writing, the weekly title achieved sales of 684,922 (July to December 2016) of which 266,000 are subscribers, and it maintains a readership of more than 2 million (*Radio Times*, 2017). By today's standards those figures are considered healthy.

So how has the magazine's reach changed and what strategies have the brand's publisher, Immediate Media, employed to ensure sustainability?

Before examining such strategies, it is crucial to first consider *RT*'s background. Initially the magazine was published by the BBC, until the corporation sold off 34 of its titles to Immediate Media in 2011 in a somewhat complex deal. *RT* was the first UK guide to radio and television in an age before the deregulation of UK TV listings and the subsequent set-up of multiple channels. Its circulation peaked in the 1950s with sales of nearly 9 million copies (Sweney, 2016).

In today's digital age, despite numerous competitors, it remains the third most popular paid-for magazine, and in 2016 it won Media Brand of the Year in the British Media Awards. On Immediate's website, under 'Key Facts', the publisher cites *RT* as "the most profitable UK magazine media brand". Yet sales and advertising aren't sufficient to sustain even this well-loved title. Most magazine readers, across all sectors, now want to engage on a deeper level; for editorial teams that means not only added-value content but also events and other engagement strategies. Hence the explosion of brand extensions across the board, at which *RT* has excelled. Yet unlike some lifestyle titles, *RT*'s team focus on innovation and excellence as opposed to mass production.

Perhaps its most promising initiative is The Radio Times Festival, an annual event which began in 2015. Why? Because, generally, while events don't make the publisher much in terms of profits, the value come in the form of engagement and raising the title's profile. In the 2017 event *RT* partnered with the BFI (British Film Institute) to produce "the UK's largest and most prestigious television festival" (BFI & Radio Times Television Festival), featuring some of the biggest names in television including Peter Capaldi and Thandie Newton.

It is initiatives such as these that go a long way to extending brand reach and audience engagement, which is perhaps why *Radio Times* remains one of the nation's favourite TV guides.

In the US *Writer's Digest* leads the way

- **Established:** 1920
- **Cover price:** US$6.99
- **Audience demographic:** ABC1 equivalent with 60% being college graduates and 70/30 female/male split
- **Brand extensions include:** digital edition, website, competitions, writing workshops and annual writer's conference

This American, bi-monthly specialist magazine (Figures 3.3 and 3.4) knows its audience and seems to have accurately assessed what readers need. In-depth analysis shows that *Writer's Digest* is not only inexhaustible in its outputs, but also actively engages readers with relevant brand extensions, appealing to writers of all levels regardless of age – a strategy that is clearly working and I suspect its British counterparts could learn much from this prolific title.

Evidence of the brand's audience reach is clearly documented in its media kit (*Writer's Digest*, 2016), which cites a circulation of 69,000, a strong iPad edition, a prolific social media following, successful eNewsletters with more than 200,000 subscribers, and a website with 1 million users each month. It also states that one of the latest brand extensions – the Writer's Digest Conference – attracts more than 800 attendees.

Having previously worked on *Writers' Forum* magazine for many years I'm curious as to why this title is so successful – and why the two leading UK writing titles can't quite achieve an equivalent footing. To investigate this I have compiled

48 Audience engagement

FIGURE 3.3 *Writer's Digest* print cover, courtesy of *Writer's Digest*

Table 3.2 to offer a comparison snapshot and identify differentials between the three brands.

The table shows there are similarities in all three titles. When looking at audience demographics it's clear that age ranges are similar, as are the male/female ratios. Looking at the UK market leader, *Writing Magazine*, we can see from the table it has

FIGURE 3.4 *Writer's Digest* iPad image, courtesy of *Writer's Digest*

an overall brand reach of approximately 102,000. Its editorial pillars are relevant, as are the brand extensions which focus on helping writers achieve their goals with courses, competitions and newsletters.

Yet, in terms of offering relevant brand extensions *Writer's Digest* stands out, although *Writing Magazine* comes a close second. The number of writing courses, groups and writers in the UK suggests that both the *Writing Magazine* and *Writer's*

TABLE 3.2 Comparison of three writing titles*

	Writer's Digest	Writing Magazine	Writers' Forum
Audience demographic	• More than 60% college graduates • Average age 50+ • 70/30 male/female ratio	• ABC1 • Mostly aged 45+ • 79/21 male/female ratio	• ABC1 • aged 25–60 • 80/20 male/female ratio
Total brand reach	> 1,000,000	102,516	21,738
Print circulation	69,000	23,000	18,000
Social media engagement	893,000	33,935	3,738
Brand extensions	Print/digital editions, eNewsletters (various), workshops, numerous writing competitions including self-publishing, an annual writers' conference and shop	Print/digital editions, eNewsletter, workshops/courses, bookshop, competitions for short stories and poetry	Print and digital edition, writing competitions for short stories and poetry

*All figures taken from each of the respective title's media kits and their social media sites.

Forum titles have unfulfilled potential. This is particularly true for *Writers' Forum*, which as the table shows is lagging behind its rival in terms of content provision, audience engagement and brand extensions.

Writer's Digest's editorial director, Jessica Strawser, attributes the magazine's success partly to the team all being writers.

> I think a big part of it is that our editorial team *is* our audience—and walking the walk speaks volumes to our readers. Our poetry editor, Robert Lee Brewer, has published collections with Press 53 and draws hundreds of poets to participate in his challenges on the Poetic Asides blog; our online editor, Brian A. Klems, leveraged his humorous parenting blog into a successful essay book, *Oh Boy, You're Having a Girl*; our managing editor, Tyler Moss, is a freelance writer who has placed work with outlets ranging from Salon to *Conde Nast Traveler*; and in March 2017 my debut novel, *Almost Missed You*, released in hardcover from St. Martin's Press. Engagement, then, comes naturally.

When asked which of their brand extensions was the most successful, unsurprisingly Jessica cites *WD*'s events programme. "We've offered conferences for quite a while but at first the format was not consistent," reveals Jessica adding that one might be in January, the next year's in May and so on, all held at different venues.

> In recent years, we've branded the *Writer's Digest* Annual Conference by sticking with key venues in Midtown Manhattan and settling in to an early to mid-August time frame, nearly tripling the size of the event (to almost 1,000 writers and industry pros in 2016, which we're outpacing so far in 2017) with better and better programming year over year. Our pitch slam draws upwards of 60 literary agents ready to meet with writers face-to-face, keynotes this year are heavy-hitters Lisa Scottoline, Richard Russo and David Levithan. We also offer occasional online conferences (via writersdigestuniversity.com) and are in our second consecutive year of a West Coast event exclusively for novel writers: The 2017 *Writer's Digest* Novel Writing Conference will be held in Pasadena, California, the last weekend of October.

Jessica says the biggest lesson from her readers was that it is more of a conversation.

> They give us as much as we give them. Some of our favourite features of the year are compilations for which we'll pose a question to our audience and collect the responses. Our most recent one, in which writers weighed in as to how their day jobs fuel their creative lives, was filled with good humour, optimism, thoughtful perspectives, and quite a lot of talent.

Despite these aspects plus the obvious differentials between the US's and the UK's population, there appears to be one crucial factor that makes it so successful – a stronger connection between *Writer's Digest* and its audience. To me this intimates a

52 Audience engagement

deeper understanding of what the reader needs and being able to bridge the gap with provision in terms of content, advice and practical help.

Summary

Audience engagement is a hot topic and something many publishers constantly agonise over. There are some good lessons to be learned from each of the magazines featured in this chapter. For me, the most crucial lesson is understanding readers and having a deeper connection with them. This makes all the difference, because one feeds the other. Without understanding there is little real connection.

We have also seen with *Radio Times* and *Writer's Digest* how brand extensions not only gain engagement but also sustain it by forging a stronger connection between the editorial team and their readers. I know from experience that meeting the readers always increases brand loyalty, but taking that a step further by developing events around content or an annual conference will pay dividends, as demonstrated by these two thriving magazines.

But what of those on a limited budget with small teams? This is where the power of a plus one comes in to play. Being creative and pairing up with a strategy partner will open up your options. Often the more challenging the lack of resources the more creative editors have to become – and that is where true innovation unfolds. As my former publisher used to say, *there is always a way forward, it is up to you to think of it.*

INDUSTRY PERSPECTIVES

Rob Attar, the award-winning editor of *BBC History Magazine* (Figure 3.5), is passionate about his readers. During his time on the title there has been a massive growth in circulation – at a time when many titles are in sharp decline.

He reveals the key to widening audience participation, engaging his readers, and explains why 'no' is sometimes the best answer ...

My proudest achievement with BBC History Magazine *has to be growing our circulation from just over 50,000 around a decade ago to almost 100,000 now – at a time when the magazine industry has largely been struggling. This has obviously been a collaborative effort, of which I'm only one part.*

There are several possible reasons and I suspect that it's a combination of all of them.

Specialist interest magazines have generally performed well over the past few years and especially current affairs titles, which is an area we're loosely connected to. Meanwhile, there has been a growing interest in popular history more generally, spurred on by TV dramas, films, books, anniversaries, a desire to understand a rapidly changing world and a desire to escape from a frequently depressing world. At the same time, I believe the magazine has become a stronger proposition in editorial and design terms as we've gradually refined every aspect of it. And though I'm not always directly involved in this, we've clearly operated very successful marketing strategies.

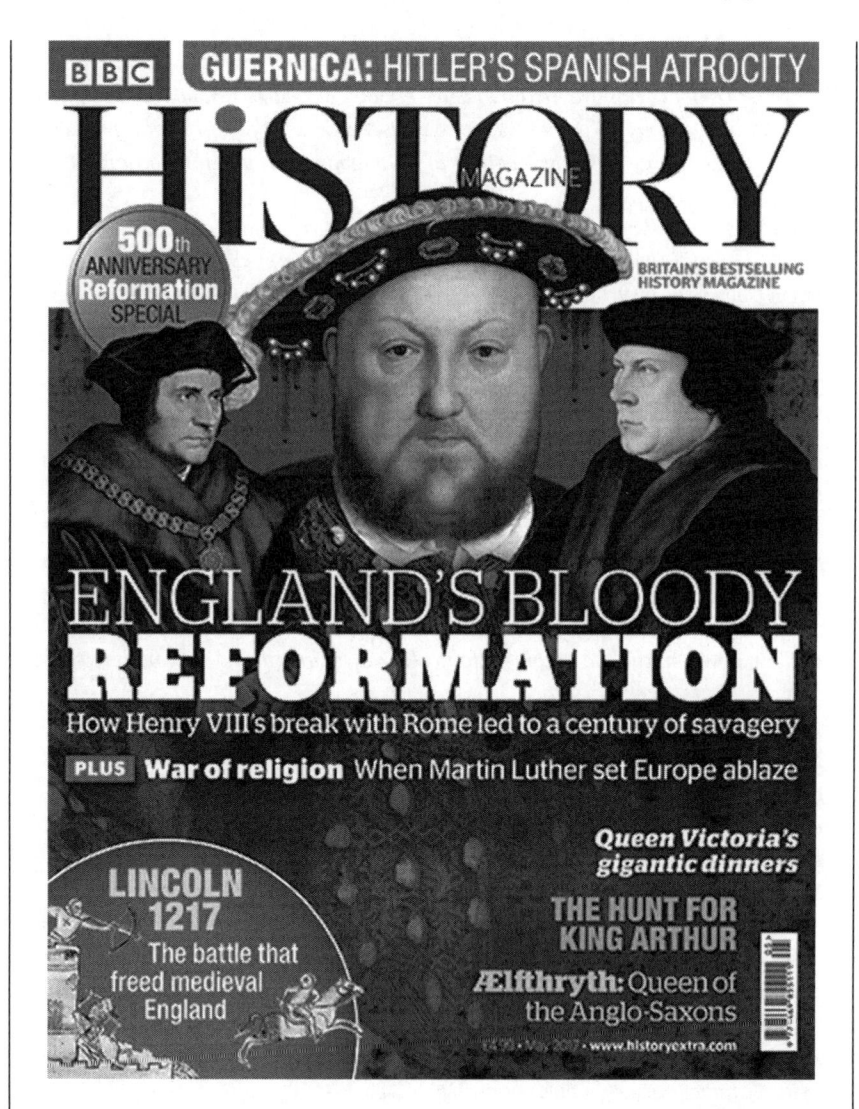

FIGURE 3.5 *BBC History Magazine cover, courtesy of BBC History Magazine*

The extensive growth in circulation has also coincided with the launch of our podcast a decade ago, and I don't believe that this is entirely a coincidence. With the global distribution possibilities of iTunes and other podcast sites, we have been able to take the brand to a large audience of history enthusiasts who either didn't know about the magazine or would not have wanted to pay for this kind of content – at least at first.

We've grown a loyal podcast audience of tens of thousands, and as they've become more acquainted with what we do, many have decided to start buying the magazine as well. Essentially it has been a brilliant shop window for our print and digital products.

Is reader feedback important? Of course, but while I don't think an individual piece of reader feedback has ever had a massive impact, as a collective our readers have shaped many things we do. We've made decisions on keeping or replacing regular sections based partly on reader feedback and our readers certainly have an impact on the topics we cover.

Much of our feedback still comes through letters to the editor – although these are typically emails now. We do also have a fair amount of social media interaction and run reader surveys every year or two. Over the years we've had some lovely letters from readers telling us how much they enjoy the magazine and what it means to them. There was one who told me how it enlivened his days while posted on a submarine for weeks on end and a few for whom it helped them get through periods of sickness.

Generally, the most entertaining feedback is of a more critical variety. I had a letter recently complaining about my 'under chin' in my editor's photo, which was quite a memorable comment.

Like many titles, we have extended our brand to widen audience reach and participation. Perhaps one of the most successful, albeit demanding, extensions has been our History Weekend events. These have been a major departure for us and taken up a fair amount of time and resources. We're working on the fifth iteration of these now and they've become a fantastic way of interacting with both readers and contributors in a live setting.

Aside from podcasting, our most successful innovation has probably been the History Extra website. We have had a website for the past 15 years or so, but it was only around three or four years ago that we decided to invest in a full-time website editor and make it into a genuine content platform rather than just an accompaniment to the magazine. Since then our traffic has rocketed, accompanied by a huge growth in social media and a much more impressive digital brand more generally.

In editorial offices budgets are always an issue, but if they weren't what would I change? On a rather prosaic level, I would like to improve the paper stock and print quality of the magazine. We've recently launched a new bi-monthly title, BBC World Histories, which is on a much higher quality paper and the difference is noticeable. However, it's obviously more expensive to produce, meaning that that magazine costs £2 more than our regular title.

Another thing I'd love to be able to do is produce more history videos, as we've still not made many strides there. Again, to do this well requires a lot of time and resources, and so may need additional investment.

Working on a magazine there is always something new to learn and during my career I have learned many lessons, but the best advice came from my boss, who I've worked with for the past 13 years. He gave me a simple, but useful, piece of advice that still pops up in my mind quite often, which was: 'just say no'. I'm generally quite an accommodating person and, especially at first, I did find it hard rejecting the wealth of feature pitches, PR advances and other suggestions that come our way.

But in the end what matters is what is best for the readers and if I, as the editor, don't think that something is going to work for them, there's no point agonising over it.

AUDIENCE ENGAGEMENT ACTION PLAN

A focus on your audience is essential – and be objective. Key questions to ask are what do readers need from the magazine and how might your team fulfil that need? That is your starting point from which to develop additional editorial pillars and relevant brand extensions.

Take the following five steps to build a feasible action plan.

1. First evaluate your competitors; look at what they are doing well and initiatives that have failed.
2. Pinpoint any gaps in your rivals' provision – particularly in terms of brand extensions.
3. Now identify three potential opportunities.
4. Research, cost and evaluate the feasibility of those opportunities.
5. Develop an action plan to implement the most suitable opportunity based on research undertaken and what is realistically achievable with your resources.

Don't forget to include a clear timeframe and set a realistic budget. And, last, do measure its success to ascertain the ROI.

Bibliography

BFI & Radio Times Television Festival. 2017. www.bfi.org.uk/radiotimestvfest accessed 17 April 2017.

BRAD. 2017. *Radio Times*. BRAD Insight. https://brad.mediatel.co.uk/profile/press/3908#circulation accessed 17 April 2017.

Good Housekeeping. 2011. The History of the Good Housekeeping Seal. www.goodhousekeeping.com/institute/about-the-institute/a16509/good-housekeeping-seal-history/ accessed 10 April 2017

Good Housekeeping. 2017a. 90 Years of the Good Housekeeping Institute. https://www.goodhousekeeping.co.uk/institute/the-institute/history-of-the-ghi accessed 10 April 2017.

Good Housekeeping 2017b. Media Pack. BRAD Insight. http://tool.bradinsight.com.libezproxy.bournemouth.ac.uk/brad/Profile/Title/a0HD000000B2bVQMAZ accessed (through Bournemouth University Library) 10 April 2017.

Immediate Media Co. 2017. *Radio Times*, Key Facts. www.immediate.co.uk/business-division/radiotimes/ accessed 17 April 2017.

Magzter. 2017. Publisher Presentation. https://www.magzter.com/publisher accessed 14 April 2017.

Radio Times. 2017. Media Kit. Hearst. www.immediate.co.uk/business-division/radiotimes/ accessed 17 April 2017.

Sweney, M. 2016. Radio Times likely to be bought by German Media Group. *The Guardian*. https://www.theguardian.com/media/2016/dec/19/radio-times-german-publisher-hubert-burda-bbc-worldwide-top-gear accessed 17 April 2017.

Writer's Digest. 2016. Media Kit. www.writersdigest.com/wp-content/uploads/WD-MEDIA-16r1.pdf accessed 18 April 2017.
Writer's Digest. 2017. www.writersdigest.com/ accessed 18 April 2017.
Writers Online. 2017. *Writing Magazine.* https://www.writers-online.co.uk/ accessed 18 April 2017.
Writing Magazine. 2017. Media Kit. https://www.writers-online.co.uk/images/files/Writing%20Magazine%20Media%20Pack%202016%20-%20Small%20file%20size.pdf accessed 18 April 2017.

4

A SUCCESSFUL BUSINESS MODEL

Defining success can be difficult, particularly when it comes to publishing. It is not simply a case of profit and loss – as with many businesses – although of course to be sustainable there must be profit. No, there are many facets to a successful magazine – a need for the title, loyal readers, quality content and a passionate editorial team who thrive on innovation.

The right editor is also a must. Magazines are a reflection of the editor in terms of voice, tone and spirit. I have long believed that an editor must love not only his/her magazine, but also the genre. An example of this can be taken from Jessica Strawser, Editorial Director of the US magazine *Writer's Digest*, who revealed the secrets of her success in the previous chapter.

Like many editors of successful titles, Jessica understands the necessity of passion and empathy in a team. When questioned on why her title was so successful in terms of circulation, she responded: "I think a big part of it is that our editorial team is our audience – and walking the walk speaks volumes to our readers." This reinforces my long-held belief. From the in-depth analysis of *Writer's Digest*, in Chapter 3, it is clear that this editor and her team are passionate about writing and helping writers achieve their goals, thereby reinforcing the point that passion and innovation play a vital role in a publication's potential for success.

However, with passion should come sound business acumen, so in this chapter we will explore successful business strategies starting with cash-flow. Time Inc. UK's *List for Life* launch in 2016 from its Innovation Lab as an online start-up will also be evaluated.

Balancing cash-flow

As every publisher knows, achieving balance in terms of cash-flow is often the difference between success and failure. The biggest challenge is to generate sufficient revenue to sustain the business and cover all expenditure – from salaries, printing, distribution and marketing to finance, professional fees and services.

Yet generating revenue is only part of the problem. Many new start-ups, as well as established magazines, have gone under because of cash-flow. Sometimes this is due to incorrect financial forecasting, unforeseen expenditure, insufficient income or simply because monies owed take too long to come in. More often than not, it is the latter.

Here are *six* tactics you can use to minimise poor cash-flow:

1. **Encourage prepayment:** offer incentives for prepayment on advertising sales space.
2. **Sell a series:** when selling advertising space, ensure your sales team always try to get series bookings with some prepayment.
3. **Strong subscription sales:** magazine subscribers pay in advance, which equals cash in the bank.
4. **Timely payments:** have systems so payments come in promptly, and don't delay dealing with bad debts.
5. **Avoid signing up to income eaters:** i.e. those monthly payments for those additional extras that aren't essential.
6. **Keep it lean:** monitor expenditure and when necessary be prepared to make cuts.

Keeping regular track of accounts helps, but ultimately it is about generating sufficient income, keeping outgoings lean and being strict with slow payees. Setting clear terms and conditions for any services or advertising sales your company provides is crucial; do offer a small incentive for early settlement – say a 5% discount – if settled within seven days. Also, keep an eye out for those slow payers whose business may be in trouble; in such instances be wary of letting them run up more debt. If selling smaller scale adverts (under a ¼ page) then it is advisable to insist on prepayment.

If cash-flow is still tight after taking these measures, then address the issue sooner rather than later by considering refinancing options or an extended overdraft. After that it might be time to re-examine your business model.

Achieving a successful model

I am often asked what a successful business model looks like, but there is no one-size-fits-all when it comes to the magazine publishing business. The key to developing a successful business may depend on many variants, such as the genre, type of magazine, market position and distribution model. However, there is one common denominator – the publisher's ability to produce a strong business plan. A business plan is after all akin to having a map for the journey because, to arrive at your destination, you first need to identify the journey's end goal, and then plan how to get there.

But what happens if the model isn't working? First, don't make rash decisions or be too quick to adopt new strategies. The first step is to undertake an in-depth analysis, evaluating both good and poor performances. Only when such an analysis has been done should work begin on restructuring the business model or plan. Two primary areas to focus on should be income and audience engagement, as outlined in Table 4.1. Evaluating the points set out in Table 4.1 is a good starting point as these factors clearly help you to identify what is working and what is not.

For example, during my time as deputy editor on *Writer's Forum* profits started to decline after the title was launched on the newsstands. Our first plan of action was to increase the cost of our advertising space by 20%. The rationale was two-fold. First, it placed a higher value on space sold; second, it provided additional funds with which to reinvest in a mini-relaunch to increase brand engagement. After initial groans from our media buyers advertising sales began to increase. At the same time, we invested in distribution strategies and in audience research with a reader survey – the data obtained from this was intended to help relaunch the magazine.

Every title suffers stagnation or a period of decline. Often, if the right strategies are employed, it can recover and become stronger as a result. A key lesson for us was to ensure that the advertising rates reflected the profile we were aiming for with *Writer's Forum*, and also that we strove to produce relevant content for our readers. As a result the magazine began sponsoring writing festivals both in the UK and overseas – then including festivals in the distribution strategy with additional copies supplied. Subsequently the title grew to a healthy circulation of just over 25,000 with around 5,000 subscribers.

However, if it's necessary to redevelop your business strategy or plan I would suggest simplifying it by utilising a Business Canvas Model, first developed by Osterwalder and Pigner (2010). The original model uses the following nine key elements:

1. Key partners
2. Key activities
3. Value proposition
4. Customer relations
5. Customer segments

TABLE 4.1 Primary areas of focus

Income	Audience engagement
• Is the current income sufficient to cover expenditure?	• Current level of engagement.
• Profit margin percentage, if any?	• Pattern of engagement in the past two years.
• Can prices (advertising sales, cover price, etc.) be increased?	• Factors responsible for the change – such as launch of new rival magazine.
• How many profitable revenue streams?	• Potential opportunities for increasing engagement, e.g. stronger editor/ revised distribution strategy?
• Can these streams be increased, and if so how?	• Is a brand relaunch necessary?

60 A successful business model

6. Key resources
7. Channels
8. Cost structure
9. Revenue streams

Keeping the model to one page means it is simple and effective – making it relatively easy to identify those elements that aren't performing and therefore need attention. But, although this model is a great starting point it doesn't cover those unique aspects of magazine publishing, as I discovered when mentoring an MA student on a publishing course who had to develop a Business Canvas Model for her new publishing concept. Therefore, I have come up with my own interpretation, a model which I have called the Magazine Publishing Strategic Quadrant, as shown in Figure 4.1.

This model is built on what I deem to be the four pillars of magazine publishing. These are:

1. Brand concept and development
2. Target audience and potential reach
3. Finance and revenue streams
4. Distribution: strategies and channels.

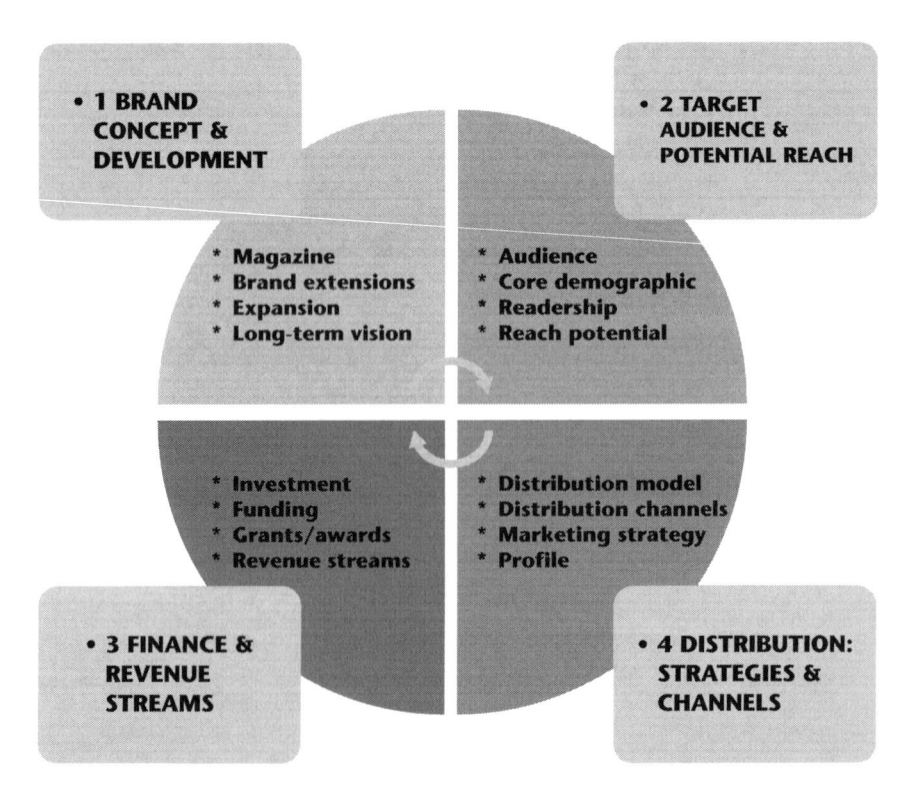

- **1 BRAND CONCEPT & DEVELOPMENT**
  * Magazine
  * Brand extensions
  * Expansion
  * Long-term vision

- **2 TARGET AUDIENCE & POTENTIAL REACH**
  * Audience
  * Core demographic
  * Readership
  * Reach potential

- **3 FINANCE & REVENUE STREAMS**
  * Investment
  * Funding
  * Grants/awards
  * Revenue streams

- **4 DISTRIBUTION: STRATEGIES & CHANNELS**
  * Distribution model
  * Distribution channels
  * Marketing strategy
  * Profile

FIGURE 4.1 The Magazine Publishing Strategic Quadrant, author's own model

Why does a quadrant work better than the Business Canvas Model? Because it simplifies content down into those four pillars. This allows publishers starting out to clearly map their journey, or those with an existing map and an already established magazine to make adjustments, identifying potential weaknesses and strengths, then developing action plans to address key problems or maximise opportunities.

However, I have not included analysis of potential rivals in these four pillars, and, no, this is not an oversight. While such an analysis is important at the initial concept stage to evaluate threats such as market saturation, it is less so with established magazines, because although rival titles may be deemed the core problem in most situations, this is not the case here. Competitors will have usually grown as a result of weaknesses within your title – be it with the product or the audience. Therefore, the answer usually lies in one of the four quadrants – it is usually either the concept or audience. Get the brand right, find the relevant audience and focus on innovation.

Innovative strategies

In this digital age, the traditional model of magazine publishing may have changed dramatically, but one thing hasn't: the need for quality content presented in an imaginative format. Technology has provided the means for such creative designs as well as new ways to bring editorial alive, with vivid layouts plus supporting audio and video too. Now publishers have the tools to innovate, but it seems that few are willing to take a risk on untrodden paths; instead many opt for a safe model or follow rival titles, resulting in stagnation in development.

One publisher, Time Inc. UK, broke the mould when it set up its Innovation Lab (aka The Lab) from which it launched *List for Life*, aimed at 18–34-year-olds, at the start of 2016. Later that year The Lab won the Association of Online Publishers' Digital Design/Product Development Team of the Year award. The publisher's strategy was to keep things simple and fluid.

Talking to me during an interview for *InPublishing* magazine, Keith Walker, digital director of Time Inc. UK's innovation group, explained that The Lab is "dedicated to a lean structure, rapid development, or rejection, and is not limited to traditional media products".

So how is such innovation possible on a lean budget? The answer is by employing low cost, enthusiastic millennials and giving them control.

While this strategy might fill some with horror, I have seen first-hand during my time at Southampton Solent University how it can work. Why? Because when those just starting out have yet to learn the lessons of failure, they are more willing to try out the seemingly impossible. Students or young entrepreneurs will focus on creativity and ignore doubts of *it can't work*. This is mostly because once a career is established the fear of failure can paralyse many – resulting in stagnation, or worse still, failure. Therefore, playing safe is often the most favoured option. Hence millennials are more likely to experiment, which is presumably why Time Inc. UK set up The Lab and invested in new talent.

During the interview Keith revealed Time Inc. UK's formula for making innovation affordable.

> We use our insight to identify an opportunity and this is then backed up by market research. This data informs the prototype which is put out into the 'real world' to test how it performs. The test cycles only last between two days and two weeks so we can either learn fast or fail fast.

He explained that more than 60 products have been tested and evaluated by The Lab to date. Out of these, only six have passed the rigid test criteria by being tested in the 'real world' and therefore are deemed more likely to succeed.

> Those six products are the *NME Daily* app, *Look's Fashion Drop*, *Now's Gossip Cam*, *Powder*, *List for Life* and the newly launched *Live-Smart* site. Some of these products are being incubated before being released to the wider business and managed outside of the Lab and some are being developed into version two and will be evolving in the near future.

A year on and *List for Life* is now part of *Look* magazine after being merged in July 2016 (see Figure 4.2). Ironically it was merged just as The Lab won a product development award and a few months after my article. In September 2016, a Time Inc. UK press release announces that 'Look Grows Reach with New Brand Strategy'. It states:

> Young women's fashion and beauty brand *LOOK* today reveals a new strategy that will grow the title's influence with a refreshed approach to content curation, digital distribution and live events, opening up new opportunities for commercial partners.
>
> Streamlining the brand proposition and reflecting the key interests of the *LOOK* audience, four content pillars – LOOK Fashion, LOOK Fit, LOOK Life and LOOK Beauty – will run across LOOK.CO.UK, the print product, social and experiential.
>
> Content will be curated by the *LOOK* editorial team and a network of over 100 'LOOK Influencers' comprised of bloggers and vloggers across the Fashion, Beauty, Life and Fit content channels. The *LOOK* audience will also be offered opportunities to become an influencer via user generated content.
>
> LOOK Life will help millennials navigate work and life, sharing inspirational stories, life-hacks and career advice. LOOK Fit will keep the audience up-to-speed on the latest in fitness fashion, women's health and workout routines, while the Fashion and Beauty channels will keep them on trend, sharing tips, tricks and inspiration.

The sell is a good one, but it does little to disguise the fact that this is a bid to increase a flagging circulation, which according to BRAD (2017d) has fallen from over

List for Life timeline

List for Life

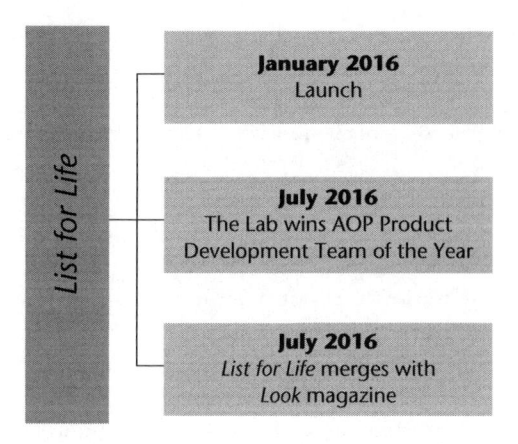

- **January 2016** — Launch
- **July 2016** — The Lab wins AOP Product Development Team of the Year
- **July 2016** — *List for Life* merges with *Look* magazine

FIGURE 4.2 *List for Life*'s timeline

300,000 in 2008 to just below 100,000. In the press release, Paul Cheal, group managing director at Time Inc. UK, gives the following rationale:

> This strategy will bring our partners closer to the audience they want to connect with. Live events will bring the brand to life and LOOK will reach a bigger audience than ever before through its new channel strategy including an influencer network contributing and promoting content.

Time will tell as to whether the latest initiative with *Look* magazine will work as there is some element of market saturation here. But this merger is a shame because in my opinion *List for Life* was a good product, but perhaps it might have been stronger if aimed at a slightly older audience. It seems a case of good product but wrong audience.

Multiple revenue streams and sustainability

Previously advertising and copy sales were the key streams of a magazine's income. Today, with falling advertising sales and a decrease in many titles' circulation combined with rising business expenditure this is no longer sufficient to sustain a title. Hence publishers and editors need to be both innovative and strategic to develop multiple income streams.

As previously stated, cash-flow is also an important consideration. Therefore, if some of a title's revenue streams can be developed as either immediate-payment or pay-in-advance, then cash-flow will be less of a problem.

Typical revenue streams for a magazine are likely to include some or all of the following:

- **Brand extensions:** such as digital editions, sister publications, books, events, conferences, courses, festivals, etc.

- **Advertising sales:** a good strategy is to sell online and print advertising as one package
- **Sponsorships/promotions and services:** facilitating strategic partnerships or third-party sponsorship of in-house events, plus selling design and content packaging services
- **Copy sales:** digital/print magazines sales on the newsstands, subscriptions, along with in-house back-issue sales and direct sales to partners/advertisers if appropriate
- **Membership schemes:** will not only help cash-flow but are also likely to increase audience reach and reader loyalty
- **Online content/paywalls:** using a micro payment system to sell additional content
- **Product licensing:** from selling the rights to content to be repurposed in an existing title to licensing the brand in terms of merchandising – particularly suited to specialist titles such as gaming magazines.

It is important to remember that every title is different and has its own identity, which must be reflected in the business model. Do not make the mistake of taking a one-size-fits-all approach as this is unlikely to work.

When developing revenue streams, always start as you would with content – with your audience. Focus on what they want and need, then figure out extensions that will provide these. For example, writing, photography and craft magazines are suited to brand extensions that facilitate learning or knowledge such as courses, festivals and conferences, whereas lifestyle and sports titles are more suited to events/merchandise type extensions.

Get the model right and profit will follow so long as you have put the right team in place.

But how do you motivate editorial teams? A strong team is an involved one, both in terms of the genre and audience. That said, giving the editor or key team members a stake in the business can be a very smart move. One example I read recently was of Jack Stack, founder, president and CEO of a US vehicle component manufacturer, SRC Holdings Corporation. Stack, author of *The Great Game of Business* (2013) and *A Stake in the Outcome* (2003), set three conditions for every employee – from the boardroom to the cleaners – thus giving them a stake in the outcome. These were:

1. Learning to read the company's financial statements
2. Being a team worker
3. Getting into the habit of asking: *what could go wrong and what are we going to do when it does?*

This revolutionary strategy has resulted in profits of US$16 million for the company, which in theory proves that by directly involving staff in the actual business, they become more invested. Talking to Peter Carbonara in Forbes about his unique HR strategy, Stack, now 68, reasoned: "Nobody knows the job better than the guy who is doing it."

I think this is a great hiring policy to adopt – one that would be particularly suited to magazines. For most of those working on a magazine it is a passion not just a job. Therefore, giving them a stake in outcomes can surely only benefit the title and the publishing company. In terms of achieving a sustainable title this would surely be a step in the right direction.

Creating relevant brand extensions

Brand extensions are a growing phenomenon in publishing. Publishers are branching out into numerous areas, from social media, online and digital editions to events, conferences, festivals, TV and radio. The opportunities it seems are endless, but are they successful?

Mostly they are, particularly in terms of raising a magazine's profile, although in financial terms events tend to be resource heavy and therefore rarely generate a decent profit. The key to getting brand extensions right is the same as good old-fashioned copy tasting – make it relevant, engaging and informative.

Events and conferences seem to be a key asset when it comes to engaging and widening audience participation. One brand leading the way in reader events is *Country Living*. This monthly title, published by Hearst Magazines UK, currently has a combined total circulation of 184,388 (BRAD, 2017b), a slight decline since peaking at just over 200,000 in 2010 (BRAD, 2017b).

Established in 1985, *Country Living* (Figure 4.3) covers all aspects of life in the countryside from homes, gardening, cookery and craft to farming and community issues, travel and wildlife. More recently it has focused on kitchen table businesses and these have now become an editorial pillar. According to the title's editor-in-chief, Susy Smith, her readers love making things and it was this that led to the launch of Kitchen Table Talent.

"They love reading about the farmers, small-holders, crafters, artisans and small producers who make a living from their passion, especially if they have left behind the rat race to do so," explains Susy. "We run a regular series in the magazine pages, talk about it online and publish books on the subject. As the interest in start-ups has grown, so too has our audience engagement."

Last year the brand launched 'Build a Business' courses and the team are now planning a series of networking events, thus building on the success of the *Country Living* Fairs, which now attract more than 1 million visitors. But do events play a crucial role in the magazine's sustainability and if so how?

Susy reveals that the fairs and other events are an essential part of the title, stating they now have 14 venues.

> Events are crucial to the brand and have been since we launched the first *Country Living* Fair over 25 years ago. Why? Because they give us face to face time with readers and a close relationship with the artisan producers we feature in the magazine and online. They allow us to bring the pages of the magazine to life and are an opportunity to introduce our audience to the other aspects of our

brand up close e.g. the licensing ranges, our dating website, our other publication *Modern Rustic* etc. We have more expansion plans for new venues and a different type of event.

When asked which of the *Country Living* brand extensions have been the most successful Susy cites the range of furniture with dfs.

FIGURE 4.3 *Country Living* cover, courtesy of *Country Living*

It's an ongoing partnership where we work very collaboratively and respect each other's areas of expertise. Both parties benefit financially and the project has allowed dfs to appeal to an audience of 'quality seekers' they were not reaching previously. We currently have plans to develop and grow the range further into new areas.

This continued reader-focused development is most likely what makes *Country Living* a sustainable title at a time when many lifestyle magazines are in sharp decline. Suzy explains,

> It is the fact that we have a true USP that none so far, despite many attempts, have been able to completely replicate. The magazine has an immensely loyal readership with around 80,000 subscribers and an audience of 180,000 in all. This has been fairly constant in the 21 years I have been editor and is growing through online engagement. But we are not complacent and move the content on all the time, thinking of new ways to present our core subjects. Below is my statement for the magazine – and by default, the website, and I think this sums it up:
>
>> *Country Living* Magazine's unique editorial package (from soft furnishings to farming) offers escapism from everyday life, transporting its audience to a world where the sun shines and the grass is always greener.

This USP, she explains, allows the brand remarkable continued successes despite changing dynamics in the market. "We describe our audience as 'Authentics' – already settled in the countryside – or 'Aspirers', waiting to make the break, but they are united in their ultimate goal of 'living the dream'."

From a publishing perspective, Susy admits one of her best lessons has been that editors need a head for business as well as leadership skills and a creative streak.

> Editors used to be regarded as wooly-headed creatives who had no eye for business. In truth, the two things go hand in hand. If you're adept enough to create something an audience wants and market it to them in a way that makes them prepared to pay well for it, you will make money. Magazine editors do this every month with content and use their covers as a marketing tool.
>
> Whilst the internet has turned this upside down by providing endless free content, there is a view that, in the midst of all the online noise, consumers increasingly search for brands they trust.
>
> Magazine brands have built huge trust and loyalty with their readers over many years, so it makes sense to make the most of this trust and move the brand into other products and areas consumers might want to pay for. This provides many more touch points and opportunities to get the brand into the hands of the consumer. *Country Living* has a global TV franchise in *Farmer Wants a Wife*,

licensing ranges that include furniture, stationery and flowers, an online dating site – Country Loving – plus a broad range of events for different audiences.

All of this creates separate revenue streams and means the brand is never solely reliant on newsstand sales.

With such a clearly defined market, strong, valuable content together with a team who are passionate in their interactions with readers developing audience-led brand extensions, *Country Living* will no doubt continue to grow despite these uncertain times. Study the formula, because this magazine is built on sound business practice, together with a passion for the content.

Thus, a key lesson for publishers here is to get the brand extensions right. This is a common denominator among successful titles – all have solid, reader-driven revenue streams. Therefore, to identify such consistencies I have evaluated three titles and their brand extensions across the sectors in Table 4.2. Each magazine targets a specific market sector therefore audience needs and editorial pillars differ significantly. Yet all three publications have a common thread in terms of brand extensions.

As Table 4.2 shows, all three magazines have different editorial priorities, yet despite the difference in sectors, events now form a big part of these titles' brand extensions and attract a high volume of visitors. From personal experience of participating at events with *Writer's Forum* I know how readers value direct interaction with the editor and his/her team. Therefore, it is no surprise that events are proving to be a popular extension.

Done well these can increase engagement thus widening participation, which ultimately leads to healthier sales and a more sustainable publication. However, it is essential that such events must reflect brand values and identity. This invariably means placing additional strain on what – in many cases – is an already stretched editorial team. The moral is proceed with caution, plan meticulously and be prepared to invest – but above all else be authentic.

The impact of targeted distribution

Increasingly specialist publishers are beginning to be more strategic with distribution by incorporating targeted distribution into their business model. Instead of just distributing via newsstand and subscriptions, publishers are now doing deals with specific retail brands.

This is potentially a great move because like all good strategic partnerships it benefits both parties. For the retail outlets stocking specific titles that fit their customer demographic – usually near the till area – this enables them to offer an additional, informative product to their customers. In turn the publisher benefits from directly reaching their intended audience and not having to compete with a mass of titles on a newsstand, where unless they pay a premium the magazine is likely to get lost in a sea of publications.

Examples of such models include retail health outlets such as Holland & Barratt who now sell a range of health-related magazines. Meanwhile farming stores such as

TABLE 4.2 Comparison of brand extensions across three sectors

	Lifestyle: Country Living *Est. 1985*	*B2B:* Drapers *Est. 1887*	*Specialist:* BBC Good Food *Est. 1989*
Publisher	Hearst Magazines UK	Ascential	Immediate Media Company Ltd
Combined circulation*	184,388	9,384	200,234
Readership	758,000	43,500	1,436,000
Frequency	Monthly	Weekly	Monthly
Audience demographics	ABC1 71% 64% women aged 35+	ABC1 50% CEO/owner	ABC1 59% 71% women, average age 45
Platform	Print, digital and online	Print, digital and online	Print, digital and online
Main social media platforms	Facebook, Twitter, Pinterest, Instagram and Google+	Facebook, Twitter, Instagram, Google+, LinkedIn and YouTube	Facebook, Twitter, Instagram, Pinterest and Google+
Key brand extensions	• Country Living Fairs – nine venues nationwide attracting 1 million visitors • Kitchen Table Talent with event days and mentoring scheme • *Country Living* shop with 11 licensed products including stationery, flowers and a range of household items • *Country Living* TV franchise, *Farmer Wants a Wife* • Bookazines	• Events including Drapers Next Generation, Digital Careers Fair and Drapers Operations Forum • Drapers Awards • The Drapers Director's Club	• Events – *BBC Good Food* shows 1.1 million visitors • Books

*Figures taken from BRAD Insight (July–December 2016).

Mole Valley Farmers in the west and south west of England sell a range of farming, country sports and food titles to directly reach their core demographic readers, from farmers to those with an interest in rural pursuits.

But how effective is targeted distribution and does it increase sales sufficiently to achieve a reasonable ROI? Keiron Jefferies, assistant circulation manager at Warners Group Publications Plc, thinks targeted distribution can be an effective means of getting your title in front of its core audience.

> In terms of ROI that can depend on the mix of sales versus the number of stores. The largest cost tends to be the carriage or drop charge to get copies to the store – if you have a few outlets and large sales per store then this can achieve a very reasonable ROI. But if you are selling a few copies in numerous stores then less so – at this point it would possibly be worth continuing only as a marketing or advertising exercise as opposed to a commercial one.

However, Keiron warns that although direct targeted distribution is a good circulation growth strategy, it is not cheaper than selling copies on the newsstand, stating that it works best for specialist/niche titles.

> Model titles to model shops, gardening magazines to garden centres and hobby/craft titles to hobby shops are some of the better options that combine stores with hi-footfall (there are plenty of others) – in most cases though this model tends to work best as an augmentation or in addition to a newstrade distribution.

Many titles have successfully adopted targeted distribution, but only as part of a wider plan. Commercially the best sales strategy is the one that maximises potential sales by placing the title in those key places where your readers shop.

Summary

While this chapter has explored the essential components of a profitable publication and given advice on good business practice, success comes down to two factors – content and the team. First class content is the foundation of any concept and it needs to evolve along with your audience.

When it comes to the team, I cannot stress enough the importance of finding the right editor, someone who has a passion for the subject and the magazine. In turn he or she will want to work alongside likeminded people. A likeminded team who communicate and gels can achieve great things with very few resources. I know, because I have been fortunate enough to have had the privilege of being part of such a team.

Get these two elements in place then focus on the business. Keep an eye on cashflow, develop relevant brand extensions and ensure innovation is rewarded. Never stagnate, because what works today might not work tomorrow.

INDUSTRY PERSPECTIVES

Independent media consultant, trainer and lecturer David Bostock has seen the industry move from print to digital – and more recently back towards paid-for content in both online and offline form.

Below he reveals the biggest challenges magazine publishers face in this tough economic climate and offers an insight into how to overcome them.

As a media consultant, I think the biggest obstacle magazine publishers face is creating viable business models. Publishers must replicate or find substitutes within their market for what was the generic – across the board – cover price and advertising model that worked so well before the 2000s. The past 15 years has really been about trying to change that business model following the technological as well as economic changes.

Those in the B2B market were hit first because their target ad market was based on classified job advertisements – one of the first types of advertising to be disrupted by recruitment moving to the digital space. So B2Bs had to adapt early, quickly evolving into events and data services provisions. Consequently, they are well ahead of other sectors when the slump hit. Having seen the B2B successfully adapt, some of my clients that sit in the consumer market are trying to replicate that model with paid-for content, but to be successful it needs be high-value, because people have been weaned on free content for the past 20 years.

The consumer sector is quite hard to monetise because there is just so much free, widespread content across the Internet. This makes paid-for content a huge challenge as the generation now in their mid 30s – many of whom are professionals in the ABC bracket – don't expect to pay for content. Added to this is the fact that much of the key consumer content has moved to the screen (and phone) – particularly in the fast moving world of entertainment news and our 24/7 culture. Previously that kind of fast moving news was the bastion of consumer weeklies but it has now moved to the digital screen. Through this medium it is much better served in the moment, particularly on social media directly from the originator – whether updates are from celebrities or fashion houses.

Cost cutting and consolidation is also a key factor in business models. In the boom years of the early 2000s publishers consolidated, acquired and launched a lot, then rapidly having come to the other side of the mountain they had to reassess – cutting costs and consolidating. Yet while new technology has disrupted the workplace, it has also created a lot of opportunities. Publishers are now able to outsource work more easily because people can work remotely, either while on the job or from home. This has resulted in major cost savings for businesses because they no longer need these big offices that were a shrine to the media industry. Also, as with most activity, this is now cloud-based, creating an easy infrastructure where workflow can be accessed anywhere, at any time.

As many publishers know, developing a sustainable business model that replicates the cover price/advertising model is not easy. Is there a secret formula? No, it's about coming up with a mix of business models that work for the reader. The old formula of a straight-A mix of cover price and advertising just isn't viable for newsstand-reliant magazines outside of the top 50 selling titles.

Today business models must be different for each title. In the past decade, I have seen the industry move from a brand/magazine-centric to a reader-centric business model – and readers are different in every market, a fact sometimes overlooked. To be sustainable, publishers must build a profitable business model around the consumer and their needs – and also for advertisers too, particularly where they see value. Often that value can be found in consumer as well as B2B data. In consumer magazines, publishers have a deep understanding of their readers, but the data backs it up. And because data is available, marketing and advertising directors now want proof of facts and figures, so when approached by the advertising sales team they will respond with: this is who you tell me your reader is, now show it to me – and I want to be able to contact all your readers too.

It is essential to realise that there isn't a one-size-fits-all model. You can't just copy a rival title's strategy and assume it will work; every magazine has a unique value proposition. Certainly, it's a lesson I've learned the hard way, so I always advise clients to focus on their readers – to talk to them and observe their habits to find out what they want. Today a reader's expectation is that someone is going to: 'serve me exactly what I want or come up with the technology to serve me what I want and cut out all the other stuff I don't want'.

While technology can do some of the editing process it takes a good editor to anticipate what people will want in three weeks, before they know they want it. Content flow and delivery needs a specialist's eye. Although those qualitative judgements have been made easier with technology, a human touch is essential to bring it all together. It's the emotional connection, that feeling that people have around news, features, fashion and beauty, that is what it's about.

Now there is a growing trend and readers want tailored content. I think we are going to see a leaner, meaner industry and the war will be won on who is the most connected with the audience. The scale war has been won by Google and Facebook, but now it's about what the magazine industry can offer in the other direction – the expertise. To evolve, publishers must aim for finite targeting and the content to be created in a way that will resonate with that audience. This is where I think the traditional magazine media will win.

But when things go wrong it's important not to give in to that first emotion – panic. In the past few years we have seen many titles close as a result of decreased circulations and cash-flow. When a magazine starts to decline, it becomes quite emotional. But whether there is a decline in circulation or revenue, it's crucial to look back dispassionately to see where the key indicators were. Go back, talk to your audience and advertisers, find out what their thoughts are and try to identify where you could evolve. At this point it's important to take a step back and take stock until you have identified all the problems.

Remember, with every problem lies an opportunity somewhere. However, although sometimes that opportunity might take too much investment to get started or it might not be something your publishing company find attractive or within your skillset, considering all the possibilities offers a stronger perspective. At least you will have a rationale for why you're not doing something.

At this stage clients often ask which revenue streams are likely to be the most successful. Again, it's not a one-size approach but about looking at your audience and ascertaining what they spend their money on. For example, can you provide the audience with that service in a better way so that they will want to spend part of their income with you? A good illustration of this can be drawn from looking at a potential magazine proposition for the fishing industry. Here lies an opportunity to sell kit and licences, and provide videos and how-to guides and perhaps weather services. Look at what readers see as value then identify revenue opportunities to be part of that passion in a different way to just providing information – that could be eCommerce, valuable content or a service/product the reader wouldn't normally have access to.

As with revenue streams and balancing cash-flow, launching a new title is always tricky, but there are early indicators to help determine whether a new publishing concept might succeed or fail. The two crucial questions should be: how is it differentiated in the marketplace from competitors and has the concept identified a new social wave within the audience? Achieving these two aspects makes it harder for competitors to react to the launch – because to do so they would either have to change their business model or abandon an existing audience to target a new one. And that can give you a good head start.

If you are replicating something on the proviso of 'we could do it better', your chance of success is reduced because this is easily replicable by a competitor who could lure your staff and writers; then it becomes a war. Aim to create the media brand version of disruption rather than a technological one.

Successful concepts are about finding a social trend to drive them. Glamour magazine is a good example. Condé Nast realised fashion was moving fast and that there was a gap in the market, and launched Glamour magazine in 2001 – filling that gap, while producing the title at half the price (and size) of its competitors, making it hard to replicate.

The most valuable lesson I've learned? Listen to people around you – particularly working in big companies – but listen to your reader harder. When surrounded by lots of smart people everyone has a vested interest in the product and they can articulate that point of view fantastically to sell it. But actually just listening to a reader – who might struggle to articulate what they think about their passions or products they like – can be more informative.

When developing any business or product you have to be brave, mindful of costs and take care not to skimp on the due diligence process.

A SUCCESSFUL BUSINESS ACTION PLAN

Business plans are a must, but sometimes having a clear snapshot of your business in front of you, rather than a 20-page in-depth plan, will make it easier to see what needs attention.

Whether you are an editor, publisher or setting up a new magazine, working on the following four steps will help you focus on the essentials.

1. Evaluate your publication to identify any weaknesses or areas of concern.
2. Next, work on your four pillars: brand development; target audience and potential reach; finance and revenue streams; and distribution strategies and channels.
3. Now map your business using my Magazine Publishing Strategic Quadrant for your title to get an overall picture of your business.
4. Last, review current revenue streams – what should you prioritise and is there room for potential development?

Bibliography

Association of Online Publishers. 2016. Digital Design/Product Development Team of the Year. www.ukaop.org/digital-publishing-award-2016-winners/digital-design–product-development-team-of-the-year-2016 accessed 25 April 2017.

BBC Good Food. 2017. Media Kit. www.immediate.co.uk/wp-content/uploads/2015/10/BBC-GF-easycook-MediaPack-2015v2.compressed1.pdf accessed 5 May 2017.

BRAD 2017a. *BBC Good Food*. BRAD Insight. https://brad.mediatel.co.uk/profile/press/4108#overview accessed 5 May 2017.

BRAD. 2017b. *Country Living*. BRAD Insight. https://brad.mediatel.co.uk/profile/press/4011#circulation accessed 5 May 2017.

BRAD 2017c. *Drapers*. BRAD Insight. https://brad.mediatel.co.uk/profile/press/4218#circulation accessed 5 May 2017.

BRAD. 2017d. *Look*. Brad Insight. https://brad.mediatel.co.uk/profile/press/23454#circulation accessed 25/4/2017.

Carbonara, P. 2017. Gaming the System: How a Traditional Manufacturer Opened Its Books and Turned Employees into Millionaires. *Forbes*. www.forbes.com/sites/petercarbonara/2017/04/18/gaming-the-system-how-one-manufacturing-company-saved-itself-with-radical-transparency-and-created-a-slew-of-blue-collar-millionaires/#47a0ab8e3f83 accessed 1 May 2017.

Drapers. 2017. Media Kit. www.drapersonline.com/ accessed 5 May 2017.

Hearst. 2017. *Country Living*. www.hearst.co.uk/brands/country-living accessed 5 May 2017.

Hogarth, M. 2016. Keeping Innovation Affordable. *InPublishing*. May/June issue.

Money Week. 28 April 2017. Give the Workers a Stake in the Outcome. (p. 32).

Osterwalder, A and Pigner, Y. 2010. *A Handbook for Visionaries, Game Challengers and Challengers*. Chichester: Wiley.

Stack, J. 2003 *A Stake in the Outcome: Building a Culture of Ownership for the Long-Term Success of Your Business*. London: Bantam Doubleday Dell Publishing Group imprint of Penguin Random House.

Stack, J. 2013 *The Great Game of Business: The Only Sensible Way to Run a Company*. London: Crown Publishing Group imprint of Penguin Random House.

5

MARKET SECTORS THAT PAY – AND THOSE THAT DON'T …

Despite cutbacks and staff layoffs in the publishing industry some sectors are doing well – in fact they are thriving. Sometimes this is due to a new trend or an interest prompted by events. For example, in 2012 following the success of our cyclists in the Olympics and a Tour de France win for Bradley Wiggins, cycling became a national passion; this was swiftly followed by numerous bike magazines launching on the newsstands. Around the same time television programmes made upcycling popular; this interest was soon noted by publishers, resulting in more craft and home magazines.

While trends come and go, magazines can thrive, providing: a) there is a sufficient demand and b) the content is trustworthy, engaging and informative. Sectors also count; while the lifestyle market can fluctuate, specialist interest, B2B and customer publishing are likely to be more stable due to demand and needs of the reader. Let us not forget the success story of *BBC History Magazine* as documented in editor Rob Attar's industry perspective at the end of Chapter 3.

Local magazines are also enjoying success – turning a profit while attracting readers who value both relevant content about their area and, therefore, the publication that provides it. The caveat here is excellent – and of course relevant – content and high-quality presentation.

In this chapter I will examine emerging trends, successes in the specialist and B2B sectors and also the failure of *Women's Cycling* magazine. I will also be looking at *Home Handbook*, a successful magazine franchise.

There are many lessons to be learned from such examples, as well as inspiration perhaps to start your own publication. But to those of you inspired with an idea to set up your own magazine, I urge caution. There is much potential for a good, new start-up – particularly from a local perspective – but you do need a solid idea, as well as a gap in the market, the ability to undertake rigorous research, plus sufficient funding to last at least six months. Skimp these points at your peril.

A healthy B2B sector

Trade journals, or B2B magazines as they are otherwise known, are one of the most sustainable sectors in magazine publishing. This is because a B2B publication (regardless of genre) has a strong business model – to provide an essential commodity, in this case information, to educate and inform the audience. However, these magazines, like other titles, have had to adapt their approach for the digital age to ensure the content reaches the reader on the most appropriate platform.

For some magazines, particularly those in the IT sector, this has meant ditching the traditional print format to move into digital and online. One such example is *Computer Weekly*, a title originally developed and owned by Reed Business Information. After being bought by TechTarget in 2011 *Computer Weekly* became a digital issue with an accompanying website, with the last print edition hitting the newsstands in April 2011. Why does this work better having a digital and online focus? Again, it's about understanding your readers' needs. By their very nature most people dealing in computers are more likely to get information via a screen – therefore it makes sense that they would prefer to access *Computer Weekly* online or via a digital edition as opposed to a print edition. This gives the brand more opportunity to further engage their audience with a variety of interactive content, which in turn opens up more advertising and sponsorship opportunities, not to mention brand extensions.

But for others print still forms a core part of their provision, while adding brand extensions such as mobile, digital and online as a strategy to strengthen brand reach as well as increase revenue streams. One such example is *The Grocer* magazine owned by William Reed Business Media. Established in 1862, the weekly title targets every aspect of the industry, from directors of large multiples to independent retailers. Despite a significant decrease in print circulation from more than 50,000 to around 30,000 in the past 20 years *The Grocer* is still sustainable. According to BRAD, the 2017 combined print and digital circulation is 30,262 (source: publisher's statement confirming the circulation sent to BRAD), while page impressions for www.thegrocer.co.uk are 526,768.

Like many titles, to survive and thrive it has had to adapt. A significant strategy has been to promote membership as opposed to subscriptions and offer readers a scale of membership from Gold (£216 + VAT) to Platinum (£414 + VAT). Both options enable members to view *The Grocer* in print, digital and of course online; however, Platinum membership includes additional content such as analysis, The Grocer Price Index and unlimited access to the magazine's archives. This is a comprehensive provision undoubtedly giving members ROI on their membership. Aside from the added value, there is another point at play here. By changing subscription to membership, the perception focuses more on community: a smart move – by a team that clearly understands what their readers want and need.

In addition, *The Grocer* has a carefully targeted selection of brand extensions from awards and events to reports and directories. Each is fulfilling a gap in the readers' knowledge. Therefore, it is not surprising this title has not only stabilised, but also begun to rebuild. Clearly the team understands the fundamentals of B2B publishing – keep your audience informed on every aspect of their business. Because if its readers thrive, then so does *The Grocer*.

Specialist titles: success vs failure

It makes sense that where there is a market specialist titles are more like to succeed than lifestyle magazines. Readers with particular interests seek expertise that will either help them progress on perhaps a career or business level or simply develop their skills. As we have seen with *Writer's Digest*, such titles can thrive if the editorial team have passion, expertise and innovation – all equally important in contributing to the success of a magazine.

As we have also seen with the emergence of numerous cycling magazines since London 2012, trends are a factor here. However, just as some trends don't last, neither do all magazines, as we will explore with *Women's Cycling*. Yet one title that is thriving is *BBC History Magazine*. This title has continued to see an upward spike – almost doubling its circulation in under ten years – something editor Rob Attar attributes to widening audience participation strategy by developing podcasts, as he reveals in 'Industry perspectives' in Chapter 3.

Although it is a history publication, Rob is quick to point out that the majority of their readers are not historians. Rob reveals,

> It's very hard to define our readers, but they have an enthusiasm that cuts across age, gender, geography so anyone who loves history. So, we have readers of school age, those who are WWII veterans. Gender wise 50/50. One thing that is clear is that our audience are not professional historians, they are intelligent enthusiasts, people who enjoy history.
>
> Although some do work in history it's not predominantly for people who are researching history, we are not like an academic journal. It's accessible history. While we do have academics writing for us, we are producing content for the general public. Our purpose is to take what academic historians do and to bring that to the wider public. Essentially we are a conduit.

No doubt television history documentaries and dramas have played a part in the magazine's success. Popular programmes have included the ITV drama *Downton Abbey* and BBC 2's *Victorian Farm* – an historical observational documentary series following a team who live the life of Victorian farmers for a year – and have helped revive an interest in the subject. However, *BBC History Magazine* has not only built on this, but also sustained it by producing lively, engaging content that appeals to all their readers, which is no mean feat. But not all magazines in this genre are faring so well.

Since 2010 at least five publications have closed, including *Ancestors*, *Practical Family History*, *Discover my Past England*, *Discover my Past* and *Family History Monthly*. This I find somewhat surprising given the interest in BBC's *Who Do You Think You Are?* – a popular programme featuring celebrities and well-known personalities who trace back their family history. Now on series 14, the programme remains popular; according to *Broadcast* (2016), despite a decline in audience viewing figures, *Who Do You Think You Are?* is still capturing more than 3 million viewers.

Yet it seems the popularity of this programme has not been sufficient to sustain the majority of family history titles. Even *Who Do You Think You Are?* magazine has seen a decline in circulation with a drop from 21,417 in 2010, to 16,000 (January – December) by the end of 2016 (BRAD, 2017a). While this is a significant drop, other remaining titles have seen dramatic falls in their circulation. *Your Family History*, launched in 2003 and published by Dennis Publishing Ltd, saw circulation peak to just over 20,000 in 2010 but by the end of 2016 this had declined to 7,346, which in my opinion is barely sustainable.

It is clear that there is a significant downturn in this sector. First, family history titles have a similar audience demographic in terms of age and male/female ratio – mostly appealing to 50+ females – yet so far the publishers haven't invested in significant brand extensions such as events or conferences. Add to this the fact that researching family history will have a somewhat limited timeframe, unlike a sports title for example, where readers are likely to have a continued interest for a longer timeframe.

Despite such a decline, I suspect that *Who Do You Think You Are?* magazine has managed to survive because it is aligned to the TV series. The question is for how much longer? Is the passion for tracing our roots waning? Given the fact that events seem to provide the life blood for specialist and consumer titles, because they widen audience participation and raise the brand's profile, publishers would do well to invest in this area. There also needs to be more of a focus on ways to widen audience participation. A tough market may make it harder to build a sustainable title, but with a little innovation I think it is possible to beat the odds.

In contrast a similar title, *Inside History*, which was launched in Australia in 2010, has closed, publishing the Autumn 2017 issue as its final print edition. Announced in *Genealogy & History News*, founder Cassie Mercer announced the closure stating:

> As a sole trader for the past seven years it's been difficult to break even, and for all the hard work I've poured into the magazine, I've never taken a salary. Rather, I've poured my own money into the business to keep it going and to make up for the losses I sustained each year, in the hope of course that the next financial year I would break even. At times, we came tantalisingly close to doing so. But while we have built up a loyal following, I have always had to prop up the business. I cannot continue to do this; to keep running into debt just because I want to keep publishing the magazine.
>
> *(Genealogy & History News, 2017)*

So what went wrong? *Inside History* was published in print priced at $9.95AUD and distributed to more than 2,500 newsagents and library and museum shops across Australia, while the digital edition costing $7.49AUD was distributed via the App Store and Zinio. However, unlike many magazines, distribution did not include the mainstream retail outlets. At first glance this title has some fantastic content and engaging covers tempting the reader in. Clearly content is not the problem.

This high-end feel and brand identity is evident in its 2016–18 media kit, which further reinforces the magazine's credentials. Yet circulation was low. According to its media kit *Inside History* had a print circulation of just 7,000 equating to 20,000 readers, while the website attracted 30,000+ unique monthly impressions and it had 7,000 Twitter followers and around 5,000 eNewsletter subscribers. Clearly the low circulation, together with a lack of brand extensions, did not produce sufficient revenue to sustain the title.

Women's Cycling

Launched in the midst of austerity in 2013 along with other bike titles following the nation's renewed interest in the sport after London 2012, *Women's Cycling* magazine looked like a good bet. Alas it was not to be. Just over a year and nine issues later, the quarterly title, published by Wild Bunch Media, closed as a print edition; although it's website remained for a while it is no longer in operation. According to BikeBiz (Sutton, 2014), no redundancies were made as a result of the closure because the editorial staff were on freelance contracts, and at the time of writing this book, Wild Bunch Media had further streamlined its brands to focus solely on running and racing.

Starting off with a conservative print run of 30,000, noted in a publisher's statement dated March 2013 at the time of the launch (BRAD, 2017c), the magazine was aimed at a wide ABC1 female demographic aged 25–49. The editorial profile noted "an accessible, motivational tone with features, news, review, travel, fashion, nutrition, health, workouts and real-life stories as well as a basic bike maintenance section" (BRAD, 2017c). All the ingredients of a successful publication – so what went wrong?

It is hard to pinpoint the exact problem and unfortunately I was unable to secure an interview with the title's former editor. However, analysing the title's lifespan, overall profile and publisher's statement – together with my expertise – I suspect that there were two key factors in this magazine's downfall: a) timing and b) distribution. In the case of the former, women's cycling had only just begun to emerge as a key sport following London 2012, but it hadn't quite gained the kind of momentum needed to ensure there would be a sufficient audience to support a magazine. Second, distribution via mainstream newsstands could also have been a factor.

This type of specialist publication would, in my opinion, have been more likely to gain a following with a more strategic approach to distribution. For example, if this had been my client I would have advised the following actions with regard to raising the title's profile and increasing circulation:

- A focus on targeted distribution via independent and bike shop chains. This might have achieved a stronger ROI than promoting the title on the newsstands because it would be directly appealing to the target audience.
- Forming strategic partnerships with key bike manufacturers that have heavily invested in developing women's specific road and mountain bikes such as Specialized and Trek with the goal of raising the magazine's profile, which in turn should impact positively on circulation.
- Linking up with groups such as British Cycling, women's cycle clubs and other similar organisations, offering their members an exclusive discount on a subscription to the magazine.

My verdict? While some might say *Women's Cycling* closed because it is more likely to be suited to digital or online, I disagree. As a keen, female cyclist I know there is a market for this type of publication. Most likely in this instance it was a case of right content but wrong time. As a sometimes road cyclist who commutes and also loves mountain biking there currently isn't a magazine that caters for me. Thus, the answer may lie in widening the editorial profile. Creating a cycling publication that covers the whole genre rather than one specific aspect instantly widens the potential for participation.

A successful franchise

Somewhat surprisingly magazines aren't exempt from the franchise model. The *Home Handbook* (Figure 5.1), launched in 2010 by regional journalist Peter Ward, is a great example of a title evolving from this method.

After taking redundancy from the *Blackpool Gazette*, Peter ploughed his savings into launching this annual directory, which is distributed door-to-door around his hometown of Preston in Lancashire. The content – a combination of editorial and photographs presented in carefully categorised trade listings/advertisements – fills the gap between those old-style free, local papers and the ever-diminishing *Yellow Pages*.

But how did the concept evolve? Peter says his idea for *Home Handbooks* was a result of a combination of three factors.

> First there was a tourism booklet whose design features I liked, then a chance conversation with a landscape gardener friend who complained of having nowhere decent to advertise and at the time I needed to find a decent roofer. These events set me thinking about starting a booklet which came out annually and would be a helpful reference book for householders, the idea being to produce something of journalistic quality – in contrast to the plethora of competing A5 booklets done by amateurs without any journalistic background.

82 Market sectors that pay

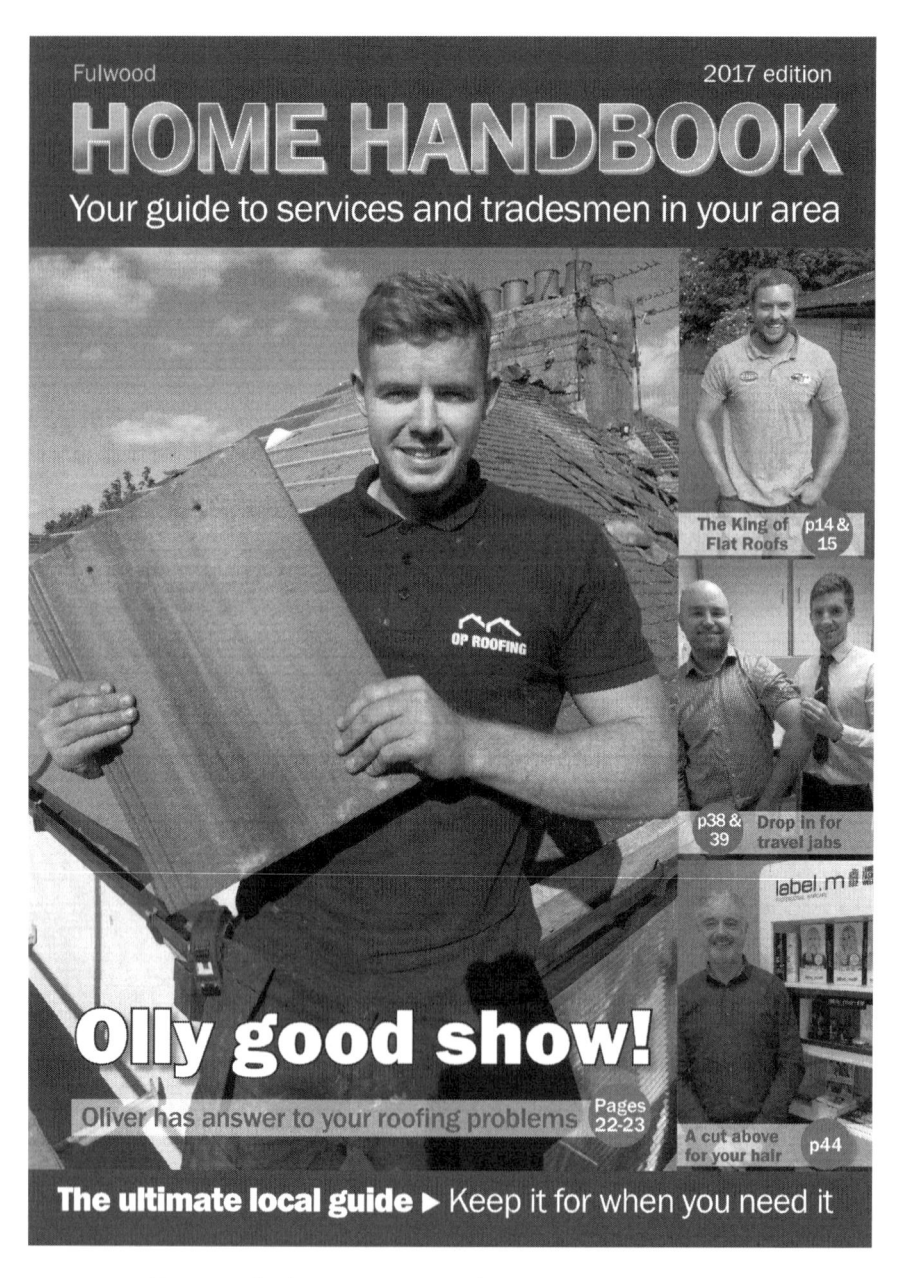

FIGURE 5.1 *Home Handbook* cover, courtesy of *Home Handbooks*

Peter admits his approach to research was simple, but effective. Having collated a dummy issue, he took a couple of days off work to research the market, visiting tradespeople and retailers to gauge their reaction, which he recalls was very positive.

The clincher was an old upholsterer who said he never advertised and then rang me back to say he liked the idea. I felt it must have merit to have persuaded him, and he continued in the booklets until he retired.

Initial set-up expenditure was minimal as the cost of his first issue was covered with pre-paid advertising revenue.

I used my existing InDesign software and computer to compile the booklet, a bit of petrol and shoe leather, and that was it. The only sizeable cost was a £600 legal bill for terms and conditions which I have never actually needed – beware lawyers.

Local independent magazines are fast becoming popular. If done well, such publications not only fill a gap in the market, but also can be an asset in sustaining a community, which appears to be the case with *Home Handbooks*. Peter is regularly asked for copies of the booklet by householders outside the free distribution area, which he sells at £3 a time.

Seven years on from the launch and this annual is a profitable title with Peter working on around a minimum 65% profit margin per issue after printing, distribution and proofreading costs. Of course, such costs vary on each issue, according to the number of copies printed.

My gross annual profit last financial year was £88,000 on a turnover of £118,000. Net profit was less after deduction of VAT payments and other costs, but not inconsiderable. I reckon to earn, as a net amount, about three times what I took home as a reasonably well-paid senior regional newspaper journalist.

The magazine is also supported by a website, which Peter says currently attracts around 1,000 unique visitors a week, most coming from Google searches from those seeking specific services.

For searches on business names, *Home Handbook* often beats Yell. And occasionally on generic searches – try 'Alterations, Preston'. Not bad for a one-man band. Imagine the potential of that, properly exploited. The website is also a valuable resource for people researching businesses and I believe it has great potential.

Not only has Peter succeeded in making *Home Handbooks* profitable as a magazine, he has also developed it as a franchise to give others an opportunity and extend brand reach to other parts of the country.

From the start, I realised that if *Home Handbooks* could work for me, it could work for other similarly qualified journalists who could write, design and

> adapt to selling – though the product does tend to sell itself. I investigated franchising and found the costs of using a franchising organisation were exorbitant, so after internet research I had a franchise agreement drawn up by a solicitor, compiled a manual myself and tested the water with my first franchisee, who is doing extremely well.

However, Peter admits initially he charged too little for the franchise.

> I sold my second and third franchises for £2,000 each plus VAT – but failed to realise how much time would need to be invested in training experienced journalists to sell. Financial necessity drove me to hammer away through trial and error until I evolved a successful way of selling my pages. My first franchisee is the son of a market trader, so the selling aspect came naturally, but the other two needed a lot of time to instil confidence and technique – time I did not have. My first franchisee and his wife agreed to invest a lot of time in this – and not unreasonably – asked for a royalty holiday, which means that so far I have lost potential income rather than made a profit on franchising.

Despite initial teething troubles, Peter believes franchising *Home Handbook* has limitless possibilities, in the UK and abroad, with journalists constantly losing their jobs. "I have a dream of partnering with a bigger media organisation better able to franchise and exploit the concept than I can as a sole trader. So far, my overtures have produced nothing – but never say never."

What would he do differently with hindsight? "Not a great deal," says Peter.

> The main lesson is not squandering your time by chasing fruitless sales leads or slow-paying advertisers. I have realised that if clients give you difficulties initially or you have reservations about them for reasons you cannot fully articulate, they are not worth pursuing, even if you want the revenue. It is better to have a portfolio of decent clients who become like journalistic contacts and even friends because it means there are far fewer copy approval/ payment hassles. And the feedback from appreciative clients is very rewarding.

From my perspective *Home Handbooks* is a great example of what can be achieved with vision, demand and a small budget. It is one to watch in the future.

Summary

There are many lessons to be drawn from the examples and stories in this chapter. But I think the biggest one is *Home Handbooks*, a local title started up from very little investment. Again, it's about filling a gap in the market and producing valuable content in the right format for that reader.

Throughout my time as a magazine consultant, while I have worked with national titles I have been privileged to be involved in some great local magazines run by small, independent publishers who are committed to their communities. There is an emerging trend here, with a growing demand for local as people move away from larger corporations and instead choose to support their area's small, independent publishers – both in terms of advertising and copy sales.

This would suggest that with so much free content available people still value strong, original editorial that is well written and most relevant to them. Yet this isn't always sufficient to sustain titles, as we have seen with Australia's *Inside History* and *Women's Cycling*. With local titles, circulation is easier to increase, as seen with *Home Handbooks*. However, to become sustainable on a national scale, publishers need to build a solid circulation and invest in raising the magazine's profile to widen audience participation. In addition, they also must include other revenue streams in the form of brand extensions to produce a strong cash-flow. A combination of these factors can make the difference between success and failure.

INDUSTRY PERSPECTIVES

Gregor Rankin, Managing Director of Green Pea Publishing, launched *Food and Travel* magazine (Figure 5.2) back in the 1990s when publishing still focused on the traditional business achieving most of its revenue through newsstand sales and advertising.

He explains how his career led to launching his own publishing company and reveals the lessons he has learned along the way.

My career essentially began in advertising, working my way up to group ad manager on two of Haymarket's biggest titles, What Car *and* Autocar. *The next logical step in my career path was to be a publisher, but at that time those positions were not open at Haymarket. Then along came an opportunity to get in and launch a range of titles for the BBC including* BBC Good Food; *it was too good an opportunity to turn down.*

After leaving the BBC I was a publishing director at what is now Wilmington – and if I'm honest information publishing took me away from the creative side of publishing, so after two years I wanted to get back to magazines. That was when, in 1995, Green Pea Publishing evolved.

Given my experience in travel and food publishing (and I enjoy my drink too) it seemed a natural area to target. At the time there was no one magazine that really addressed my combined passions for these naturally inter-linked areas. I thought, 'I should launch one and hopefully there will be enough similarly minded people out there to buy it.' I was lucky enough to join forces with my creative partner Angela Dukes, who was creative director on BBC Good Food *and shared similar passions. She is an incredibly talented designer and without her we would not be here today.*

As with all new start-ups, it took a lot of investment, basically everything we had and then some, more than once . . . Securing funding is never easy, but I was lucky enough to have developed some good relationships with similarly minded people in the industry over the years who were incredibly supportive and continue to act as sounding boards for our plans.

FIGURE 5.2 *Food and Travel* cover, courtesy of Green Pea Publishing

> Why did I opt for the food and drink sector? It's about doing what you know and love – having a passion is essential. Also, this was an area I had prior knowledge of, having launched BBC Good Food and BBC Holidays, but the most important factor was my passion for food, drink and travel.
>
> More than 20 years after the launch the magazine is profitable and those profits are growing, although it hasn't been an easy journey, especially having to navigate our way through the digital age. But for me the key to profitable magazines lies in understanding your consumer and delivering the right products to them in the format they are willing to pay for. Growing an audience is hard, especially at the beginning, and our brand extensions have been critical in terms of widening audience participation and generating meaningful profit.

The economics of publishing are very heavily skewed towards scale (rather than skill in some cases . . .). We have extended our brand into seven international markets – Mexico, Turkey, Italy, Arabia, Portugal and Germany – which has been key to our success. The local-language editions are all licensed apart for the German edition, which is now owned directly, and we have a small office in Hamburg. In addition, we launched the Food and Travel Awards which have become the Blue Riband event that both destinations, the hospitality industry and chefs really strive to win.

Success is a combination of experience and sometimes getting good advice. My most important lesson in magazine publishing has been to have a very clear vision of who your (target) readers are, be willing to go the extra mile and never say 'That'll do' – you have to make your magazine the very best you can. Equally, the best advice I was once given was: don't buy what you can borrow; don't borrow what you can get for free.

Is Food and Travel *magazine sustainable in the long term? Yes, we all need, want and use the Internet relentlessly, searching for everything from train journeys to bed and breakfasts. But you have to know what you are looking for (there are a lot of bed and breakfasts in a lot of places). And if there's one thing that* Food and Travel *magazine provides to our readers, it's ideas. People want to know inside information such as great places to eat, where to visit as well as what to cook and drink.*

Most of all it's important to remember that we are here to inspire. Journalists are those in the know, and we know the places a gourmet traveller would want to visit. So, while the Internet has an awful lot of information, it's hard to search when you don't know what you're looking for in the first place. Whereas if it's food and travel inspiration you're looking for, we'd like to think there's only one place you need to look.

People will always buy quality and hopefully still appreciate well-written, well-designed magazines.

MARKET SECTOR ACTION PLAN

How often do your measure results in terms of your market sector? As a publisher or editor, it is essential to continually monitor whichever sector and genre you publish in – be it specialist, B2B or consumer.

The following five points will help you keep ahead of the market and spot downturns or a potential saturation early.

- In general, how are magazines performing in your sector? Look for patterns.
- Have your rivals seen a spike or downturn in circulation recently?
- Note any recent news launches or magazine closures in this sector?
- Be aware of any emerging trends resulting in a series of new launches. How will you ensure your magazine doesn't become a victim of market saturation?
- Last, continually review performance indicators and directly measure these against your rivals.

Bibliography

Blazeby, M. 2016. Who Do You Think You Are? Slips to 3.3m. *Broadcast*. www.broadcastnow.co.uk/ratings/overnight-tv-ratings/who-do-you-think-you-are-slips-to-33m/5112069. article accessed 3 July 2017.

BRAD. 2017a. Family History Titles. BRAD Insight. https://brad.mediatel.co.uk/profile/press/15293#circulation accessed 11 July 2017.

BRAD. 2017b. *The Grocer*. BRAD Insight. https://brad.mediatel.co.uk/profile/press/5503# circulation accessed 16 May 2017.

BRAD. 2017c. *Women's Cycling*. BRAD Insight. https://brad.mediatel.co.uk/profile/press/29288#circulation accessed 13 July 2017.

Doug. 2013. New Women's Cycling Magazine. The Cycle Hub. http://thecyclehub.net/new-womens-cycling-magazine/ accessed 13 July 2017.

Genealogy & History News. 2017. Important Announcement from *Inside History* Magazine. www.gouldgenealogy.com/2017/04/important-announcement-inside-history-magazine/ accessed 28 July 2017.

Home Handbooks. 2017. About Us. www.homehandbooks.co.uk/about-us/ accessed 14 July 2017.

Inside History. 2017. About Us. www.insidehistory.com.au/current-issue/ accessed 28 July 2017.

Inside History. 2017. Media Kit. www.insidehistory.com.au/media-kit/ accessed 28 July 2017.

McQuaid, D. 2016. Former Daily Star Sub-editor more than Doubles Salary Launching Local Magazine. *Press Gazette*. www.pressgazette.co.uk/former-daily-star-sub-editor-more-than-doubles-salary-launching-local-magazine/ accessed 14 July 2017.

Ponsford, D. 2014. Chief Sub Made Redundant by Johnston Press Doubles his Earnings by Launching Home Handbook Booklet Series. *Press Gazette*. www.pressgazette.co.uk/chief-sub-made-redundant-johnston-press-doubles-his-earnings-launching-home-handbook-booklet-series/ accessed 14 July 2017.

Sutton, M. 2014. *Women's Cycling* Magazine to Close. Bikebiz.com. www.bikebiz.com/news/read/women-s-cycling-magazine-to-close/017025#after-ad accessed 13 July 2017.

TechTarget. March 2011. TechTarget to Acquire Computer Weekly, the UK's Most Respected IT Media Brand, from Reed Business Information. www.techtarget.com/press-release/techtarget-acquire-computer-weekly-uks-most-respected-it-media-brand-from-reed-business-information/ accessed 2 June 2017.

William Reed. 2017a. *The Grocer* Magazine. www.william-reed.com/Brands-and-markets/Grocery-Retail/The-Grocer/The-Grocer-Magazine accessed 17 May 2017.

William Reed. 2017b. *The Grocer* – The Grocer Gold Membership. https://shop.william-reed.com/brands/thegrocer/the-grocer-gold.htm accessed 17 May 2017.

6
SEE YOUR READERS AS STAKEHOLDERS

In the tough economic climate of the digital age, making a profit in publishing can be difficult. With growing costs from all aspects of print and digital copy sales combined with a decline in advertising revenue, publishers are having to take an innovative approach to ensure their magazines are sustainable. Such approaches include looking at new ways to sell copies and content while building other revenue streams to offset any potential losses.

So far in this book I have demonstrated many examples of innovation and profitable titles showing that while it may be difficult to achieve sustainability it is not impossible, as we have seen with Peter Ward's initiative *Home Handbooks*. This model makes money because a) the emphasis is on local, where the editor/publisher becomes known to both the reader and the advertiser, and b) it meets a need by both parties. Simply, it is a case of supply and demand – give the readers what they need, focus on quality and keep your costs low.

Yet with other titles the model isn't so straightforward because to produce and distribute nationally or globally requires significant investment and a long wait before an ROI is seen. Therefore, publishers need to see their readers as consumers by creating a sustainable title that is valued by all its stakeholders. This means embracing change: looking for new ways to move away from traditional distribution models and developing relevant brand extensions that readers not only want, but need.

Creating a community

At the start of the millennium print was the defined driver of information. Yet while information is still invaluable, some of its mediums aren't necessarily so. Today those seeking local or world news, study material, how-to problems and the like will go online first via a mobile device, tablet or desktop computer. Despite the doom and gloom about the digital age, it shouldn't mean the end of print

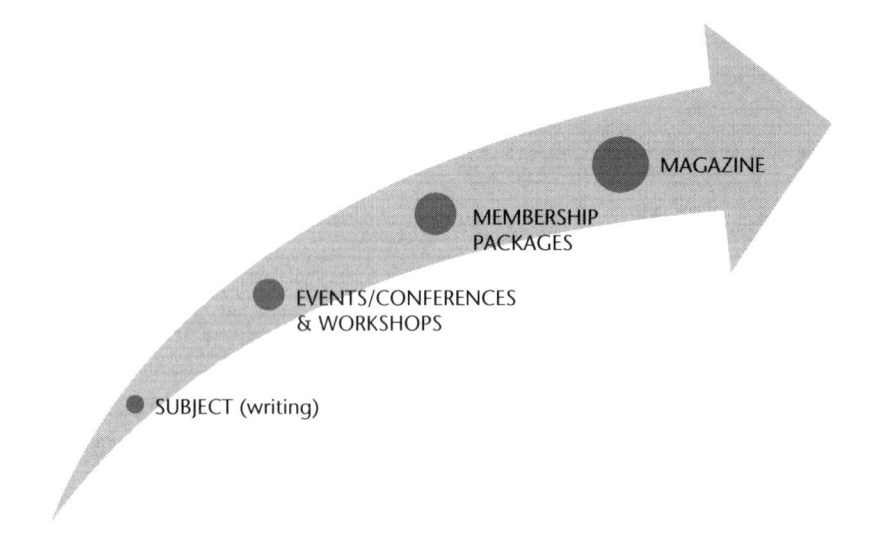

FIGURE 6.1 Membership model, author's own model

publishing. But you do need be smarter by packaging your content in a way that creates revenue streams.

Creating a community via a membership package is such an option and one I have recommended to a few clients now, particularly those launching a magazine to run alongside another venture.

The membership model I have created (see Figure 6.1) demonstrates how this works. As with any magazine concept this too is built around the subject/genre. In this instance I have chosen writing to demonstrate the model because many writers need support and are therefore drawn to groups. Events, workshops, etc. are developed on either a national or local scale from which a membership package with various tiers can be created. Once members are signed up the magazine is launched – paid for by the membership packages.

Perhaps my best example of the membership package to date is *The Mint* magazine – a concept that came to light a while ago when I was approached by a new client wanting advice on the launch of a new digital magazine on the economy. The following case study explores how *The Mint* evolved from concept to publication – its core objective and sustainability have been based on the membership model.

CASE STUDY: *THE MINT* MAGAZINE

Inspired by the campaigning genesis of *The Economist*, Henry Leveson-Gower had passion for new economic thinking and a solid background knowledge but knew little of magazine publishing. His goal was to launch a new digital magazine to promote fresh thinking in economics. So, after reading my first book, *How to Launch a Magazine in this Digital Age* (2014), he got in touch.

Initially Henry was focused on launching the title through digital newsstands and commissioned me to write a business plan. Overall his instincts were good – a major rival and source of his inspiration, *The Economist*, was thriving.

Yet digital distribution needs serious backing. After demonstrating that such a model was prohibitively expensive, a rethink was needed. As he had also set up NEKS (aka New Economic Knowledge Services) owned by his non-profit company Promoting Economic Pluralism (PEP) around the same time, I suggested he shift the focus to creating a community with events and developing a magazine for members. After a series of NEKS events with high-profile speakers, including Sir Vince Cable and Ann Pettifor, director of PRIME, *The Mint* (Figure 6.2) was launched to members of NEKS through its subsidiary Knowledge Network, using the digital platform Joomag early in 2017.

At the time of writing this book, the magazine had recently produced its third issue and currently reaches around 950 readers. It's a slow start but building a community takes time. Below Henry reveals his journey from concept to publication.

The Mint evolved because I wanted to raise awareness and develop a deeper understanding of economic systems and how they interact with political, social and physical systems. A magazine seemed the perfect platform to share knowledge and ideas.

Start-up costs were minimal, around £5,000 to produce and launch the magazine with £1,000 spent on the launch party. Funding came from a personal business loan and The Cambridge Trust for New Thinking in Economics, which helped finance initial research into the viability of the concept.

Finding an editor was tricky but luckily I found one quickly, along with a designer to lay the magazine out. In the run-up to the launch we spent a lot of time developing content but not enough on getting the layout right so the magazine could be viewed on a tablet, phone or laptop. Hence it has taken about three issues to get it right. Of course, there were a few teething problems such as Joomag using the Adobe Flash player; this meant the magazine wouldn't run on some devices. However, just as we were about to move to another digital platform, Joomag resolved the issue by switching to HTML5.

With regard to sustainability the magazine has yet to become profitable. Looking back, I realise it was a mistake to initially target personal businesses and the finance sector as a potential audience; while we had some response, overall this had limited success. I've realised that promoting the magazine to those more 'converted' to economic reform and pluralism for non-profit organisations is potentially a more successful approach. A key element of this is linking it to the 10 Years after the Crash network that PEP coordinates.

Subsequently my thinking now is to create a paid membership system for PEP, the non-profit company which owns NEKS, and give members access to The Mint *for free as part of a range of membership packages, while starting to charge a small amount for the magazine to those who are not members.*

Overall the experience has been a steep learning curve. One of the biggest lessons has been not to forget about the user interface. Magazine publishing is not all about

FIGURE 6.2 *The Mint* cover, courtesy of New Economic Knowledge Services (NEKS)

content, because if people find an interface difficult to use or it doesn't work on their laptop, tablet, phone, etc. this will impact on engagement and uptake. I have also realised that the content needs to have a stronger link to the community, so from the second issue we included a News from the Network section and now are trying to build it into part of network hub.

Within the next five years I hope to make The Mint *a monthly title, but obviously, it's got to pay for itself. Currently costs are low at around £4,000 an issue, as the only*

> people who are paid are the editor and the designer who does the layout, with both working on a freelance basis. Currently the content is created by a network of writers who volunteer their services to gain a voice and ensure knowledge is shared. However, once the frequency expands the magazine will need to sustain at least one full-time salaried position.
>
> Long term I'm aiming at a much higher readership and international distribution – creating a global community within the next 18 months to three years. The idea is to grow events on a global basis all under the '10 Years After' logo on the same URL but with different country versions of the site. Building a community and magazine in tandem is essential to ensure both become sustainable.
>
> Although it is too early to tell if the magazine will succeed, initial indicators are favourable. Essentially the membership model is about seeing your readers as consumers and providing services that will benefit them and enrich their world – either professionally or personally, or sometimes both.

Meeting a need

Like *The Mint*, if magazines can fulfil a need or hit the right note then they have a much greater chance of succeeding. An ethical, current affairs magazine, *New Internationalist*, is a good example of this. Founded in 1973 this was a long-standing title, but – as widely reported – by the start of 2017 with a circulation of around 25,000 (BRAD, 2017) it had run into financial difficulty.

For some publishers options might have included a merger, sell out or closure. Instead *New Internationalist* turned to its readers with a community-share offer to sustain its independence and achieve financial security. The magazine used community-issue shares – a structure aimed at raising capital for charities, community benefit societies and non-profit organisations in the UK. Clearly loved and valued by its readers *New Internationalist* raised more than £200,000 according to *Press Gazette*, with actress Emma Thompson among the first to invest along with musicians Jarvis Cocker and Billy Bragg.

In the article, *New Internationalist* co-editor Hazel Healy told Dominic Ponsford, editor of *Press Gazette*, that the move was necessitated by the fact that it was getting hard for independents to survive.

> We have always written about other people coming together to change things, now it's our turn. It felt like we needed to do something big. Fear, and mistrust are rising all over the world, and misinformation along with them. Meanwhile, the media's broken business model is making it harder than ever for independents like us to survive. We want to scale up and get our stories out to more people than ever before. Our slogan #FactsAndHeart says it all. This is journalism that has the power to bring people together. We think that is something worth buying into.

Whether this will be sufficient to sustain this magazine in the long term remains unclear. Currently published around the world ten times a year, it is now co-owned by workers and more than 3,600 investors. However, although funding helps in the short term, the title will most likely need to rethink its revenue strategy to survive into the next decade. Yet what this level of support demonstrates is that when a magazine is as dedicated to independent journalism, particularly socially conscious content, then people do recognise its value, supporting it in any way they can. A parallel can be drawn here with *Private Eye*'s model examined in Chapter 1. Readers regularly send the *Eye* donations to help fund its numerous legal battles.

The moral of the story is that people value trustworthy content and independent coverage and, therefore, are more likely to be prepared to actively support such coverage with hard cash donations or crowdfunding campaigns.

Blurred lines

Earning sufficient revenue to be sustainable is a major problem with many publishers; this has resulted in some blurring the lines between editorial and other content, thus risking losing the trust of one of the major stakeholder groups – the readers. This is occurring with more frequency, particularly in the lifestyle market as increasingly lifestyle titles are developing strategic partnerships with advertisers to grow revenue streams while providing an additional service for readers with partnered brand extensions.

Generally, these come in the form of product endorsements whereby a magazine will support a product. Hence the lines between editorial and content marketing can become blurred. One such example is Eve Cameron, *Good Housekeeping*'s beauty director, endorsing Olay Regenerist three-point night cream in a TV advert. Inviting viewers to "try it for yourself" she cites positive findings from independent testing at the Good Housekeeping Institute. Now for me this is a step too far as I've always believed that those magazine writers/editors who review products need to be independent. Writing honestly about an experience or product is a must – there can be no influences or blurred lines. Therefore, I believe that endorsing your advertisers' products nationally on TV clearly crosses that line of independence.

That said, I must state that the Good Housekeeping Institute maintains the highest testing standards and continues to remain independent.

Decreasing advertising sales has no doubt been a factor in the temptation to explore opportunities to offer services to readers or advertisers, which may blur lines and thus compromise brand values to a degree. This may include offering paid-for product reviews as part of an advertising package or developing a reader testing facility, which *Glamour* magazine has recently launched.

In 2017 *InPublishing* reported that *Glamour* magazine had launched its own Beauty Club with free membership. The report stated that the new club provided:

> the opportunity for beauty clients to sample their products with *Glamour*'s audience and get crucial product feedback, members of the Beauty Club

will have access to some of the most exciting new beauty products from some of the magazine's favourite brands, say the publishers.

(InPublishing, 2017)

According to *InPublishing*, Glamour Beauty Club gained 19,000 members in the first few days of trialling. Clearly readers were interested and the *Glamour* team had launched this latest extension in a quest to raise the title's profile and widen participation. But does it blur the lines? Perhaps, as while the club offers a genuine opportunity to try products it could be argued this is tantamount to product placement. Furthermore, the magazine can also make the following gains:

- **Valuable research data:** by signing up for membership new members are giving *Glamour* a wealth of data on their skin and hair types.
- **Contact details:** a database that can be shared or sold to advertisers and product manufacturers.
- **Audience participation:** readers are likely to see this as a benefit to them, and therefore the extension may increase brand loyalty.

Considering these points, that line is a thin one. It must be remembered that readers are consumers of what should be unbiased editorial content so it's crucial to be mindful of blurred lines.

Figure 6.3 illustrates key themes which can result in readership trust issues arising if the balance between advertising and editorial content isn't clearly defined. Content marketing has become a key theme in recent years with many PR firms now producing features to sell or place with magazine editors, who may be short-staffed with a limited editorial budget. Moreover, in a bid to sell advertising space, invariably advertorial articles under the guise of promotional content will also be offered as an incentive.

The model demonstrates how the balance has changed. Content previously defined as advertising now has the potential to be repurposed under editorial along with partnered themed features or, as we have seen with *Glamour*'s Beauty Club, product reviews. It is a fine line and one that must be trodden with care. Yes, you need to make money but maintaining strong editorial values is a must, otherwise it could be a case of short-term gain but long-term loss as readers may become disenchanted with a change in brand values – however subtle.

Keeping up with demand

Having solid brand extension adds value to your magazine proposition, as demonstrated in previous chapters. Yet before jumping on to the next big thing to widen participation or improve revenue, take a step back. Sometimes it is better to wait and see how things pan out, especially with social media platforms, before overextending or populating areas your readers don't use. It's always better to keep your focus somewhat narrow and focus on producing high quality across your brand,

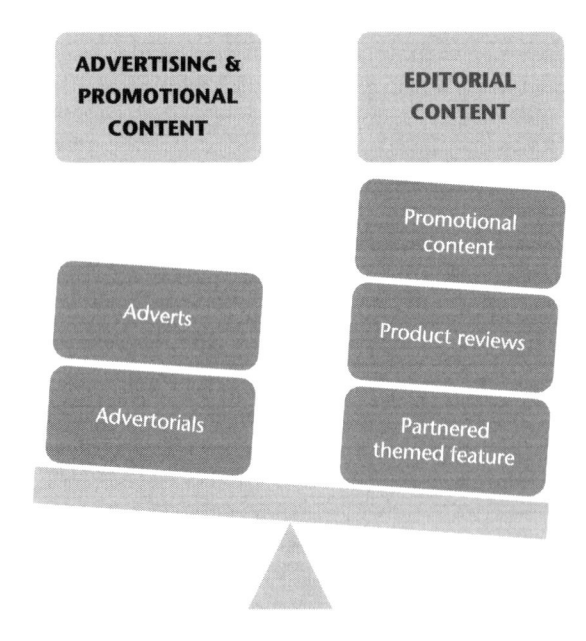

FIGURE 6.3 Balancing the scales of advertising and editorial

because over extending usually leads to under performance, which risks disappointing your audience.

But continued development is a must, because not to evolve is to stagnate and, as examples of history have shown, with stagnation comes a fall. Therefore, publishers need to continually evolve to thrive. In my *Writer's Forum* days, I realised it was essential to keep an eye on trends and technology while ensuring that we didn't do what had always been done – because therein lies the pitfall of habit. Hence we were one of the first magazines to publish a website guide for writers and were also pioneers of self-publishing – launching the *Writer's Forum* Write A Novel competition.

Today things are perhaps not so straightforward. Advertising has, up until the last decade, been the main source of revenue for magazines and newspapers, but now publishers face a huge challenge of balancing increasing costs against ever-decreasing advertising sales revenue. Fighting for survival can have a huge impact, as I have seen with some of my clients who before calling me were focused on finance, but had little or less interest in evolving their business and forward planning.

As a result I have compiled a list of five points I think should be key focus points for magazine publishers during the next few years.

- **360-degree content:** print is becoming more interactive with links that can be scanned with a phone or tablet to access additional content. This will move away from QR codes.
- **A high focus on print quality:** layouts will be more spacious and image-rich with high-quality covers.

- **Goodbye content marketing:** readers want in-depth, independent content so editors will return to old-school rules of clearer boundaries in features.
- **Sustainability:** readers will want more eco-friendly products; therefore publishers will move towards using sustainable materials when producing printed magazines.
- **Fewer social media channels:** less will be more here as major players facilitate audio as well as video uploads, resulting in more content on fewer channels.

To keep up with demand make sure your content moves towards these points, but do your research before any major developments – remember that old maxim *less is more*. Avoid content marketing-style features and make sure your print products are sustainably produced. For those of you who argue this isn't cost effective, think again. As the organic food market has shown, there is a demand for quality and people will pay for it.

Summary

As demonstrated throughout this chapter – and the book – it is possible to create strong magazine propositions. Meeting a need, developing a community focus and avoiding blurred lines are all fundamental factors when building a sustainable product.

As we have seen with *The Mint*, being passionate about a subject and wanting to share that knowledge with others is a good starting point. However, given that the cost of a national or global launch is somewhat prohibitive for smaller, independent publishers another route needs to be found when developing a new title. The concept of developing a community first and then delivering the magazine to serve it is likely to work well for *The Mint*. However, one size does not fit all. So, if considering a community membership option you must have a solid foundation on which to build.

Whatever the genre, magazines must remain true to their values. Avoid scenarios that might create blurred lines, because in the long run such projects are likely to erode trust which will subsequently impact on sustainability. Remember your readers are stakeholders too, so my advice would be to keep that as the centre focus for every brand extension you create. It may seem obvious, but it is easy to forget when trying to balance cash-flow against poor or decreasing advertising sales figures.

INDUSTRY PERSPECTIVES

Ben Budworth, owner and publisher of *The Lady* (Figure 6.4), was somewhat new to magazine publishing when he took over in 2008. Coming from a background that included 12 years as an MD at radio stations and stints as a helicopter pilot, taking over his great grandfather's magazine was a steep learning curve.

Below he reveals the challenges along the way and how he sees the magazine's future in the long term.

98 See your readers as stakeholders

FIGURE 6.4 *The Lady* cover, courtesy of *The Lady*

Taking over The Lady *was a huge challenge, circulation was at an all-time low and there were few subscribers. It was a steep learning curve and very clear that drastic action was needed or the publication would become another statistic.*

My most successful business strategy? Taking an axe to not only the personnel but also the costs. Another way of having done it would have been to have closed the magazine down for a week, made all of the staff redundant, then started again.

It would have been considerably cheaper, properly considerably more efficacious, but as we are The Lady *it just couldn't be done.*

Almost a decade later we now have a turnover of around £2.8 million per year. Roughly speaking we are selling £1.3 million of advertising, while our print and subscription sales are producing about £1.3 million per year. Other revenue comes from brand extensions such as events and the like; although popular, the profit from these is negligible, and as a result, our turnover is constantly declining. I can't remember a year where we have not had to manage reduced turnover – the management of that is a skill in itself.

That said, we are making in-roads in the recruitment business. In addition to the advertising we now have a very successful agency where, careful though we are not to tread on other agencies' toes, we have the benefit of being able to see all the applicants for all jobs in The Lady. *This is likely to become a key focus in the future. The recruitment agency is for the long term and I would like to square the circle so that we can train or be involved in training domestic staff and ultimately certificating them using* The Lady*'s brand.*

That way the magazine becomes involved full cycle in sourcing staff, training, certificating, placing and recruiting them. Maybe it might move towards managing staff, but this is more to do with the larger households with whom we deal. I can see there are elements of households now that aren't run as effectively and efficiently as they might have been years ago, so there is an opportunity for us to get involved in household management.

One of the most important lessons I have learned about magazine publishing is in editorial. It's not quite publish and be damned but . . . I believe it is far better to take an editorial standpoint and publish than not to take any standpoint at all – and hope that by being nice people will flock to the magazine. Although we haven't done that yet, it is something I have learned and am internally frustrated that we haven't put it in place yet. Just writing nice articles is not enough in this day and age. Being nice doesn't make anyone – let alone everyone – happy.

Another important lesson has been that in this market there is never a price that could not be bettered, but if you have agreed on a price and term then you must see it through. Dictum meum pactum *(my word is my bond) – if I agree to pay the printer x amount for y amount of time then I'll do it, but I will always know that in this market that next time I come to negotiate it may well be a lower price.*

Magazine publishing is facing challenging times and the electronic magazine market is going to be every bit as difficult as the print market with each having similar challenges. I suppose radio has it easier than magazines. If you compare the Internet with magazines and radio with apps such as Spotify or Tidal: the app doesn't decide what it is going to play or take an editorial position – it is simply there as a repository of music – whereas with radio someone else is making the decision, and you buy into that editorial choice. And so it is magazines with strong editorial versus the deluge of material available on the Internet.

> *A magazine must have a club following and the reader has to be part of a conspiracy of agreement.* The Lady *will always be here; it's just a question of in what form. My predictions for the future of magazine publishing are pessimistic in terms of print because I believe that the moment when the iPad or tablet becomes larger than A4 in terms of size, it effectively becomes a reader. As soon as I have a tablet of that size I can read a page as easily as I can from the printed edition. The tablet could be mounted under any number of tables such as train tables, breakfast tables or restaurant tables and I could have any degree of magazines served to it. So why would I ever need to pick up magazine and take it on a train/bus to a guesthouse? In the not so distant future, I suspect table-style readers will be incorporated into anything, wherever we go.*
>
> *This makes me think that* The Lady *has a future for subscribers because we know our subscribers are loyal followers of the editorial. But does it have a future on the newsstands? It's a dwindling market and we have to support the retailers more and more every year. Whether* The Lady *will remain on the newsstand for more than three or four years I seriously doubt. I think the magazine will be printed for subscribers only and be available electronically for everyone else. The jobs and recruitment side will all go online. But up to that time we will have a damn good fight to keep it on the newsstand.*
>
> *Distribution must work for all the stakeholders of* The Lady. *It may be that we keep it targeted at retailers such as Waitrose. But what we can't do is to continue to supply it to independents where we provide two copies a week to each of them and either both copies get sold, in which case they sell out, or no copies get sold and they come back and get pulped. It's far easier to put 50 copies into a Tesco and know that you are going to sell 38 of those copies – allowing you a little bit of leeway.*

EVALUATION ACTION PLAN

Evaluation of your title should be a continual process. Here are three key aspects you should review, analyse and test; then make revisions where necessary.

- **Community engagement:** if you haven't already created a community around your magazine do some research to determine whether an opportunity exists.
- **What your readers (stakeholders) need:** are you meeting all their needs? Evaluate your current provision to explore potential development while considering what needs to be revised.
- **Ditch the blurred lines:** develop a clear set of guidelines from the outset around editorial vs content marketing. It's crucial when developing any strategic partnership/brand extension/reader service to ensure it won't compromise your brand values or editorial boundaries.

Bibliography

BRAD. 2017. *New Internationalist*. BRAD Insight. https://brad.mediatel.co.uk/profile/press/6526 accessed 3 August 2017.

Glamour Beauty Club. 2017. www.glamourbeautyclub.com accessed 8 August 2017.

InPublishing. 2017. Glamour Beauty Club Launches. www.inpublishing.co.uk/news/articles/glamour_beauty_club_launches_11149.aspx accessed 8 August 2017.

Kamps, H. 2017. *New Internationalist* Magazine Turns to Crowdfunding to Secure Independence. Tech Crunch. https://techcrunch.com/2017/03/07/new-internationalist-crowdfunding/ accessed 3 August 2017.

NEKS. 2017. www.neks.ltd accessed 3 August 17.

New Internationalist. 2017. https://newint.org accessed 3 August 2017.

Olay. 2017. Three Point Night Cream. tellyAds. www.tellyads.com/play_advert/?filename=TA19963&advertiser=Olay&type=recent accessed 7 August 2017.

Ponsford, D. 2017. *New Internationalist* Magazine Raises £200,000 in Two Weeks in Crowdfunding Bid to Secure Its Future. *Press Gazette*. www.pressgazette.co.uk/new-internationalists-raises-200000-in-two-weeks-in-crowdfunding-bid-to-secure-its-future/ accessed 3 August 2017.

7

THE 360-DEGREE APPROACH TO CONTENT

While editors and publishers understand the importance of creating great content, putting it into practice – when there are so many other demands such as budget, time and staff – can be a challenge. In reality, editorial often achieves an 80/20 ratio where the majority of content is high quality, but sometimes the odd page filler (in print and online) slips through the net. But as readers become more demanding in their expectations standards must be raised to keep pace. Enter the 360-degree approach to content, because it is no longer acceptable to produce content in one medium.

Today a magazine's features should be multi-faceted across print, digital and online with the latter incorporating a video or audio element. Each version should contain different strands to create a content-rich experience; thus, taking a 360-degree approach with a feature package as opposed to repurposed content. The emphasis needs to be on creating crafted editorial that works for its intended platform. However, this presents many practical challenges, such as ensuring editorial teams have the necessary training to produce such content. There is also a question of financial viability.

Taking such an approach inevitably puts a strain on editorial budgets in terms of creation and production. So how do you make it a financially viable proposition? The answer lies first in creating a strong brand, then focusing on providing valuable content. Once those aspects have been achieved, then the publisher must develop strategies to successfully monetise the brand in a variety of forms and widen audience participation as highlighted in previous chapters.

Start with a strong brand

Gone are the days when a magazine was simply a publication; today it's about taking a multi-platform approach, which is where branding comes into play. To be successful a magazine must become a brand with a strong profile that is easily recognisable across platforms. It must have a consistent brand identity – from the printed issue (if there is one), digital edition and online provision to brand extensions and social media. This is the key criteria when moving from product to brand.

But what makes a strong brand? In my estimation, there are four key factors that determine whether a magazine brand will be successful, which is illustrated in my 'Components of a successful brand model' (Figure 7.1).

In my opinion each of these four key factors contributes equally to making a strong magazine brand that is sustainable. However, problems in developing a strong brand can appear where there are too many products on the peripheral of a market sector.

Such examples can be seen across many sectors including cycling, parenting and running – all of which have similar titles all competing for readers. When this happens, brand consolidation can be a solution. This is the option that *Running*, a magazine published by Kelsey Publishing Ltd, has opted to take. In the September/October 2017 issue, editor Amy Curtis announced in her Editor's Letter that: *Running is about to merge with our sister magazine,* Outdoor Fitness! (Curtis, 2017). A smart move as currently – according to BRAD – there are seven magazines in this sector, four of which are print titles and three digital.

Initially the title was known as *Running Fitness*, but it was then relaunched as *Running* in 2016. The relaunch being followed by the consolidation of two titles indicates that the relaunch didn't quite achieve the ROI targets. That said, this latest consolidation makes sense as it is likely to give the brand a USP which will be hard for competitors to recreate from their existing provisions.

The forthcoming case study, exploring Bauer's parenting provision, illustrates how clever consolidation can build a stronger brand, increase audience engagement and achieve long-term sustainability.

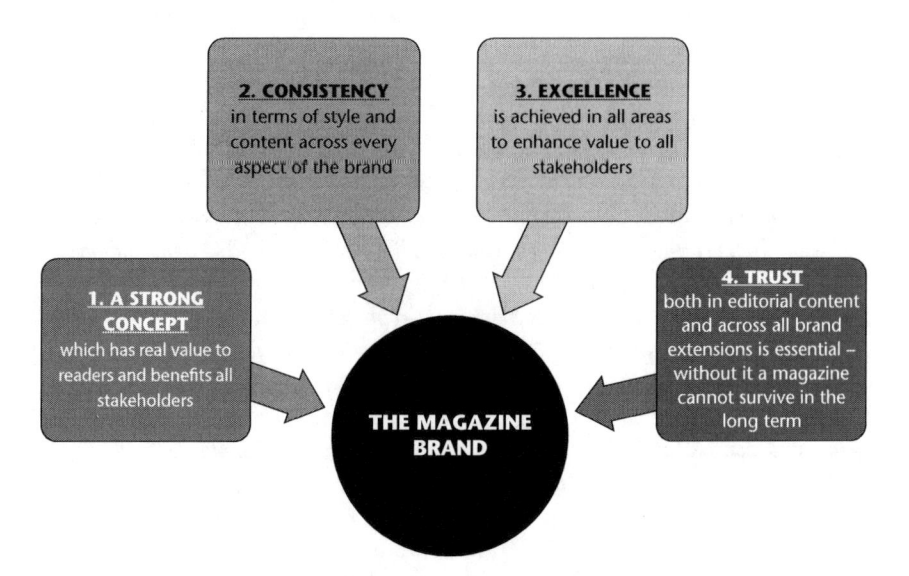

FIGURE 7.1 Components of a successful brand model

CASE STUDY: BAUER CONSOLIDATES ITS PARENTING PROVISION

David Bostock, then brand publisher at Bauer, faced a similar dilemma to *Running*, with titles targeting the parenting market. At the time Bauer had three brands aimed at the different stages of parenting – Pregnancy & Birth, Mother & Baby and an online site called AskAMum. With the technology disruption hitting the newsstands in 2010/11 David's teams' solution was simply to talk to the readers and consolidate.

Below he reveals how he identified the strongest title of those three provisions and consolidated it into one brand to become a market leader in the parenting sector.

The parenting market is a very competitive one. Working for a legacy magazine brand business where the main aim was to dominate the market in the 1990s and 2000s by producing a lot of print products segmented around niches like Pregnancy & Birth, Mother & Baby and AskAMum forum-based site. But because of a digital disruption with sites with massive start-up investment such as Mumsnet and Netmums evolving, the market changed rapidly.

At this point, it's important to remember that the average age of a mum ranges from 28 to 32 – a generation who had been brought up with technology. Unsurprisingly they were early adopters of the social media space. Instead of turning to their favourite parenting magazine as the previous generation had done, Mums began to log on to Facebook and other platforms including Mumsnet to seek advice. As a result, parenting was one of the first genres to be disrupted by the phone/iPad.

In 2010/11 our research revealed that the iPad was one of the key big purchases mums bought before going on maternity leave. Mums were getting teched-up as they wanted to stay communicated with the world, friends and work. Therefore, our strategy for moving into that space focused on brand consolidation. From the research data we identified Mother & Baby as the strongest of our parenting brands so we put everything into it, turning the team into a one-brand team which operated across different platforms. The idea was to have one audience, because at that time there were so many other brands in the parenting market many readers found it confusing.

During the consolidation stage talking to our readers was key. As a new parent, the reader needs to work out the best buggy, while getting advice on their concerns and anxieties. Our readers told us that as new mums they didn't have time to trawl through numerous platforms looking for information. We realised that editors needed to do the job for them – our parenting brand would become a reader-centric model. Tapping into our audience's needs was crucial, as was having a talented editorial team to turn the content into something compelling. It was these aspects that helped us dominate in such a competitive market.

Today's mums are digitally savvy because they have to be. A smartphone or tablet enables them to keep in touch with access to a massively convenient source of information. This has impacted on the print products, which now struggle in this

> market. Through research, we found that a lot of online activity happens at around 2am because mums often seek information when they are feeding. New mums often find it difficult to leave the house in the early stages due to all the preparation involved. Therefore, the idea of our readers going out to buy a magazine was no longer viable, so we revised our strategy – driving online users to subscriptions. And we did this quite successfully too.
>
> Over the past 20 years the first big specialist content sites – and success stories – were all in the parenting market because it is full of ever-green content such as baby sleeping patterns and has lots of tools for fertility, baby names, etc. As a result, the parenting market was one of the first to really have a massive success digitally, not just because of the audience, but also because parents are faced with all these new brands – which are often brands they've never heard of before. Mother & Baby had a lot of success in that area.
>
> There is money to be made both from the traditional advertising model and from the eCommerce side. Yet despite its challenges – particularly as seen in the parenting market – print is not dead, but it's changing rapidly. I think it's moving to a different space and place. An interesting trend – and one to watch – is the big success in high-cover-priced, specialist, gorgeous print products which small publishers can make money out of, although it's not currently an attractive sector for a big publisher. Very few of these high-end, niche titles have the same distribution model as the consumer magazines. Instead these are sold through specialist shops or bookshops relating directly to the marketplace they are in – having found a new route to market. They are highly targeted, bespoke, tailored magazines which have very clever routes to audience as opposed to high street retailers and supermarkets which focus on mass distribution often resulting in massive un-solds.
>
> Perhaps the hardest lesson today is about timing, knowing when to launch digital products – do you want to be an early or late adopter? With the parenting market, it was easier to move into digital as we were driven by trends and used data to support brand consolidation. But for many publishers it is often tempting to jump in before there's a revenue stream. Knowing when to launch is a core skill – it's about having a strategy to convert those mass eyeballs into revenue.

Create effective feature packages

While consolidation is a good business strategy, your brand is only as good as the content it provides. Essentially all content needs to be reader-centric; the simple feature is no longer sufficient – either for the reader or in terms of creating a sustainable title. Enter the feature package, a mix of written content, short audio or video clips and maybe some data visuals in the form of info-graphics.

Today publishers need to create a content-rich experience for readers across platforms – from the print and digital editions to eNewsletters, events and online. But remember it is crucial that the print and digital angle differs from the online so the reader sees fresh content on each platform. A temptation to produce articles written for the magazine's print edition then simply repurpose these for the brand's online pages must be resisted.

To further demonstrate this point, I have created the 360-degree feature package model (as shown in Figure 7.2) whereby the content goes full circle, developing different angles to suit each aspect.

My 360-degree model illustrates how a successful feature package can be created in three stages. First comes the theme, which in this case will be *Living with dementia*. A key factor in delivering a successful reader/user experience is to start with the theme, then develop a different angle for each platform to achieve an 80/20 ratio so the majority is new copy with a small amount of repetition to link back to the theme and facilitate signposting.

Stage 1 of the model focuses on the print/digital angle *Getting the right care*. This uses a mix of research, quotes and anecdotes to develop a strong, informative article; however, it should also include sufficient images and some form of info-graphic to further enrich the readers' experience. Next, in Stage 2, the online approach uses the angle of *A daughter's experience*, which is a mix of written, audio and visual content, thereby maximising the user's experience by using a wealth of mediums. However, you can – and should – also include an audio or video clip in digital editions, where appropriate. Last comes Stage 3 – a promotional opportunity to facilitate widening audience participation by driving readers and users to each of the theme's angles, thus increasing engagement through sharing opportunities. All these aspects can impact positively on circulation.

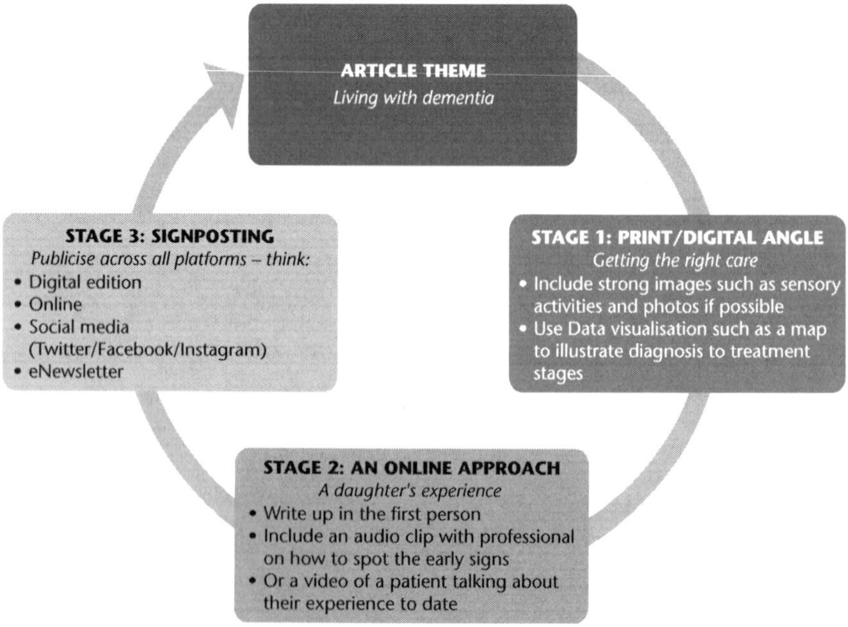

ARTICLE THEME
Living with dementia

STAGE 3: SIGNPOSTING
Publicise across all platforms – think:
- Digital edition
- Online
- Social media (Twitter/Facebook/Instagram)
- eNewsletter

STAGE 1: PRINT/DIGITAL ANGLE
Getting the right care
- Include strong images such as sensory activities and photos if possible
- Use Data visualisation such as a map to illustrate diagnosis to treatment stages

STAGE 2: AN ONLINE APPROACH
A daughter's experience
- Write up in the first person
- Include an audio clip with professional on how to spot the early signs
- Or a video of a patient talking about their experience to date

FIGURE 7.2 The 360-degree feature package model

Of course, every magazine is different; therefore editors are likely to have their own take on the feature package and how it should be structured. However, once it becomes part of the editorial provision, the concept can then be adapted to explore both data and content opportunities as demonstrated in the Bauer case study, which while focusing on consolidation also increases content provision.

Through accrediting bodies such as the PPA (Professional Publisher's Association), the NCTJ (National Council for the Training of Journalists) and BJTC (Broadcast Journalism Training Council) the concept of a feature package is also feeding into the next generation of media students. Today's journalism students are fast developing an understanding of the importance of a user rich experience. Students know how to produce quality content across the key platforms because many university courses are now building the feature package into their undergraduate curriculums.

For example, at Bournemouth University those final year students who opt for magazine major projects must produce an investigative feature that takes the 360-degree approach – including text, audio and video components to maximise content potential. Therefore, when those journalism graduates start their first job they understand that a feature no longer just involves writing a 1,200-word article.

Maximise content resources

As with the parenting market, which we know provides a rich source of ever-green content, editorial in all sectors needs to pay its way. A good example of this is the B2B market, particularly those titles that sit in the corporate sector. Much can be gained from analysing publishers' strategies and resourcefulness in this market.

Two magazines stand out for me as having achieved sustainability through diversity and packaging their content in an articulate, user-friendly way. These are *The Lawyer*, which until recently was a weekly title, and *The Economist*. Both titles are evaluated in Table 7.1.

The table demonstrates parallels with these two titles in terms of both targeting a high end audience and utilising data to provide specific, high-value reader services. However, while *The Lawyer*, which has recently become a monthly magazine, published by Centaur has a much lower print circulation, it stands out as a great example of developing profitable content despite the challenge of having a much smaller target market.

Established in 1987 in the heyday of print, *The Lawyer* has successfully navigated its way through the digital disruption of the 2000s. According to BRAD, a publisher's statement hasn't been submitted since July 2012 when the average net circulation was 89,158 (BRAD, 2017c). However, *The Lawyer*'s (2017) Media Pack (Figure 7.3) states that the magazine has 25,000 print readers every week and achieves 1.2 million page impressions a month, not to mention 120,000+ daily newsletter recipients, 343,000 registered users and more than 3,000 annually attending the brand's events. Its readership credentials are equally impressive with 24% being FTSE 500 in-house counsel and 48% holding senior management/partner positions in their firm.

TABLE 7.1 B2B vs consumer

	The Lawyer B2B Est. 1987	*The Economist* Consumer, news Est. 1993
Publisher	Centaur Media Plc	The Economist Group Ltd
Formats	Print, digital and online	Print, digital and online
Magazine frequency	Monthly from May 2017	Weekly
Cover price	£5.70 Controlled Circulation	£5.00
Readership	25,000 (source: Media Pack)	162,431 (source: BRAD, Jan–Jun 2017)
Total audience	More than 1 million (source: Media Pack)	3.7+ million (source: BRAD)
Distribution strategy	Mostly subscription-only through membership-style packages	Subscription and newsstand
Target audience	High flyers in the legal profession, which includes the top 200 UK law firms (source: BRAD)	Board directors, financiers, administrators, opinion formers and politicians (source: BRAD)
Advertising page rate	£4,750 (source: Media Pack)	£21,300 (source: BRAD)
Brand extensions	• Digital and print content • Events • Data services	• Digital and print content worldwide • Events – more than 70 worldwide • Data services

In other words, this audience has serious spending power – and therefore is more likely to pay for knowledge that will further enhance their profile or progression, an observation that Centaur has noted from the outset and made it a core part of its revenue strategy. Thus, it has developed impressive brand extensions or in this case product services. As well as print and digital editions of the title, other products include data-driven services including research and briefings, events, awards and invitation-only roundtables.

More notable is *The Lawyer*'s membership-style subscription packages posted on its website, from which subscribers can choose one of the following four options:

1. **Registered – FREE includes:** latest headlines, job boards, selected career insight, Lawyer 2B, briefings from law firms
2. **Premium Individual online – £440 + VAT – includes:** exclusive news, in-house interviews, managing partner interviews, latest panel reviews, latest deals and cases, long-form analysis of market trends, in-house appointments, *The Lawyer* archives
3. **Premium Individual online & print – £550 + VAT – includes:** all of the above, plus the printed issue

FIGURE 7.3 The *Lawyer* media pack

4. **Premium Corporate – rate not specified – includes:** exclusive news, access for all employees, access *The Lawyer Market* Intelligence (LMI), access market reports, managing partner interviews, latest panel interviews, long-form analysis of market trends and data, UK and global, latest deals and cases, in-house appointments, *The Lawyer* archives.

Steve Newbold, Centaur Media's divisional managing director of media and events, has played a key part in the brand's transformation and admits that the digital disruption did present some challenges. The main challenge was sustaining and building revenue opportunities as previously *The Lawyer* and many of Centaur's other B2B titles were dependent on revenue from recruitment advertising.

However, whenever there is a challenge it is crucial to take stock and look for opportunities, which is exactly what Centaur did. For Steve, the digital age provided the chance for him and his team to turn the problem into an opportunity by maximising the title's existing resources and strengths to breathe new life into declining revenue streams.

> We were brilliant at reaching high-value audiences in significant volume via controlled circulating print whereby we collected print registration details and sent out high-quality, weekly magazines for free. For these we would attract both display and recruitment advertising – *The Lawyer* used an advertising model – that was our main revenue stream. Conferences have played a key part and yield good data as we collected registration details. Revenue from this was achieved through sponsorship with some paid-for delegate revenue.

The problems started when the digital disruption started to kick in, probably around the dot.com era, recalls Steve.

> Publishers rapidly started to see those revenues migrating on to digital platforms and also our advertisers started finding other ways to recruit such as LinkedIn. Despite this *The Lawyer* has held up well from a recruitment perspective, whereas there are other markets – not just within Centaur – titles have disappeared in the space of a few years. We still get decent recruitment revenues, not as good as we used to get.

However, he admits that the brand's biggest challenge was the on-demand element and finding a route to market demands, as well as from *The Lawyer*'s readers who wanted to consume things in a multimedia way – not just waiting once a week for a weekly magazine to drop on the mat.

> Today's readers want daily news updates and regular content. It has changed the dynamic but from a business perspective we recognised quite early on that advertising was likely to decline in print and therefore you have to find other ways of diversifying revenues.

To overcome these challenges Steve and his team used several strategies but he cites Centaur – and many of their contemporaries – as being behind the drive to initiate paid-for content in recent years.

> That challenge resulted in us creating new forms of content which we wouldn't have done before, such as information and analysis. For example, we did a series of reports for *The Lawyer* and started selling them. What we quickly realised was that the value of such is quite high because they are information products as opposed to news artefacts. We produced a series of reports such as *The Lawyer* Top UK 100, which became the 200 report, then the Euro 250 and the China report. These were analytical reports full of data and analysis, therefore they were high-value products.

Essentially, *The Lawyer* utilised its brand as a brand extensive, using the route to market as a way to promote its additional products and services. Their existing sales team were then tasked with selling the reports. Steve explains,

> We had to bring in certain skillsets around content such as research, data and analytical skills to blend in with our market research and editorial team. But we soon realised that particularly in the legal market there is a need for this type of analysis. People trust *The Lawyer* as a brand to deliver that type of information – and on that journey we have started to become less newsy and more feature/analytically driven.

Steve reveals that they are moving way forward by recognising and delivering on what people expect from *The Lawyer*.

> Our audience expects expertise, for *The Lawyer* to have a definitive opinion on things and be a trusted source of expert information. So, for example, if there is a piece of news breaking or a story it is crucial to ensure that people will want to know what *The Lawyer*'s point of view is on the story.

Surprisingly he admits that in the past *The Lawyer* has somewhat undervalued its content. "We will be developing even more analytical, data-driven research on the website and putting it behind a paywall."

As we have seen from my earlier analysis of the title, *The Lawyer* has embraced the membership strategy. Moving forward the content will become more tiered, with less copy being free to view. The next level will require users to register to access it, thus facilitating data capture – and then there will be the premium content, where users must pay a subscription fee to access. So far, says Steve, this has been very successful. "Initially we perhaps undervalued our own content, but over time more will be behind the paywall leaving very little that users can access for free."

Unlike consumer brands, who struggle to achieve success for paywalls, *The Lawyer*, like *The Economist*, has succeeded. Steve admits that with B2B it is generally easier to get your audience to pay for specialist knowledge than in other market sectors.

As with many B2B titles, it's all about the data. Rather than react impulsively to the digital disruption, Centaur Media has taken its time to develop a strong brand with a clear value proposition. It started with the readers' needs and worked outwards as every publication should. It is an excellent example in terms of developing revenue and content strategies.

My verdict? *The Lawyer* is a strong brand with a great future – and there are many lessons to be learned from this brand's journey.

Summary

While it may seem obvious that the focus should be on content, with so many brand extensions and other demands on today's editors, editorial is in danger of taking second place. During the past few years a few magazines have not evolved much in terms of their features list – instead preferring to follow their rival rather than focus on creating a reader-centric editorial profile unique to their publication. This, together with market saturation in some sectors, I feel, has been a contributory factor in circulation declines among many key titles.

Why? Because today's readers know that they want. They are also far more informed than any previous generation, have more choices and – perhaps most importantly – have 24/7 access to information. Some editors and publishers need to fully grasp the impact of these cultural and technological changes to build sustainable publications. However, some forward-thinking editorial strategists have adapted well, as we have seen with Steve Newbold and David Bostock. By focusing their efforts on what readers need and want – then finding a way to provide it – they have succeeded in building sustainable, reader-centric and value-led titles.

Therefore, to conclude I would say that the solution lies in not only creating valuable content that readers both need and want but also packaging it in a highly visual, imaginative way. It is also crucial that each aspect of a feature is specifically created for its intended platform as demonstrated in my 360-degree feature package model with all content carefully signposted at each stage to drive the audience to it.

Get the basics right, watch your timing and don't invest beyond what will achieve a reasonable ROI. As we have seen throughout the examples in this chapter – and the book – readers will support a magazine which has valuable high-quality content and offers relevant brand extensions.

INDUSTRY PERSPECTIVES

Steve Newbold, divisional managing director of media and events worked across numerous market sectors before joining Centaur Media Plc. With a wealth of experience and an innovative approach, Steve has steered *The Lawyer* (Figure 7.4) through the challenges of the digital age only to emerge even stronger.

FIGURE 7.4 *The Lawyer* cover, courtesy of Centaur Media Plc

Below Steve reveals the changes that have seen the title evolve into a brand leader – which now has a high-end, luxury print edition – and how he sees it evolving in the next five years.

Achieving a strong subscription base is one of the biggest challenges magazines face, but at The Lawyer, *we focus on membership-style packages primarily because we want to create a community. Subscription is really just a payment method whereas having a membership makes you feel that you belong to something. What we want people to feel about* The Lawyer *is that they belong to The Lawyer premium – to that community.*

Increasingly as we take the brand forward on our journey, membership will become more important because it will entitle members to certain other privileges such as giving members early-bird rates or invites to our events or award ceremonies. Primarily it's about being valued as a customer and that will be the same for all our brands at Centaur. We want to make our audience feel they are part of something, that they have access to exclusive content.

In addition to membership, we have decreased the frequency of the print edition. Previously it had always been a weekly print title, then in May (2017) The Lawyer *went monthly, which so far has been tremendously successful. Because if I think about why it was weekly (going back to 30 years ago when it first launched) it was largely because of the recruitment advertising, whereas all of that is now daily on the website. Also, nearly all of our recruitment revenue is digital so in that respect print was kind of redundant and the same is true of news. Pretty much everything we were producing is on the website and we were just packaging up a weekly.*

Moving to a monthly title, the magazine's editorial focus has had to change, shifting from a news emphasis to taking an analytical approach. The monthly edition now targets a discreet, more senior audience and gives readers an analysis of what's gone on the previous month. In the near future, we plan to filter in there some of our proprietary data and report summaries. Ultimately, our strategy is about positioning The Lawyer *as an opinion forming, high-value brand.*

Part of this strategy also meant creating the right design, moving from saddle-stitched to a perfect bound, high-quality big monthly of around 80 pages – and bigger in some months. Because of this people are keeping their copies now. It reinforces everything that we stand for as a brand. It means that we can have long-form features rather than news type stories, which is perfect for this sector.

Another change is that we have introduced themed issues – such as technology, ambition and diversity editions. This means we can have elements of features so we are covering a constant theme. And that works brilliantly in monthlies, but not so well in weekly titles. It may seem surprising, but the advertising revenue is doing as well as when the magazine was weekly. People like the idea that they can place a page in a magazine that is around for a month or longer rather than having to place one or two pages in a weekly, which is more disposable. So, it suits The Lawyer *better.*

In recent years, there has been a huge shift in our focus, when I think about what we used to do and where we are going in terms of moving towards paid-for content. Much of the content is all going on digital channels as that's where we live and breathe so it makes perfect sense because there is broader reach in terms of audience and locality – instead of national it becomes international. Digital provides the opportunity to do more things such as combining long-form with short-form; you can package it into emails, add video and have webinars. It also allows you to set up paywalls or isolated membership areas. Digital also facilitates great search options.

But to set it up properly is hugely expensive in terms of both labour and infrastructure. Behind the scenes – and it should not be underestimated – is Centaur, which as a company, was able to invest in research and development. Investment is at the core, you can't just switch from being a publisher to doing what we are doing without investing heavily. The journey needed a product development team, investment in platforms and to bring in new skillsets. There is a lot of stuff that needs to come together.

It's quite a transformation; you can't take your existing team and flip them on to digital. That wouldn't work because it's essential to keep the essence of those core brand values, particularly the editorial strengths. But at the same time, these need to be surrounded with new and different skillsets and that's not cheap to do. Unfortunately, digital in many ways is more expensive than print.

Digital is the journey we are on – the rewards for getting there are massive. Our plan for the next five years is to maximise the opportunity to grow significantly. I would say that there will be much more focus as a brand on information. Although there will still be news and analysis, it will have a whole suite of info services which people will pay for and I think we can do that through launch and acquisition. I also believe it can be more international, which is really exciting – Laywer.com for example, what a fantastic name. We already have a lot of US subscribers. The two big centres London and New York have many international law firms with offices in both regions and already we are covering that ground brilliantly.

Realising those expansion opportunities into international territories will probably be the main area of focus, mainly through online digital services, and, of course, brand values and maintaining our reputation. Ensuring we remain our members' primary source of intelligence will be at the heart of our journey.

AN EDITORIAL PACKAGE ACTION PLAN

Previously editors had strict guidelines for articles; however, in today's digital age articles should be thought of in terms of feature packages, which should start with a theme instead of an angle.

Consistency is crucial; to achieve this you need to develop specific editorial guidelines for these packages which should be given to staffers and freelances.

Here are four key components your guidelines should contain.

- **Print and digital content:** set a basic word count (700–1,000 words) and the minimum number of images needed and encourage the use of info-graphics to present the data visually. It's particularly worth having specific instructions for profile/interview pieces such as the inclusion of timelines. Note, for digital the info-graphic should be interactive and images should be in the form of a slide show.
- **The online story:** stipulate that this aspect needs to take a different angle; suggest a word count (300–500 words) and number of images and hyperlinks along with an audio or video clip.

- **Signposting and social media promotion:** include guidelines for signposting all content across platform. For example, at the end of the print article direct readers to the online aspect and vice versa. Also, staff should post previews on the title's social media to create a buzz. Signposting needs to be a must-do within the editorial team so that it becomes second nature.
- **The journalist's responsibility:** ensure all journalists – whether staff or freelance – tweet and post spoilers for their feature from their own social media accounts.

Bibliography

BRAD. 2017a. List of Running Magazines. BRAD Insight. https://brad.mediatel.co.uk/search/browse/title?Submit=Go&searchTerm=Running accessed 30 August 2017.

BRAD. 2017b. *The Economist*. BRAD Insight. https://brad.mediatel.co.uk/profile/press/6314#circulation accessed 8 September 2017.

BRAD. 2017c. *The Lawyer*. BRAD Insight. https://brad.mediatel.co.uk/profile/press/6664 accessed 5 September 2017.

Curtis, A. 2017. *Running*. Sept/Oct issue. Kelsey Publishing Ltd (p. 7).

FIPP. 2016. Centaur Media CEO on Innovation in B2B Media. www.fipp.com/news/features/centaur-media-ceo-on-innovation-in-b2b-media accessed 5 September 2017.

Norris, A. 2016. Centaur MD on Company's Digital Technology Journey. FIPP. www.fipp.com/news/features/centaur-md-on-companys-digital-technology-jou accessed 5 September 2017.

The Lawyer. 2017. Media Pack. https://s3-eu-central-1.amazonaws.com/centaur-wp/thelawyer/prod/content/uploads/2017/03/14101517/TL_Media-Pack.pdf accessed 5 September 2017.

The Lawyer. 2017. www.thelawyer.com/subscription-plans/ accessed 5 September 2017.

Thorpe, E. 2017. How the Lawyer Implemented a High-Value Subscriptions Strategy from the Start. The Media Briefing. www.themediabriefing.com/article/how-the-lawyer-implemented-a-high-value-subscriptions-strategy-from-scratch accessed 5 September 2017.

8
MONETISING ONLINE CONTENT

Steve Hill

The Times has been rolling off the presses for over 200 years. As with many legacy print newspaper and magazine brands, it can be forgiven for being slow to adapt to the challenges presented by digital publishing. Compared to *The Times*, the web is in its youth – little over 20 years old. Yet since its birth in the early 1990s it has been highly disruptive, causing chaos to traditional media revenue sources.

During this time magazine publishers had to launch new platforms in rapid succession, and latterly that has included the growing number of social media platforms and digital expansion. These are:

- **Websites:** in the 1990s publishers first had to invest in setting up websites as audiences accessed content on desktop and laptop computers.
- **Smartphones and tablets:** post 2000 we saw the rise of smartphones and tablet computers – markets where Apple and Google dominate. Although smartphones existed before, it was the launch of Apple's iPhone in 2006 that led to investment in apps and publishers had to redesign websites to cope with smaller screens and touchscreen access.
- **Social media:** Facebook launched in 2004 as a small university website. Who would have thought it would become the dominant way that people access news content in nearly all major media markets worldwide?
- **Digital editions:** Digital editions of printed magazines became popular with the launch of Amazon Kindle e-reader devices in 2007. A number of 'all you can read' pricing models exist for digital editions. For example, Readly (www.readly.com), launched in the UK in 2014, provides access to over 2,000 top titles for a single monthly subscription of £7.99 (see 'Industry perspectives' later on).

The pace of change hasn't stopped. Publishers must take into account the rise of new devices based around virtual reality (VR), augmented reality (AR) voice control and artificial intelligence (AI). The cost of investing in new technology and retraining staff is immense. New staff may be needed in roles such as community manager, data analyser, mobile editor, video editor, etc.

In this chapter we will explore the economic challenges and the value of print media and look at solutions to generate revenue.

The economic challenge

Let's get straight to the point – the biggest challenge that all publishers face, regardless of sector, is how they monetise digital content. Magazine brands must grow digital revenues fast enough to at least match a decline in revenues from print. Unfortunately, in many sectors this simply isn't happening.

Forward-thinking magazine brands operate a distributive publishing strategy, outputting content on a wide range of new platforms. This chapter will consider how magazine brands can generate revenue from their main digital outlets. These are likely to include:

- **Platform (outlets the magazine brands owns and runs):** the magazine's own website or own app. The publisher usually gets to keep all or most of the revenue generated.
- **Off-platform (external platforms that may host the magazine brand's content):** social media, e.g. Facebook, aggregator services such as Apple News/Flipboard and sales of digital editions on the Apple Store and via platforms such as Readly.

Off-platform publishing gives magazine brands huge international exposure, but publishers have to compromise when it comes to revenue. Julia Greenberg (2015) in *Wired* writes:

> As on Facebook and Snapchat, Apple News offers publishers another venue for serving content to readers in exchange for surrendering a degree of control. The trade-off may be worth it; news organizations will keep 100 percent of the revenue for ads they sell on Apple News, while Apple will pocket 30 percent if it helps sell ads using its iAds ad tech.

For those looking for easy solutions to generating revenue, we need to point out that the business models around digital publishing remain extremely challenging – to put it mildly. A report from global consulting firm OC&C Strategy Consultants in 2016 found that 'online disruption' has already cost the industry an estimated 46% in revenue within the last ten years and warns online platforms are set to become "more powerful in controlling the flow and consumption of news traffic" (Mayhew, 2016).

On the positive side, online digital publishing has enabled magazines to reach new audiences and overseas markets. Digital technology is relatively cheap and is infinitely more environmentally friendly than paper publishing – so there are cost savings to be made in the production process.

However, the key social media metrics of 'reach' (how many people see content) and 'engagement' (how many people interact, e.g. like, share or comment) sadly don't necessarily lead directly to monetisation – if only it was that easy. For example, Facebook Live streaming videos launched in 2016. Trials suggest such videos are often very popular with users, but it can be very hard to generate revenue from them directly.

Pockets of success exist. *The Economist* magazine is a name that crops up time and time again and we will discuss this later in the chapter. Current affairs publications with older, wealthier and international audiences are doing well online.

There are other successes in B2B and contract aka customer publishing. In the online world, niche content is good and in this respect magazines have the upper hand compared with newspapers with general news. However, consumer magazines are most likely to struggle online – particularly those in the most competitive sectors such as general lifestyle and teen magazines.

Why print publishing has been so good

To understand how publishers can generate money on the Internet today, it helps to look to the past. Many print models have solid advantages such as:

- **Scarcity of content:** in the 1980s if readers wanted their fill of pop music news and gossip they had to wait up to a fortnight for a magazine like *Smash Hits!* to hit the newsstand or land on their doormat. As anyone old enough will recall, in the pre-web days you spent a long time just waiting for content to be delivered to you. There were only four TV channels and no international media. Today we have an abundance of content in digital formats.
- **Control over the platform:** control of the platform and distribution *is* control over the audience relationship – this is the classic rule in publishing. Dead tree distribution was, and remains, a very expensive business; this meant that a few large publishers dominated the market. For advertisers, there are only so many ways for them to reach a target consumer sector. Today, the strength of the web is anyone can publish, but this meant massive global competition in publishing.
- **Gatekeeping:** in the 1980 and 1990s magazine journalists were the content gatekeepers and were often key opinion formers in the sectors they operated in. They acted as controllers of information appearing in the public domain. Today celebrities and businesses communicate with their audiences directly via social media taking journalists out of the information loop.

The pre-web days of the 1980s and 1990s were good times for publishers who controlled the platform and distribution. But a small number of large publishers dominated the sector and the reality was that audiences lacked choice. Where print advertising was once lucrative, online banner advertising brings in less revenue for publishers. Then there is the problem of Facebook and Google's dominance in online advertising. Dominic Ponsford (2017a) of *Press Gazette* writes: "In the UK the current size of the digital advertising pie is £10.3bn (2016) with most of that money going to Google and Facebook." According to Ponsford, the two Internet giants alone take a massive "80 per cent of new money coming in." Such is their dominance; *Press Gazette* has launched a campaign to end what it calls an advertising duopoly.

Solutions to generate revenue

It is easy to be disheartened by the economic challenge of digital media. However, in this main part of the chapter we propose eight key solutions to help increase revenue and achieve a higher level of sustainability for your publication.

1) Do more that is unique

The web is a competitive and noisy environment where numerous amateur and mainstream brands compete for attention. Academic Ian Hargreaves (2003) describes a modern phenomenon he terms 'ambient news'. He states:

> News, which was once difficult and expensive to obtain, today surrounds us like the air we breathe. Much of it literally ambient: displayed on computers, public billboards, trains, aircraft, and mobile phones. Where once news had to be sought out in expensive and scarce news sheets, today it is ubiquitous and very largely free at the point of consumption.

Content comes to us via news alerts on our mobile devices or via news streams – such as Facebook, Twitter and Instagram feeds. The rise of digital media led to an abundance of content that is distributed, copied and stored at minimal cost. Economics theory suggests that when you have too much of any product available – wherever it is bananas in a supermarket, music on the Internet or even magazine content – the price will fall. Indeed, it may even fall to rock bottom – i.e. a price point of zero. This is something that has happened in the most competitive sectors in newspapers and magazines.

So publishers need to think about the value of their content. To put it bluntly – is it really worth paying for? It is likely that some of it is and some of it isn't.

Action point

There is a lot of text online, so it can pay for magazines to experiment in more interactive outputs including audio podcasts and streaming video that engages mobile users.

2) Facebook is *the Internet (for many users)*

We have stated that forward-thinking media brands have adopted a distributed publishing strategy – using websites, apps/digital editions, social media and aggregators. Content should be available on all the platforms that the magazine's audience is likely to access. However, not all platforms are equal and it is harder to monetise some types of content over others.

According to a survey of Internet users in 26 countries carried out by *The Digital News Report* 2016 from the Reuters Institute (Newman et al., 2016), Facebook is the top social network for news consumption by some margin. An average of 44% of people in the countries surveyed obtained news from Facebook; Japan was the only country where it wasn't number one. YouTube, owned by Google, came in second (average of 19% of users accessing news) and Twitter third (10%).

In the past, users discovered news on such services and then followed the links to the website of the media brand. However, Facebook and Apple News are tools for 'direct consumption', i.e. users consume content without leaving what is known as the 'walled garden' of the platform. While this is very convenient for users, it means that content providers on these services must do a deal with the platforms to take a cut of the advertising revenue.

Snapchat and Instagram, while popular as a general social media service, have struggled to become tools for content consumption. Snapchat's Discover service, which has brands such as *Cosmopolitan* and *National Geographic*, has 12% of users among 18–25 year olds in the US, but only 1% in the UK.

That said, *Cosmopolitan* estimates it achieves 3 million views each day on its content. *The Economist*, with its older readership, doesn't necessarily sound like a natural fit for Snapchat, yet it joined in 2016. "Joining Snapchat Discover is the latest initiative in our *Read, Watch, Listen* strategy, allowing *The Economist* to adapt its highly regarded content to new platforms as a way to grow reach and awareness with key audiences," said Lydia Kaldas (2016), senior vice president of strategy and channel relationships at *The Economist*.

Twitter, whose audience has been falling in recent times, still remains an important tool for news discovery in many countries. The rise of social media poses specific challenges to brands aimed at the young (18–24) and women. Women were the most likely to go on social media sites to read, share and comment on news. Men, while still heavy users of news on social media, were more likely than women to go to a direct news website or app/digital edition, stated *The Digital News Report* 2016.

Mobile is an important tool for consumption of content for all groups, but tablets (a market dominated by Apple's iPad) are more popular among older groups. Smartphones dominate among the young and beat every other platform for content consumption, including TV.

Action point

Publishers are wise to publish on Facebook, as it is popular with all social groups. When it comes to other social media platforms, be wary of the hype. For instance, while journalists are often fans of Twitter, its impact can be overstated among audiences.

> **CASE STUDY: *GLAMOUR* MAGAZINE**
>
> Condé Nast's *Glamour* has embraced both a mobile-first and a social media strategy. Of course, this makes complete sense; it's where its young female audience spends most of their day, on Instagram, Snapchat and the rest! Speaking to *The Drum* (Goodfellow, 2016), *Glamour*'s publishing director Jamie Jouning states:
>
>> With distribution, it really is a question of making sure and acknowledging that content has to go everywhere where our readers are spending their time, who might not necessarily traditionally buy print, and are more likely to be on social platforms.
>
> *Glamour* journalists handpick content they think will work best on each social media platform. "That is our underpinning strategy for everything that we do with our content," Jouning says.

3) Keep investing in the brand

"Our audience tells us that they're drowning in information, much of which is manipulative clickbait, irrelevant, or junk," says Caroline McGinn, Editor-in-Chief of *Time Out*, London. In an online world of amateur reviews, few would doubt that *Time Out* is a strong magazine brand. "They trust us to help them find something genuinely excellent. That's been *Time Out*'s aspiration since it was founded in London in 1968," she says.

The Reuters Institute report (Newman et al., 2016) noted that in news consumers still view the big names such as the BBC and *The Guardian* as their primary sources of news. The report states: "Main usage online remains with brands that have a strong news heritage and have been able to build up a reputation over time." The success of some digital editions, which is a very different content consumption experience compared with social media, suggests there remains a thirst for curated product over raw and often untrusted online news feeds.

In this era of fake news and filter bubbles, magazine brands need to invest in their brands to differentiate themselves. To cope with the economic challenge, some media publishers have recruited teams of low paid journalists to churn out clickbait style stories – these can include outlandish headlines that have little to do with the actual story. However, audiences are increasingly getting wise to this and returning to those trusted magazine brand names they respect.

In our view the Facebook and Twitter newsfeeds do not highlight strongly enough the branding of the media organisation behind the content. This can frustrate users who are seeking out high-quality content. Thus, we much prefer Apple News' aggregation service that highlights the logo of the leading news source – *Vogue*, *Radio Times*, *National Geographic*, *T3* are just a handful of trusted names on the platform.

Action point

Media buyers haven't taken kindly to having their client's adverts appear next to extremist videos on YouTube and other dubious online sites. Increasingly, they only want to be associated with trusted magazine brands.

4) Learn from digital-only rivals

BuzzFeed is frequently highlighted as a success story in both hard and soft news. It is way past being 'web first' in its approach to journalism and now operates mobile as well as social media first. It is surprisingly happy with the fact that visitors engage mostly off-platform, i.e. via Facebook, Instagram and Snapchat, rather than going directly to its own website.

The traffic to its own website is small. "Of the five billion interactions BuzzFeed has with its public each month, only one billion occur at BuzzFeed.com; the rest occur on Facebook, YouTube, Instagram, Snapchat, and platforms yet to be invented," states Jeff Jarvis in the Tinius Report 2015.

And who can forget BuzzFeeds's exploding watermelon? In April 2016 BuzzFeed experimented with the newly launched Facebook Live streaming video service and had 800,000 viewers watch as the drama unfolded. As we write this, it has since been watched over 11 million times. BuzzFeed takes an experimental approach to new technology as soon as it launches, which is good practice for all magazine brands. It was one of a handful of media partners who were paid to use the service at launch.

BuzzFeed runs an ad format called Swarm at South to allow marketers to run campaigns that simultaneously reach all of its web and mobile outlets, as well as six of its social media platforms, including its Snapchat Discover channel, Tumblr, YouTube, Instagram and Facebook.

Action Point

Follow your digital-only rivals in taking an experimental approach to online distribution and remain nimble on your feet.

5) Take a user-centred approach

We can't emphasise enough the importance of developing an approach to monetisation that is user-centred – which means putting the needs of the audience and the online community first.

The first rule in UX (user experience) design is to do no harm. Online adverts present serious problems for a website's user experience as most advertising is designed to interrupt the content consumption process. Looking at display adverts in a printed magazine or on commercial TV is acceptable because readers expect to be interrupted by them. But online ads have a very poor reputation. One report estimated 32% of under 35-year-olds use ad blocking technology in the UK, such as AdBlocker Plus, on their computers. Worryingly, the latest trend is still to install it on phones.

Mark Zuckerberg, founder and CEO of Facebook, has adopted an attitude to online banner advertising which appears informed more by his experience as a user than that of someone who wishes to make pots of money. In the first few years of Facebook a note stating "*We don't like these either, but they help to pay the bills*" appeared above its tiny display ads. Soft drinks company Sprite in May 2006 offered to pay US$1 million if Facebook allowed it to turn its homepage green for a single day. Facebook turned it down. This type of 'takeover advertising' while very lucrative does immense damage to a website's brand and users hate it.

What unites Apple, Facebook and Google is they are deeply focused on the user experience – something that all media players can learn from. It's because of the same principle that Google allows it users to skip pre-roll adverts after just a few seconds. It's the principle that states that annoying the user is always bad.

As long it is clearly identified as such, a less intrusive advertising option is to encourage advertisers to create branded or sponsored content that is highly shareable. Some magazine publishers have set up internal agencies that create multimedia content or microsites for advertisers in their magazine style.

Another source of annoyance to users is slow access to content. Fast loading articles generate more engagement and sharing. Bounce rate, the speed people leave a site, can be as high as 58% on pages that take more than ten seconds to load.

To speed things up, some publish on Facebook using its Instant Articles technology launched in 2016. This is essentially publishing directly on to the Facebook website and mobile app and, as the name suggests, articles appear very quickly – perhaps instantly. Publishers can include auto-play videos and interactive maps as well as text and images. The key negative is that this is the walled-garden approach of Instant Articles – Facebook does not allow users to visit the magazine website and keeps users within the Facebook app.

Some, such as Katharine Viner, Editor-in-Chief of *The Guardian*, find moves by social apps to keep people away from the open web concerning; Katharine states:

> The old idea of a wide-open web – where hyperlinks from site to site created a non-hierarchical and decentralised network of information – has been largely supplanted by platforms designed to maximise your time within their walls, some of which (such as Instagram and Snapchat) do not allow outward links at all.

When it comes to user-centred approach, the principles are simple. If your website frustrates you, then chances are it will be annoying your users. A poor UX (user experience) will prevent monetisation.

Action point

Controversially, Google in June 2017 warned publishers the next version of its Chrome browser will come complete with an ad blocker and, to make matters worse, it will be switched on by default! However, it won't block all adverts, just the ones it deems to be intrusive. The Coalition for Better Ads (www.betterads.org/standards/) has advice on how to prevent your site from being blocked.

6) Know the user

In 2005, just as Facebook was starting out, Interscope Records released a single by Gwen Stefani called 'Hollaback Girl'. Stefani, in a sort of cheerleader's chant, sings:

> A few times I've been around that track
> So it's not just gonna happen like that
> 'Cause I ain't no hollaback girl
> Ain't no hollaback girl

The ridiculously catchy, pom-pom inspired, single was a massive hit. Interscope marketers promoted the digital download exclusively to cheerleader groups. The hope was these groups would adopt the chant, use it during their routines and this would act as viral promotion. Facebook ran promotions exclusively appearing on the profiles of young women who were either cheerleaders themselves or had expressed an interest in it. The results were impressive and it was the first song to sell more than 1 million digital downloads.

Now this type of advertising scares the heck out of many in publishing. Yet they forget that this type of advertising – where the consumer is being informed of new products which they don't yet know about – was once dominated by print magazines.

But now a digital camera manufacturer takes out sponsored content campaigns on Facebook targeting new dads in their thirties and forties – essentially the typical consumers of new cameras. This is remarkably efficient for advertisers and cheaper than taking out display ads in hobby magazines.

Google, with its AdWords network, is particularly strong in the sector of consumers who know what they want to purchase – this is known as 'demand fulfilment'. Say I want a plumber, I do a Google search and AdWords for plumbers appear next to search listings.

This level of targeting on Google and Facebook certainly has its critics. Tech journalist John Naughton, writing in *The Guardian* (5 March 2017) noted:

> The data is sliced, diced and sold to advertisers in a vast, hidden – and totally unregulated – system of high-speed, computerised auctions that ensure each user can be exposed to ads that precisely match their interests, demographics and gender identity. And this is done with amazing, fine-grained resolution: Facebook, for example, holds 98 data points on every user. Welcome to the world of 'surveillance capitalism'.

So it is no surprise therefore that a huge amount of advertising spend is moving from print to online. However, it is where it is going online that matters. The twin threat of Google and Facebook snapping up ad spend is a key problem for all media brands – but there are few easy solutions. These companies simply know more about users than magazine brands do and they are harvesting data on an industrial scale.

Action point

Magazines must follow in Facebook's footsteps and focus on building closer relationships with the online audiences and communities they serve.

7) Generating revenue from apps and digital editions

There is mixed news when it comes to generating revenue from digital editions. A quick look at the Apple Store shows that current affairs magazines from *The Economist*, *The Week*, *Forbes*, *The Spectator* and *Newsweek* are dominating the charts.

According to the *Press Gazette* (Ponsford, 2017b), the latest ABC figures (taken from July to December 2016) of digital editions now account for 2.5 per cent of the total circulation of audited titles. Table 8.1, with figures taken from *Press Gazette*, outlines those magazines which are achieving strong sales with their digital editions.

The Economist leads the sector in the UK by some margin. Only the free magazine of the *Camping & Caravanning Club* comes close. One rationale may be because *The Economist* acknowledges that readers will have different consumption preferences. This is reflected in its subscription options which has three rates – print only (just the magazine delivered by post every Thursday), digital only and, the most expensive, print/digital combination. The list of services that come as part of *The Economist*'s digital package is impressive:

- The app edition (app for Android or Apple tablet and phones)
- Audio edition (listen to each week's issue of *The Economist*, read by professional broadcasters)
- *The Economist Espresso* (morning briefing distributed direct to smartphones)
- Economist.com website and its online archive since 1997

TABLE 8.1 Magazines achieving high sales

Title	Total	YoY%
The Economist – UK edition	79,853	8.5
Camping & Caravanning	71,378	76.1
The Week Magazine	36,765	6.1
The Spectator (excluding Australia)	22,034	43.7
Time Magazine – EMEA (excluding BI/SA)	17,288	13.1

It is clear that *The Economist* has a sharp focus on getting people to subscribe – everything it does on the web and on social media has that single objective in mind. It knows it must convert free readers to subscribers.

On a digital edition, it is possible to create a linear reading experience that is very similar to accessing a traditional print magazine. It is a bounded experience, that is to say it discourages users going on to the open web and encourages loyalty to the brand. People spend longer with apps than they do on websites. Sales of digital editions are by no means pure profit. For example, Apple's cut of profits was in the region of 30% on sales going through its now closed Newsstand platform (www.macrumors.com/2015/06/08/newsstand-discontinued/).

In order to achieve higher digital sales, publishers must move away from the idea of adapting the issue's PDF. Thus, we would like to see the sector focus on thinking more creatively in terms of apps. Apps encourage publishers to create content and services that exploit the unique functionality of handheld devices.

App services can include:

- Touch screen
- Voice control
- Camera
- Accelerometer
- Bluetooth
- GPS/location-based services.

We see particular potential for growth in personalised location-based content services based around GPS, although app production can be expensive and magazine brands have not been particularly strong in developing interesting services. There is growth in voice control – using Amazon Alexa, Google Assistant or Apple Siri. Amazon's Echo device has no screen, is voice operated and media brands such as Sky News, BBC, CNN and *The Guardian* to name a few distribute headlines in this way. As we write, Amazon Echo does not include audio adverts, although rumours persist that they may well be introduced.

When Apple launched its first iPhone in 2007 it not only invented a new marketplace of downloadable apps; it also made an often-ignored breakthrough – a new system of micropayments. It is easy to forget that paying for very cheap items, like a single news story or single issue of a magazine, was a pain until Apple made it convenient and even, dare we say it, fun.

It is perhaps surprising that with such easy systems few people appear willing to pay for magazine subscriptions. The UK has one of the lowest rates of people willing to pay for news online. When it came to newspapers, The Reuters Institute Survey (Newman et al., 2016) found that only around 7% of Brits pay for online news content through subscriptions. *The Times* and, yet again, *The Economist* are most popular. Yet 27% pay for content in Norway.

Many people have speculated about the lack of uptake of subscriptions compared to some other countries – one theory is that the English magazine market is just so competitive with users being spoilt for choice with content from mature media markets of the US and Australia. In countries where there are fewer magazines in the local language, those that are often have higher digital subscriber numbers.

For magazines, bundling digital with paper subscriptions is usually a sound idea. In some countries, sales of individual magazine issues or even individual articles are much stronger. In other countries a 'freemium' model exists as well, where free users get a cut down version of the newspaper, while paid members get extra perks. It is possible in the future that such models could become popular in the UK.

'All you can read' for a monthly fee, also known as the 'Netflix model' of magazine publishing are being developed by rivals Magzter (www.magzter.com) and Readly (www.readly.com). For publishers, every download of their magazines contributes to their ABC figures. "Many aspects of entertainment consumption such as music and film have already demonstrated the effectiveness of the subscription model and magazines are a natural development of this trend," states Per Hellberg, CEO from Readly (HUFFPOST, 2016).

Action point

Apps and digital editions can be profitable if they offer genuine value to the audience.

8) Revenue streams of the future

It's hard to generalise, as magazine publishing is so broad. However, despite an onslaught from Facebook and Google, magazines are still well positioned in the so-called 'discovery to transaction funnel'. That is to say magazine publishing remains an important medium for readers to hear about new products, perhaps read reviews of them, and then go off to buy them.

As we have said, a focus on the user experience and building new online services is the best approach. Sponsored or branded content, where clearly identified, can appeal to the user and be informative.

Magazine publishers have developed trust and authority over many years and this puts them at some advantage over newer digital-only players. It is perhaps rational that traditional media publishers like selling banner adverts – it is a world they understand. However, it is clear that this model is breaking down in many areas of publishing – if not entirely broken. They perform poorly on smartphones and users often find them intrusive. The social media platforms have always known they are in the user relationship business, not the content business. They leave the expensive business of content creation to others. The social media providers soon realised the more information they know about their users the more it can serve them for better-targeted commercial content. They share some audience data with publishers, but magazines are right to feel concerned that their relationship with the audience is slipping away as more people access their content via social media sites, and in some cases, never visit the magazine's website directly.

It has become a cliché for media publishers to complain at industry conferences about a poor revenue split with social media and aggregator platforms. Well, it is highly unlikely that publishers would shout about it if they secured a good deal. Under pressure from publishers, Facebook promised in July 2017 to improve the revenue share it offers publishers. Its head of news partnerships for EMEA, Patrick Walker, states: "The publisher can sell its own advertising against Instant Articles (and keep all the revenue) or else allow Facebook to sell the ads and keep 70 per cent of the revenue." This is a considerable improvement on previous revenue share schemes from the company (Ponsford, 2017a).

Walker said it will allow publishers to advertise within video, even though YouTube had allowed it for some time and is also introducing technology that promotes digital subscriptions, something publishers have been demanding for some time. We know very little about how Facebook promotes or downgrades news content at will. Publishers are right to demand far more transparency from the social media companies about precisely how these algorithms operate.

Action point

Social media sites offer an unprecedented amount of global reach and audience engagement opportunities, although this isn't enough. Publishers are right to insist on a better deal from the Internet platforms.

Summary

We said at the start that control of the platform and distribution *is* control over the audience/user relationship – this is the classic rule in publishing. But the balance of power is clearly in favour of the big online names. However, the social media sites know that content from respected magazine brands brings loyalty and repeat visits. This is at a time when the personal stuff (gossip, pictures of friends, etc.) which they were once best known for is moving to private messaging services such as WeChat and the Facebook-owned WhatsApp.

It is important that publishers do not relinquish control of what they do well. A strong brand and a reputation for independence and trust are important more than ever. Reducing standards in quality or the creation of cheap clickbait style stories will only damage things.

One of the wonderful things about the Internet is how quick and easy it is to launch products – 'fail fast and fail well' is the Silicon Valley motto. Developers talk about apps as being in 'constant beta'. Never fully complete – always a work-in-progress. Publishers can learn from this approach – new opportunities emerge all the time and media publishers are advised to take an experimental approach, while remaining focused on the user and brand values.

If there's one lesson you should take from this chapter it is that which *The Economist* does well – focus on your audience and their needs. Think about how they consume your product and offer a tier-based subscription model. Last, remember trust and reputation are key – this is where publishers will always win the long game.

> ### INDUSTRY PERSPECTIVES
>
> We meet Ranj Begley, Readly UK's (www.readly.com) managing director, at her central London office. From a user perspective the Readly model is highly compelling. Its 'all you can read for just £7.99 a month' price gives access to over 2,600 digital magazine editions on tablets and phones.
>
> The roll call of big magazine names is impressive and includes: *GQ, Elle, Stuff, Heat, Men's Health* and *Grazia* – and the list goes on. It is fair to say there is something for even the most discerning reader. But Begley isn't resting for a moment and is signing up yet another big magazine title as we start the interview . . .
>
> *Readly started in Sweden, but the UK is the flagship store and also our largest market. We know the pricing model is quite disruptive and it took a long time to get to 2,000 magazines. The magazine industry really wasn't sure about us when we first started. They thought it would cannibalise their existing readership.*
>
> *The reality is that the overlap between their subscribers and Readly users is less than 0.8%. We view our users as 'entertainment junkies', exactly like the people who use Netflix and Spotify, rather than people who would subscribe to a single monthly magazine. What they are after is really good value.*
>
> *We reveal all the data to publishers about who is reading their magazines, but there really isn't much overlap. When they realised how much money they are making and the fact we are doing all the marketing for them, the publishers have been really impressed.*
>
> The technology behind the Readly app is incredibly impressive. You collect a huge amount of data about how users access magazines. That must be very useful for publishers?
>
> *Magazine reading is changing throughout the day and Readly is reflecting this. We know because our recording demographic tells us that people are downloading magazines in the morning, so they can read them offline on the train during the commute to work. During the day readers are 'time deprived', but they will go in and perhaps email interesting articles to friends and family. I have done that with recipes from* BBC Good Food *magazine that I send to my husband.*
>
> *One of the most popular times is in the evening when they are sitting back with a glass of wine and reading, while watching TV. This is where you get into second screening.*
>
> *When we started, our user base was heavily male dominated. These were early adopters – the techy types! But our audience demographic today is really wide – its 35/60.* [This is based on who pays the Readly subscription – a whole family can share an account and set up individual profiles.]

Stats show that 40% of the audiences use it every day and this is on a par with Netflix. We give access to back issues, and what publishers need to understand is that its money for old rope.

We also see the 50 Shades of Grey effect – the book was a massive hit on Kindle as nobody knew you were reading it the train. On Readly we see that men read women's titles and vice versa. Those cheap 99p women's mags are really popular. You also get older people reading younger titles and vice versa. It is changing people's magazine habits.

Publishers really like the platform as it is superfast. Readly Analytics shows lots of data. People read on average 33 titles per month, per household for an average of 21 minutes at a time. We can track everything users read – Top Gear *is read for around 45 minutes. On* Newsweek *there are average reading times of 15 minutes per article. You just don't get that level of granular detail from any other system.*

The technology can see what cover-lines most appeal to people. Psychologies magazine put Felicity Jones [the actress] on the front cover and it did really well. In fact 20% of readers of the interview were male, which is interesting as Psychologies is aimed at women.

We can see when a magazine is being read from cover to cover and where people drop out. You get car magazines where those classified adverts at the back are really popular and we can see what adverts are getting most read.

Are covers as important for digital magazines as they are in print?

Yes, covers really do still matter. It is human nature that covers pique our interest. Those that stand out do well. We can tell even what cover-lines appeal to our users – often it's a tiny cover line in the corner that is getting people to download the magazine.

The revenue share with publishers is the classic 70/30 split; 70% of the £7.99 goes to the publisher and we never touch ad revenue. The 70% is based on dwell time. So, if a user reads three magazines and spends more time on one than the other, more of the money goes to that magazine title. I should say, we can track how people are reading magazines, even when they are offline. The second they get Internet access the app reports back to us.

We don't offer magazines preferred positions within the app, although there is a whole lot of stuff we use to promote the magazines via email. It is in our interest that people read magazines so we can pay the publishers.

I can't tell you how many subscribers we have. However, we are tripling the digital edition revenues of some of our publishers. I can also say that the Apple Store is not always number one [in terms of digital magazine downloads] *– it really depends on the magazine title.*

To begin with it was imperative to get ABC on side, so they can accredit the data. We appear in the number of digital reads, beneath regular subscription rate. However, we notice that publishers are not chasing the ABC as much as they used too.

We don't take free titles. Readly is a premium product. The free titles want to be sat next to premium titles like Marie Claire, but the free business model is very different.

> Back in 2014 we really had to knock on publisher doors to persuade them to give us access to their titles. There was a time when publishers wanted to keep the big-name titles to themselves. But now they look at the data and they see it is so strong. They really like the platform and the money they are making. So now we have publishers knocking on our door and we actually have to say 'no' to publishers.

MONETISING ACTION PLAN

Achieving revenue from your digital outlets is crucial to generate a return on the substantial investment needed to create these platforms. With each platform or digital brand extension it is necessary to have a clear monetising strategy – ideally from the start.

However, before implementing any new strategies make sure you cost every expense first, including a contingency budget of around 20%, and remember the ROI potential must far outweigh the initial costings.

The following three steps will help you develop an effective plan to generate more revenue from content.

1. **First undertake a comprehensive analysis:** to explore untapped revenue potential you first need to evaluate your digital platforms, looking at the user stats and evaluating the potential value of content.
2. **Next identify three ways of monetising existing content:** take an innovative approach here, consider creating paywalls around high-value content, creating value add-ons for membership packages or developing a directory/information source.
3. **Then explore potential additional advertising revenue through digital channels:** with a focus on native advertising and collaborative campaigns, it is worth exploring if there are opportunities around strategic partnerships or collaboration opportunities.

Bibliography

Dixon, C. 2012. BuzzFeed's Strategy – Citing Peretti, J. BuzzFeed CEO Email to Staff (July 2012). http://cdixon.org/2012/07/24/buzzfeeds-strategy/ accessed 3 April 2017.

Goodfellow, J. 2016. Conde Nast Redesigns Glamour, Moving the Title to an Integrated Print and Digital Team. THE DRUM. www.thedrum.com/news/2016/04/15/conde-nast-redesigns-glamour-moving-title-integrated-print-and-digital-team accessed 24 August 2017.

Greenberg, J. 2015. Apple Finally Kills Newsstand to Make Way for Apple News. *Wired*. www.wired.com/2015/09/apple-finally-kills-newsstand-make-way-apple-news/ accessed 24 August 2017.

Hargreaves, I. 2003. *Journalism: Truth or Dare?* Oxford: Oxford University Press.
HUFFPOST. 2016. Readly: 'Spotify for Magazines' Launches in the UK. www.huffingtonpost.co.uk/2014/03/27/readly-spotify-for-magazines_n_5041214.html accessed 24 August 2017.
Jeff Jarvis Tinius Report. 2015. https://tinius.com/blog/death-to-the-mass accessed 3 April 2017.
Kaldas, L. 2016. *The Economist* is joining Snapchat Discover. US Daily Review. http://usdailyreview.com/the-economist-is-joining-snapchat-discover/ accessed 3 April 2017.
Mayhew, F. 2016. UK News Industry Could Lose £500m in Revenue to Online Platforms Over Next Decade, Report Warns. *Press Gazette.* www.pressgazette.co.uk/uk-news-industry-could-lose-500m-in-revenue-to-online-platforms-in-next-decade-report-warns/ accessed 24 August 17.
Naughton, J. 2017. Bad News for Online Advertisers – You've Been 'ad. *The Guardian.* www.theguardian.com/commentisfree/2017/mar/05/online-advertising-social-media-facebook-google-youve-been-ad accessed 22 October 2017.
Newman, N., Fletcher, R., Levy, D. and Nielsen, R. K. 2016. *Digital News Report 2016.* Oxford: Reuters Institute for the Study of Journalism.
Ponsford, D. 2017a. Duopoly: Facebook Tells Press Gazette How it has Changed to Share More Revenue with News Publishers. *Press Gazette.* www.pressgazette.co.uk/duopoly-facebook-tells-press-gazette-how-it-has-changed-to-share-more-revenue-with-news-publishers/ accessed 24 August 2017.
Ponsford, D. 2017b. Magazine ABCs: Digital Editions Account for 2.5 per cent of UK Mag Sales with Economist Leading the Way. *Press Gazette.* www.pressgazette.co.uk/magazine-abcs-digital-editions-account-for-2-5-per-cent-of-uk-mag-sales-with-economist-leading-the-way/ accessed 3 April 2017.
Reynolds, J. 2016. *Time Out* Editor Says Title Makes a Profit and Predicts that More Magazines will Go Free. *Press Gazette.* www.pressgazette.co.uk/time-out-editor-says-title-makes-profit-and-predicts-more-magazines-will-go-free/ accessed 24 August 2017.
Viner, K. 2016. How Technology Disrupted the Truth. *The Guardian.* www.theguardian.com/media/2016/jul/12/how-technology-disrupted-the-truth accessed 24 August 2016.

# 9

AN INSIGHT INTO ADVERTISING

Since the decline of revenue from print advertising sales as the digital revolution began to seriously disrupt the traditional magazine business models, publishers have been looking for new opportunities to replace it. Today there is more emphasis on content marketing, strategic partnerships and of course native advertising – the latest trend to publicise a product or service using an editorial approach either in terms of story or promotional article.

The latter is becoming a key focus across all mediums from magazines to broadcasting and social media. But what is native advertising and how does it differ from its traditional predecessor? First, it is defined by the Native Advertising Institute as: "paid advertising where the ad matches the form, feel and function of the content of the media on which it appears" (Vinderslev, 2015). Furthermore the Institute goes on to cite the key formats as:

- Advertorials in newspapers and magazines
- Advertiser funded programming on broadcast or web TV
- Promoted or sponsored posts on social media like Facebook, LinkedIn and Twitter.

Essentially native advertising takes a creative approach to selling instead of a direct sales message because today's readers are more media savvy and thus less inspired by traditional adverts. Therefore, response rates in traditional advertising formats have been in decline since the digital disruption. And as every publisher knows, a poor response is likely to equal a low ROI, thus resulting in advertisers using more creative strategies to sell their products or services. What native advertising does is create a story or personalised approach to which the reader (or user if online) can relate.

In this chapter I will be examining the evolution of traditional advertising as well as strategic partnerships and of course going native. There will be an evaluation of key examples, while also exploring the boundaries looking at how far a magazine can go before its brand values are compromised.

The evolution of advertising

When I first began my career in magazine publishing back in the late 1990s the revenue model was more straightforward with most proceeds coming from copy sales and display advertising. Today it is more complicated. While advertising sales still make a significant contribution to a magazine's core business model, revenue has significantly declined across the sectors, mostly as a result of the digital disruption era that began back in the early 2000s. But even before the big 2008 crash it was clear a rethink was needed.

During this era, I was working at a small publishing company which published two national, newsstand titles. As we were a small team I oversaw key aspects of the business side of publishing, therefore, in my concurrent roles – deputy editor of *Writer's Forum* and managing editor of *Weddings Today* – this meant being involved in advertising sales targets and looking at maximising opportunities for promotional content.

While the latter magazine focused more on display advertising and promotional pages, *Writer's Forum* had lots of potential for advertorial copy. To fully explore these opportunities, we developed five key strategies to maximise revenue and support our advertising sales team. I should stress at this point that publishers should never underestimate the value of supporting their advertising sales teams with initiatives. This not only makes their job easier, but also helps to build team spirit, which in turn will impact positively on sales targets.

The five developmental strategies we employed were as follows:

1. **Themed issues:** we began producing themed issues at key points in the year. Themes included self-publishing, holidays for writers, writing courses and a festival guide.
2. **Advertorial space:** to support our advertising sales team we included a small amount of advertorial content in every issue.
3. **Supplements:** to further boost our ad revenue we developed an annual *Website for Writers* guide, which I wrote. In addition to editorial, it carried both display advertising and advertorial copy.
4. **Classified section:** This gave smaller companies or individuals an opportunity to advertise their services from proofreading and editing to word-processing and weekend workshops, all achieving a decent page yield. This initiative evolved following a meeting with our sales team who made the point that some contacts couldn't afford a quarter or half page advert, but would pay for classified.
5. **Writer's web directory:** An extension of our classified section, but themed. This evolved following the success of our annual Web Directory.

All these strategies worked exceptionally well. Supplements and themed issues boosted advertising revenue, sometimes by as much as a quarter of the basic sales target, while the classified section widened advertiser participation and at the same time provided a directory of services to our reader. These strategies rejuvenated our sales team who in turn felt more supported. This resulted in the overall advertising revenue tripling between 2001 and 2005. However, I should stress that these strategies worked well because of being in the pre-digital age when the Internet was evolving; social media and more sophisticated online sites were yet to be invented.

What would I do differently at *Writer's Forum* in the digital age? A few things would change, but essentially the basic model of attracting the right advertiser with products or services that are relevant to the audience remains key in my opinion. Advertisers need high response rates whichever medium they use. Despite much of the recent doom surrounding print advertising I believe that print and digital content can work together. I see the digital age as an opportunity to be explored – thus innovation and providing relevant content should be the starting point.

Therefore, to make those initial development strategies for *Writer's Forum* suitable for today's digital era I would implement the following changes:

- Take a complete approach by offering advertisers a package rather than separating advertising space into print, online, social media and eNewsletters.
- Move the classified advertising and Writer's Web Directory online to enable more immediacy and up-to-date content, while providing users with easy access. This space would then be sold separately under a specific title such as Services for Writers.
- Expand on the themed issues by offering sponsorship opportunities as opposed to advertising display.

Remember that every publication is different; therefore the approach to advertising revenue must be unique to that brand, its audience and their needs. That said I do feel that taking a 360-degree approach to advertising sales is the way forward and have advised my clients accordingly. Essentially this is because when you give advertisers a choice of platforms it is likely that they will only opt for one. By offering your media buyers an appropriately priced, multi-faceted package you are providing them with a much wider exposure to their target market – making advertising a much more attractive value proposition and therefore counteracting a decline in sales.

The wider the market, the more likely clients are to spend their budget. However, it is crucial to provide an attractive media kit detailing the options. Skimp this last point at your peril.

Creativity and storytelling

Advertising is no longer a basic format. Over the past few years it has got creative, making adverts entertaining, seemingly more relevant and, in a few cases, poignant. Step forward native advertising, a clever trend which in the digital age has taken the media and its buyers by storm. Going native is not just about blending into the magazine's brand identity with the presumption of product endorsement; it's also about being creative.

The focus here is on developing a strong storyline or angle with which readers, users or viewers can identify – and of course the ability to create a story around that product or service. A story or article built specifically around a product is always going to have more of an impact than a standard advert. As advertising guru David Ogilvy famously pointed out in 1963:

> There is no need for advertisements to look like advertisements. If you make them look like editorial pages, you will attract about 50 per cent more readers. You might think that the public would resent this trick, but there is no evidence to suggest they do.
>
> *(Gabay, 2015, p. 56)*

Native advertising should be seen as a progression of this concept, taking Ogilvy's idea to the extreme. But how exactly does the native advert differ from its traditional counterpart? Essentially it is more of a merger between an advert, advertorial and editorial content that uses a creative, but tailored, approach.

Previously advertorials were a necessary bane of an editor's life, he or she stood between the advertisers and the readers to ensure editorial standards were upheld. However, with the decline of ad revenues together with the emergence of native, boundaries are not so clear cut, meaning that editors must be more flexible, particularly if the magazine in question is struggling. Blurred lines make it harder to police. Unlike a straightforward advert, its native sibling will either reflect advertorial content using a more sophisticated, blended approach or it will revolve around a story.

As these adverts are likely to be a collaboration between three parties – the advertiser plus the magazine's editorial and advertising sales team – boundaries could come into question. Thus, it may be hard to differentiate between actual editorial and promotional copy because the magazine's brand values are more likely to be embedded, making it hard to distinguish from editorial copy. Figure 9.1, my native advertising model, demonstrates how the process works.

THE CONCEPT
native content featuring a product or service

CONTENT ANGLE OR STORY
developed specifically for the magazine's target audience

DISTRIBUTION CHANNELS
including the magazine (digital/print), its online and/or social media plus the advertiser's own channels

FIGURE 9.1 A native advertising model – from concept to platform

My model shows the framework and order of development. First comes the concept for the native content to promote a product or service; next the angle is defined to directly relate to the target audience. Finally, the most appropriate platforms must be chosen through which it will be distributed; this might even include the advertiser's own channels such as social media or, if retail, instore promotional opportunities.

The key to successful native advertising is ensuring that:

- copy is relevant to the audience
- it is blended so it doesn't appear as a normal advert
- it maintains careful boundaries and doesn't challenge editorial brand values.

While not appearing as a normal advert, the native content should still be recognisable as promotional content to ensure brand values aren't compromised. However, there has always been a fine line between editorial and promotional content – native advertising has the potential to cross that line if clear boundaries aren't set. Anything that has the potential to jeopardise a magazine's brand values should be approached with caution.

I know from experience that this is an area where key boundary and brand value issues surface, as we will explore later in the chapter.

The impact on revenue streams

During the last decade, the decline of revenue from print advertising has sent shockwaves through the industry and resulted in a few magazine closures. Today publishers are more likely to adopt a build, fix and grow approach, both in terms of advertising and by seeking other revenue streams – as examined in previous chapters.

Part of the build, fix and grow strategy has been focused on maximising relationships, with magazines seeking to develop strategic partnerships with some of their advertising buyers. This has led to more opportunities in terms of promotional content as well as taking a more creative approach to developing adverts – all centred on the goal of boosting revenue.

As we know, achieving strong audience or user engagement in terms of editorial can be a tough call, but ensuring that advertisers gain the necessary response rates to make advertising in a publication viable is much harder. When ad revenue streams – and in some cases response levels – hit an all-time low it was clear that both the business model and the industry needed to evolve.

But before exploring ways to evolve it is essential to objectively look at why advertising revenue has declined. Is it simply a case of the 24/7 updateable content, or is this only part of the reason? In my opinion, this very much depends on the sector and the publisher. The examples we have seen in previous chapters show that in some areas advertising is in fact thriving – particularly in the B2B sector with regard to digital. It is also clear that print is here for the foreseeable future, although this may be in a more discerning, luxury format; therefore it makes sense that print advertising will remain a key part of this business model.

So, how can magazines achieve a sustainable and strong revenue stream from advertising? I always advise a client that:

1. They need to ensure there is a three-way synergy between the publication, its advertisers and the readers.
2. Advertising should – where possible – be across all platforms to maximise response opportunities.
3. All advertisers need to get a strong ROI and that means a good response rate – but if point 1 isn't taken into account or the magazine's circulation is dropping substantially, then they probably won't and will stop advertising.

The bottom line is if advertisers can see a good ROI from buying space, then they are more likely to remain loyal and keep a regular slot. Poor response rates will never result in long-term retention. The market sector can also be a crucial factor. Those sectors that are currently on trend – such as iGaming and sports for example – are more likely to achieve stronger advertising revenue than those that aren't.

Stewart Darkin, editor of iNTERGAMINGi magazine, says advertising revenue on his publication is holding steady and hasn't declined since he joined the magazine in 2010.

> Overall revenues have grown as the title has but the proportion that comes from advertising remains high. Revenue from copy sales is low. There are subscriptions available and these are popular for other titles we publish but for the online gaming mag, readers favour the free-to-read model, either via print copies picked up at trade events or, more commonly, the digital version online or via our app.

Stewart admits he enjoys a strong relationship with his advertisers but is careful to maintain boundaries.

> I think that advertisers – indeed all sector professionals we enjoy strong relationships with – like the consistency of dealing with a stable team, both on sales and editorial sides. I have been the editor for around five years and the change during that period has come from the maturing of the relationship between editor and market. I know a lot of people in the sector and many know me.

He feels that the value of having that personal connection cannot be underestimated and says there is no doubt that consistency transmits to the bottom line.

The other key change Stewart has seen more recently is the move towards content marketing.

> Advertisers rarely want 'traditional' brand advertising as it doesn't enhance their multi-thread marketing strategies. So, we find there is a much greater emphasis on placing editorial that explains a product or service in detail or, more commonly, it is a chance for a named contributor to show off his or her knowledge.

Given the financial constraints in recent years the lines between content and promotional copy can become blurred. As an editor, it can be hard to define those boundaries between editorial and advertorial/promotional content. Stewart is passionate about putting his readers first and takes a hard line on advertorial.

> Simply put, I don't think it offers much value for the reader. But of course, contributors – and savvy PR firms – know that offering a piece of engaging editorial is tempting for the editor. He or she just must be careful that the piece adds enough for the reader as well as the originator. If someone writes something good, it can go in and I'm happy to give them credit. However, not everyone gets that. A few push very bland copy, while asserting that they have 'no advertising budget' for their client.

He does, however, acknowledge the necessity of advertorials.

> We tend to allow our advertisers to contribute editorial but if that is a standalone piece we add a discreet note that 'This content has been supplied by an advertiser'. This is just to be transparent and resist accusations of cronyism. The middle ground is asking advertisers (and others) to contribute to longer roundtable-style articles. This carries no such notes, which many see as a caveat on quality, and I often discuss the topics in advance with the contributors to ensure their interests are served. Ultimately, we need to keep our advertisers happy but it does no one any good if we are simply a mouthpiece for their claims to be the best thing since sliced bread. It is a balancing act and sometimes you have to hold your nerve and tell someone (who may be paying a lot of money for an ad campaign) a firm 'no' on an editorial matter. In truth, they tend to respect that.

Although iNTERGAMINGi magazine has not taken on native advertising or personalised advert delivery, revenue remains constant and Stewart doesn't see that changing radically in the short term. However, he feels that the focus on the need to tell stories through campaigns will continue to grow.

> Advertisers are realising that a series of full-page or DPS spreads showing off their corporate colours in full bloom doesn't really represent value for money anymore. Not least because in an online age of page impressions and click-throughs, value from print media can be very hard to demonstrate. Also, readers expect more. And readers should be respected – they get the subtlety and appreciate not being force-fed company names and achievements. They want to learn something from the content. So, advertisers – or those seeking to run marketing campaigns in whatever format – need to recognise that readers expect and deserve more.

According to Stewart, the trick for editors is to find a place for those stories. In other words, content that pays the rent mustn't compromise journalistic integrity, as that is a core breach that readers will never forgive.

Selling display advertising is never easy but at its heart remains a fairly straightforward transaction. Sharing corporate artwork across six industry magazines is easy – just rinse and repeat – but six pages of unique editorial, each a thousand words in length with a by-line attached? It is much more work and advertisers need to be convinced it is worth it. So it starts with the editors and the journalists. We need to drive change and demonstrate there is value to be had.

Stewart's is an excellent perspective – editors and journalists do need to be the drivers of change where content and content marketing is concerned. He clearly supports his sales team – both in terms of content and by forging relationships with existing and perspective advertisers.

However, some editors are not so forward-thinking and believe – rightly or wrongly – that they should keep their distance. Yet in today's somewhat difficult climate, that extra support can be a lifeline. When asked by my clients how to best support their sales teams I have advised them to take the following three steps:

1. Set realistic and achievable sales targets with incentives for extra achievement.
2. Facilitate good communication between the editor and advertising sales manager with clear boundary guidelines on advertorial, promotional and sponsorship content.
3. Share knowledge in real time. For example, at the start of each issue the sales team should be given a flat plan (with subsequent updates) and a list of key editorial content with potential leads.

One tool used by a few of my clients is an ad sales pipeline which they say helps their teams achieve sales targets. This tool is basically a spreadsheet that clearly sets out the sales forecast for each issue, listing pages booked and rates achieved. It can also include updates on sales leads as well as list bookings for forthcoming issues. The format can be compiled as a spreadsheet or as a table in Word.

To demonstrate how this might work I have created a basic overview of an Advertising Sales Pipeline as shown in Figure 9.2. In this example I have created this overview for a bi-monthly writing magazine, but the model can be applied to any publication.

Creating a tool such as this which can be shared on any docs drive such as iCloud, Dropbox or Google gives the editor and the team a clear picture of advertising at a glance. Hopefully it will also impact on motivation, which in turn will be reflected in the sales figures. Experience has long shown me that working as a team is a core requirement to achieve sustainability in publishing.

The value of strategic ad partnerships

With the traditional advertising model being somewhat less popular, publishers have been looking for new ways to secure revenue from their advertisers.

ISSUE: August/September
COPY DEADLINE: 10th July
ISSUE THEME: Self-publishing

ISSUE FORECAST

- Sales target – £14,000
- Advertising currently booked – £10,900

LEADS & STATUS

- Jo Bloggs Publishing Services – status: contacted, may book into next issue
- 123 words – status: contact, booked in for 1/4 page in Oct/Nov issue

SPONSORSHIP OPPORTUNITIES

- Write-A-Novel competition – status: MEH Publishing considering proposal
- Short story supplement – status: sponsored by ABC Writing Academy (£3,000)

BOOKINGS FOR FORTHCOMING ISSUES

- Oct/Nov £4,575
- Dec/Jan £2,960

FIGURE 9.2 An advertising sales pipeline

Previously these might have focused on sponsorship, a joint event or promoting the magazine to an organisation's members such as the subscription campaign I organised between *Vegetarian Living* magazine and the Vegetarian Society. The deal here was that the society gave us space in their newsletter and on the website in return for offering their members an exclusive subscription deal to the magazine. Both parties gained from this initiative, and more importantly so did the Vegetarian Society members.

Fast forward a few years and the bar has been raised because advertisers need to be tempted to spend their media budget by bigger ROI. Through such necessity has come innovation and some clever strategising, resulting in some interesting campaign partnerships. These have the potential to work fantastically well, but – as with the *Vegetarian Living* example – only when a campaign benefits all stakeholders.

Bauer and Matalan's joint fitness campaign is one such example. In January 2016 Bauer's weekly glossy magazine, *Grazia*, unveiled a multi-platform campaign with Matalan to publicise the brand's exclusive fitness wear range, Souluxe. A press release issued by Bauer (2016) at the time outlined how together the brands produced a 40-page fitness supplement which was inserted into *Grazia*'s 26th January issue. As well as being in *Grazia*, 500,000 copies of the supplement were distributed through Matalan's UK stores accompanied by the magazine's unique branding.

This advertorial partnership worked well in my opinion because it tapped into the growing fitness trend, while at the same time fulfilling the needs of all parties involved who benefited as follows.

- **_Grazia_ readers:** as well as being exposed to fashionable fitness wear, readers gained useful and relevant content advising them on key aspects of fitness including apps.
- **Matalan:** Matalan gained access to _Grazia_'s readers – the 20-something, stylish, affluent women on a professional career path. Perhaps not quite Matalan's usual demographic, but certainly an aspirational market with potential. After all, who doesn't love a bargain?
- **Bauer:** the campaign enabled the publisher to raise _Grazia_'s profile with instore branding plus it provided the opportunity to widen audience participation at the same time with the targeted supplement. It gave Matalan customers, who may not have read the magazine, a taster of _Grazia_'s content in the form of this joint supplement.

Key words for achieving a successful partnership like this one are 'ROI', 'relevant and useful, informative content'. Ensuring that all stakeholders' needs, especially the readers', are met is the key to a successful partnership that won't compromise brand values.

Another example is the Very campaign. To raise awareness of its brand Very, Shop Direct also opted for a strategic advertising partnership and chose to work with a range of consumer titles including _Marie Claire_, _Cosmopolitan_, _Heat_, _Closer_ and _Elle_. Writing on marketingweek.com Leonie Roderick reveals how each magazine developed its own campaign tailored to audience requirements. "While _Heat_ and _Closer_ developed native in-mag content and branded cover wraps, _Elle_ partnered with Very to 'take over' its fashion cupboard – a permanent bricks-and-mortar space," says Roderick (2017).

Roderick goes on to point out how during the take over, _Elle_ and Very curated the most relevant items from the V range for its readers with the activity supported by video, print and digital.

> Elle opened a 'pop-up' fashion cupboard to allow readers to browse a V collection that had been curated by the magazine's editors. The pop-up also offered a VIP area, where readers could have one-on-one styling sessions with the Elle fashion team.

Clearly the Elle campaign was the most innovative and therefore likely to be more successful than the others because it clearly focuses on Elle's readers' needs. This innovative approach gave both _Elle_ and Shop Direct clear benefits, which it would seem resulted in a strong ROI.

So advertising partnerships can work well, as we have seen through these examples. However, not taking into consideration brand values and readers' needs could jeopardise a publication's sustainability. Get it wrong and not only is the campaign liable to flop; it could also cause irreparable damage to a magazine's hard-won reputation.

Caution is advised

As we have seen, due to the changes in approaches to advertising – together with the emphasis on native and emergence of strategic partnerships – those once clear-cut lines between editorial and promotional content are becoming less defined. Now a few savvy publishers are starting to realise that the curse of blurred lines is a serious threat to editorial integrity and needs to be managed with care.

So how do you define where the line is? I advise my clients to always put their readers first and never compromise their brand values. Lose your audience's trust and you may never get it back. Building up strong advertising revenue is crucial, but as a publisher it is equally important to weigh up the true cost of every action. Readers will see through advertorial disguised as editorial or poor content eventually, resulting in a decline in circulation or, worse still, closure.

Although there are no clear directions from its UK counterpart, the American Society of Magazines Editors (ASME) published guidelines for editors and publishers in 2015. The ASME clearly sets out key criteria to maintain editorial integrity citing "The primary responsibility of the editor is to serve the interests of the reader" (ASME, 2015). It also states editors and publishers should:

- Avoid conflicts of interest
- Differentiate editorial content and advertising
- Not trade editorial coverage for advertising
- Not submit editorial content to advertisers for approval
- Disclose eCommerce partnerships to the reader.

These criteria are a good starting point. But to me if an opportunity is too one-sided then reject it as it is bound to disappoint your readers. A fast buck strategy is never a good thing; on this point editors should be unyielding when it comes to their brand's values.

My advice? Focus on maintaining the highest editorial standards and keep your readers at the heart of everything you do.

A word about media kits

One key aspect I haven't dwelled on is media kits, aka the rate card, but as a core part of any advertising sales team's resources it should not be ignored. Therefore, it makes a fitting point to end the chapter on because having a strong, iconic media kit is one of the best ways to support your team as it provides an opportunity to demonstrate your brand's creativity and uniqueness.

Giving media buyers clear pointers as to your editorial pillars, readers and brand's reach can be the difference between success and failure in terms of ad sales. However, publishers are becoming a little reticent about publishing media kits, citing concerns that their rivals will then have access to their key selling points, not to mention advertising rates. Yet the audience – in this case media buyers – are worth considering as it can be frustrating by not having access to a media kit within a couple of clicks. This is why I advise my clients to publish their media kits. Media kits should at least be on BRAD, even if publishers don't want to make them available on their brand's website.

Summary

As I have documented throughout this chapter, advertising as an industry is evolving in terms of creativity, design and focus. No doubt this is both an exciting and nervous time for many publishers too as they begin to focus on collaborations and strategic partnerships. Those who have embraced the digital age are at last starting to see those investments pay dividends, particularly in the B2B sector. Now perhaps it is time for more publishers across other sectors to explore how digital platforms can best serve their advertisers.

But first perhaps it would be prudent to consider what the drive towards content marketing and native advertising really means for publishers and their audiences. The answer depends on clear boundaries being set within the publishing industry. Blurred lines are never good. Yet at the same time it can be hard to achieve that balance, with editorial integrity taking priority above all else. I think the answer lies in one of the industry bodies, such as The British Society of Magazine Editors, publishing a set of clear guidelines on advertising and content marketing similar to those of its American counterpart, the ASME.

Ultimately, those publishers and editors who put their audience at the centre of all their activity will, I suspect, not only survive but thrive in this digital age.

INDUSTRY PERSPECTIVES

Terri White joined *Empire* (Figure 9.3) as Editor-in-Chief in 2015. Since then she has been named among Folio's top women in media and has taken *Empire* from strength to strength.

Here she shares her career journey as well as her thoughts on advertising, promotional campaigns and how to avoid blurred lines in publishing.

I've been in magazines since 2000, beginning as a (truly terrible) secretary having worked my way up through news and features desks on both monthly and weekly titles, before becoming editor of ShortList at 29. Since then I've been lucky enough to edit Buzz magazine with The Sun on Sunday, Time Out New York *and now* Empire.

The latter was always my dream job and I would often stare at previous editor (and lovely human being) Mark Dinning across crowded rooms, plotting his demise. There are only a handful of brands, anywhere in the world, that have the power, influence, reach and heart of Empire. *It's a once in a lifetime editing gig, so when the*

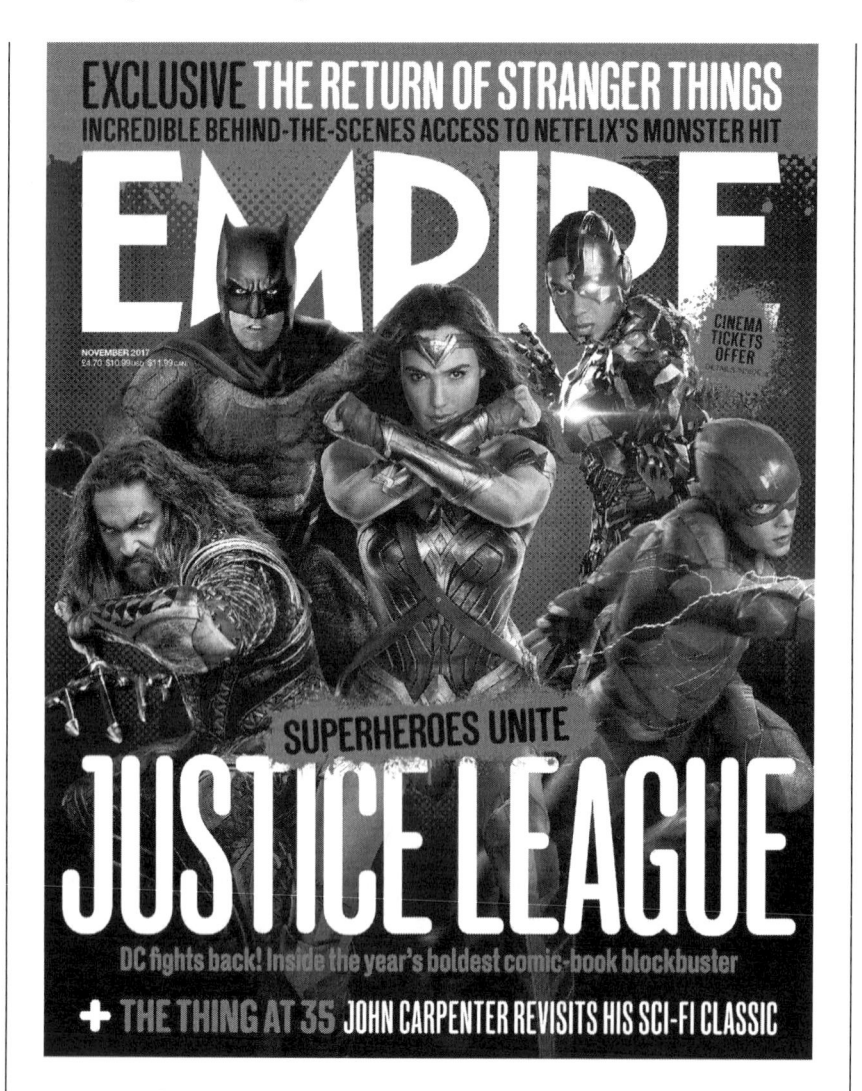

FIGURE 9.3 *Empire* cover, courtesy of Bauer Media Ltd

big chair became available, it was inevitable that I'd leave New York and return to London.

Two years in the job and I am still as passionate about Empire as that first day I sat in 'the chair'. Since then I have made many changes; the most crucial was the redesign. This was a very visible change to the magazine giving it a new dynamism, energy and modernity and it was incredibly well received by the readers. I put my email address in the first redesign issue and am pleased to report that I had overwhelmingly happy readers.

We have also made strides into the new cinematic world – reviewing TV shows and original content on platforms such as Netflix and Amazon alongside movies for the first time. Maximising digital opportunities has been a key challenge. While some titles struggle with that fine line between editorial and promotional content, for me it's about keeping the reader at the heart of everything you do. As Editor-in-Chief I'm involved in ideation for all advertorials. Creating Empire's content day in day out means my team and I are perfectly placed to know what our audience will engage with and how brands can really connect with them. Content is content, whether it's paid for or straight editorial – the reader still demands the same level of excellence. They want to immerse themselves in great storytelling, whether that's straight from Empire or from Empire and a partner.

Many magazines are struggling in terms of advertising revenue but in my opinion, there is absolutely no reason to compromise editorial standards to achieve strong ad revenue. I've actually found the opposite to be true – if you don't have integrity and authenticity in your editorial, why would a brand trust you with theirs?

I firmly believe that if you create a strong, compelling editorial product that deeply connects with and resonates with your audiences, the advertisers will come.

It's about having integrity and excellence as an editor and about being transparent with your audience. It's about applying rigour and high standards to everything you put your hands on – whether that story has been paid for by your publisher or by an advertiser.

Is native advertising a good thing for magazines? Yes, I think it is – but there needs to be a true understanding of what native is. Native, to me, is not promotional content that isn't labelled as such. We have complete transparency with our audience in terms of what is paid for. To me, native is great strong content that has been created with the help of the biggest and best brains on the editorial team. It packs the same punch as editorial, but it has been done in partnership with a brand.

Again, our audience don't care as long as the content is of the same quality as everything else in the mag.

The best career advice I have been given came from my old boss Phil Hilton. After I explained once again why I'd executed a cover (that wasn't working) a certain way for the sixth time, he stopped me and told me that it didn't matter. It didn't matter what had gone wrong, what the process was, why I couldn't get the picture I wanted, how hard it had been to reach the execution we arrived at. All that matters is what the reader finally holds in their hands and what they see. And all they see is what's on the page; they have no knowledge (or care) for how you arrived there. So never explain, never try to rationalise, never try to give excuses: the reader won't get to hear them, so it doesn't matter. It is the most liberating and focusing thing I've ever been told.

Experience also plays a part in developing your skills, but as an editor, instinct and passion are the most important things. While data and research are vital tools (I can spend an eye-watering amount of time in an analytics rabbit-hole), these should be used to inform, not dictate. When I started out, I didn't trust my gut as much as I should have – which was probably to be expected as a young woman in men's magazines – but now, if my belly is shouting something, I listen up and speak up. Our instinct and all-consuming passion are what makes any editor great. If you're *not banging a table and pulling at your own hair at least once a day, you're not doing it right. Oh, and surround yourself with great people. I make it my mission wherever I work to drag the best talent out there along with me.*

No editor can, or should, do it alone and the thrill of working with the best in the business cannot be beaten. And quite frankly, your audience deserves nothing less.

ADVERTISING ACTION PLAN

Innovation and integrity are the key to maximising and maintaining advertising revenue. Here are four essential action points to ensure that your publication fulfils its advertising sales potential.

- **Create and publish a strong media:** this must not only reflect your brand's values, but also demonstrate its creativity while setting out a clear rationale as to why media buyers need to invest in advertising space. Do make it easily accessible.
- **Develop advertising packages:** a focus on 360-degree advertising exposure in the form of a package is more likely to appeal to media buyers as it has the potential to offer a stronger response rate, resulting in a good ROI on their initial outlay.
- **Set out a clear advertorial policy:** guidelines are essential; the policy should cover advertorials, native advertising and content marketing. Both your editorial and advertising sales teams must be clear on what is acceptable and what is not. Do not be tempted to break these by agreeing to a potentially lucrative deal.
- **Design an advertising pipeline:** this document will give you and your sales team a snapshot of advertising sales in both the current and future issues.

Bibliography

American Society of Magazine Editors (ASME). 2015. ASME Guidelines for Editors and Publishers. www.magazine.org/asme/editorial-guidelines accessed 15 October 2017.

Bauer (26 January 2016) Bauer Media and Matalan join forces for *Grazia* Fitness Supplement. Bauer Press Release. www.bauermedia.co.uk/newsroom/press/bauer-media-and-matalan-join-forces-for-grazia-fitness-supplement accessed 14 October 17.

Gabay, J. 2015. Lies, Excuses and Further Justifications for Inconvenient Truths. *Brand Psychology: Consumer Perceptions, Corporate Reputations*. London: Kogan Page (p. 56) Google Books. https://books.google.co.uk/books?id=2lXHBgAAQBAJ&pg=PA56&lpg=PA56&dq=There+is+no+need+for+advertisements+to+look+like+advertisements.+If+you+make+them+look+like+editorial+pages,+you+will+attract+about+50+per+cent+more+readers.

&source=bl&ots=el7rTqzX2G&sig=3CRUAPzup2aYDaBmCIxug9Mb-o0&hl=en&sa=X&ved=0ahUKEwjXp9XRhbHWAhVDPVAKHXU2BrUQ6AEINjAD#v=onepage&q&f=false accessed 19 September 2017.

InPublishing. 2016. Bauer and Matalan Join Forces for Grazia Fitness Supplement. www.inpublishing.co.uk/news/articles/bauer_and_matalan_join_forces_for_grazia_fitness_supplement_9733.aspx accessed 14 October 2017.

Roderick, L. 2017. How Brands are Switching up their Approach to Magazine Advertising. *Marketing Week*. www.marketingweek.com/2017/08/23/brands-magazine-advertising-change/ accessed 14 October 2017.

Vinderslev, A. 2015. Native Advertising Definition. The Native Advertising Institute. https://nativeadvertisinginstitute.com/blog/the-definition-of-native-advertising/ accessed 14 September 2017.

10
A SUSTAINABLE FUTURE?

Overall there is a growing confidence in magazines, perhaps more so now than in the past five years. While there have been some unexpected closures, particularly among the print lifestyle sector – *Nuts*, *Easy Living*, *Company* and more recently *Glamour* to name but a few – there have also been a few launches and mergers. From those interviews I have conducted while researching this book and the survey I undertook, I have found some great success stories – it's perhaps just a question of getting the model right.

As I write this Brexit has yet to be fully defined, so yes, these are still uncertain times. Before you are tempted into doom and gloom, it's prudent to remember that every generation of publishers have faced – and survived – economic challenges. No doubt there are more crashes to come as we approach the next decade, as well as disruption from emerging technologies.

Yet as we have seen throughout these chapters, those magazines that are thriving have adopted a reader-centric model. Get the basics right – and that means not skimping on content by hiring experts to write an engaging, informative and relevant editorial. This maxim should be every magazine publisher's priority.

Also, be wary of being too quick to adopt a new trend. Although an eye on the future is always prudent, it is always good practice to wait a while before jumping on bandwagons. Therefore carry out due diligence checks, undertake a risk analysis and have a clear ROI strategy before investing hugely in new platforms.

In this concluding chapter, I will evaluate the results of my recent survey, which was distributed to both academic practitioners and industry figureheads to gain their perspective on magazine publishing, including whether print magazines will be available in 2027. I have also included quotes from a few of my contributors and academic colleagues on how they see magazines evolving in the next 10 to 15 years.

Finally, as this is a book primarily aimed at undergraduate and postgraduate students, it seems only right that I should give the last word (at the end of this chapter) to my former magazine journalism student, Alice Freeman.

Print will survive

To gain a wider insight into the future of magazine sustainability and revenue streams I surveyed 48 magazine publishing experts – a mix of academic practitioners and industry figureheads in both the UK and the US. The results of that survey are as follows.

Unsurprisingly (to me), an overwhelming 87.50% of those respondents thought that the printed magazine would still be available in 2027. Out of those remaining only 2.08% thought the printed format would cease to exist, while 10.42% weren't sure. Interestingly, those who felt print is on the way out cited the following reasons:

- A few very niche titles, yes, but overall they will decline into obscurity.
- Media companies' current business models are simply unsustainable. Note the revenue shortfalls at Time Inc/IPC for just one example. Shrinking trim sizes, higher costs at newsstand, lower reader engagement and the resulting advertiser exodus are endemic. Magazines could survive *if* media companies can find a way to be profitable within the changes of the industry. And *if* social media companies are treated and taxed like the media monoliths they have become.

Personally, I'm with the majority on this, but I do feel there does need to be a market correction across some sectors – and of course a greater emphasis on quality editorial. But what does make a successful, sustainable magazine in the eyes of academic practitioners and industry figureheads? When asked to identify the three most essential components of a successful magazine I was pleased to see that quality content, a strong brand identity and trustworthiness topped my respondents' list.

Other re-occurring responses included:

- Informative articles that cannot be accessed easily elsewhere
- Close alignment with interests of readers
- An understanding of the audience
- A brand that goes wider than just the print magazine
- Clear market niche
- Engagement with the community
- A brand that goes wider than just the print magazine
- Expert contributors
- Strong imagery, identity and design aesthetic
- Interaction with readers, including via various digital platforms, and social media.

Targeting the next question at publishers and editors, I asked where their strongest revenue streams had come from in the previous two years. Responses, shown in

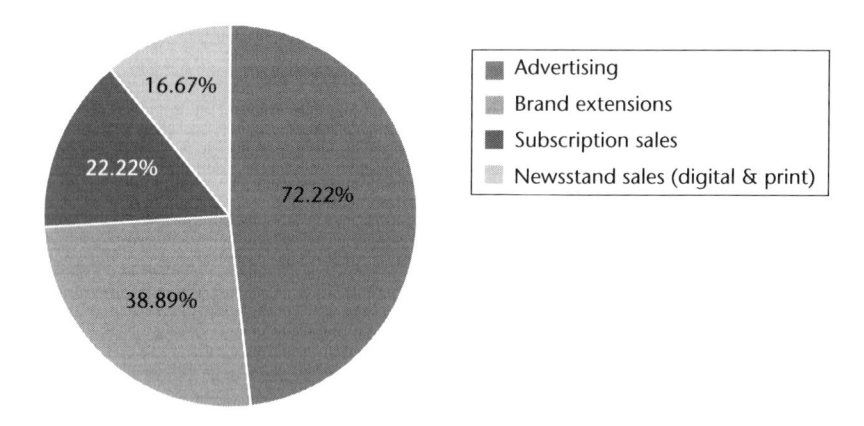

FIGURE 10.1 A survey of magazine revenue streams

Figure 10.1, were somewhat surprising given recent doom and gloom surrounding advertising sales.

As the pie chart illustrates, an overwhelming 72.22% cited advertising, while 38.89% attributed brand extensions and 22.22% said subscription sales. Only 16.67% identified newsstand sales (digital and print) as a strong revenue stream – not a surprising result given the exorbitant retail distribution costs.

Those 38.89% who cited brand extensions as driving revenue identified reader events, awards and shows as being among the key income earners from this stream.

From a personal standpoint, I'm not in the least surprised that advertising came top followed by brand extensions. Working with clients from across the sectors – who publish local and national titles – has provided sufficient insight to know that if it is a quality product with a strong reach, then advertisers will buy space. When it comes to revenue, it's about getting the model right, building a strong reputation and of course being a trusted brand.

I also wanted to gauge market confidence with regard to new launches with the next question, which was also aimed at editors and publishers. This time responses were far more conservative. Asked if they planned to launch a new concept in the next year, the majority said no, with only 17.65% saying a new launch was likely.

Last, all respondents were questioned on how they saw magazines evolving in terms of revenue and sustainability. This provoked some interesting answers; although some were pessimistic I was heartened to see that overall there is optimism for the future.

Thoughts on revenue and sustainability included:

- The new USP for magazines will be one of consolidating issues and creating specific campaigns that readers want to know about. The lead times are so long that they cannot compete with 'news features' like online offerings can. Therefore, magazines will find a niche which will be about aesthetics, feel good 'flipping' and gorgeous visuals – whether through info-graphics, photography or content driven and contextualised articles. If the offerings are strong and unique, there will always

be a place for something to flip through during our life-stages. It must also be remembered that – with the current infrastructure – online doesn't always work so well if on the move, such as taking a journey for instance. Therefore, it could be argued that in a digital world where worldwide Internet access is not consistent in terms of reliability and speed, the print magazine still has the edge.
- Extinction looms, except for those with unique, high-quality content.
- More digital magazines with twice-yearly collectable print editions, almost like the old-fashion Christmas annuals which were gift material.
- Revenue will fall across the board, some will fold but that will allow others to continue.
- More events focused, monetising social media, eCommerce, brand extensions.
- Revenues in the print sector will continue to go down. Digital niche enterprises will provide revenue but not as high in comparable terms – sustainability may mirror Internet outlets, i.e. short life, three to five years.
- More small magazines covering an ever wider selection of niches within niches, and combining their print publications with other activities to create small, sustainable businesses.
- Magazines are essential reading for many people. I think there will be more print tie-ups with digital to maximise advertising revenue.

Overall the survey data yielded some key insights. Despite the seemingly pessimistic attitude to advertising, it seems publishers are still making money from this once thriving income source and I suspect they will continue to do so, provided they rethink their sales strategy. There is also a general consensus that audiences will continue to support high-quality print products. However, I think publishers are aware that the market corrections we have seen over the past decade are set to continue. When there is saturation a correction is usually around the corner.

Looking to the future

But what does the future hold and how accurately might we predict it? I asked some of my industry perspective contributors and contacts plus a few academic colleagues how they see magazines evolving in terms of revenue streams and circulation in the next 10 to 15 years.

Their thoughts are as follows, starting with **James Evelegh**, Editor of *InPublishing*, who believes that in the long term only strong, original titles will thrive. However, he does see a future for printed content.

> *Specialist and niche sectors will continue to develop their highly desirable content and, for them, the immersive print experience will remain a successful part of the publishing mix.*
>
> *Reader/content revenues will come more to the fore as publishers of all titles seek to build communities and then monetise those communities in all number of ways, including events, eCommerce, product and merchandise sales.*

Advertising will remain a key revenue stream, and I see a significant proportion of the advertising budgets that have migrated to the social platforms returning as advertisers come to appreciate and value the trusted environments that quality publishers, with their engaged audiences, provide. I think there will become an increasing awareness and appreciation of professionally produced content, in contrast to the free-for-all and extremely open to abuse environment that the social platforms provide.

For mainstream titles, I think that there will be further closures as the me-too generation of magazines, especially in the celebrity, women's and real-life sectors, close because they have nothing distinctive to offer. Strong, differentiated titles, even in those sectors, will survive and, after the clear-out, even thrive. Quality, in all areas, is the key to future success. Lazy, poorly thought-through, me-too titles that don't deliver value for money will close, and maybe that's not such a bad thing . . .

Carole Watson, Programme Leader, BA (Hons) Fashion Journalism, University of Sunderland – and former Deputy Editor of *Grazia*, Head of Features at the *Daily Mirror*, as well as an editorial consultant on *Woman* magazine – thinks many titles will close.

Sadly but inevitably, as we have seen with the likes of In Style *and* Glamour, *more mainstream titles will close.*

In my opinion, the most saturated market in 2017 is the weekly showbusiness/women's genre which is struggling to find cover-worthy stories in an age when celebrity news can be digested 24/7 on a smartphone via Twitter, Instagram, et al.

Those brands which do survive will need to find more innovative creative solutions to satisfy both brand partners and readers with engaging content across all platforms from the printed magazine through to their website and social media platforms.

Finding the next generation of readers and where they want to consume content will be key. As Cosmopolitan *discovered, readers can be driven to print by smart use of Snapchat. Always being on top of what is the next zeitgeist go-to platform will become part of the business model.*

As circulation revenue declines, revenue streams will be driven less by mainstream adverts and more by sponsored content and long-term brand partnerships with those decision-makers being more shrewd about only buying into editorial that is seen as authoritative and entertaining and cleverly targeted at the right demographic, rather than just gushing advertorial.

Sponsored podcasts, events and other brand extensions will all become a crucial part of the mix in trying to discover new ways of making money and raising brand awareness.

While I'm more optimistic about the sustainability of niche magazines and B2B titles, they must also be more forward-thinking about where their readers are engaging with the media in decades to come.

What this means for journalism educators like myself is arming our students with a toolkit of futureproofed skills from video and mobile journalism, social media engagement, to thinking of brilliant multimedia editorial ideas which satisfy both readers and sponsors.

Liisa Rohumaa, Senior Practice Fellow in News Journalism at Bournemouth University feels there is a market correction looming with regard to print magazines.

I think the big publishing companies won't let their print magazines die out completely, they will just invest in fewer of them. Many combine print and digital as part of their strategy and will be also thinking in terms of new revenue streams and how they can diversify. Subscription strategies could be new offers such as an app, exclusive access to archives, 'club' memberships, tangible products or experiences as part of a reader bundle.

David Bostock, independent media consultant, trainer and lecturer at Birkbeck is optimistic about the future and sees a growth in events, data, commerce and other near market adjacencies.

The seismic shift will be in the area of tech, which is on the move again. Over the next five years readers will move from a mobile-first to an AI-first world. This change will bring both the biggest opportunities and primary threats to publishers. The challenge will be ensuring that the big four – Facebook, Google, Apple and Amazon – who are already first out of the AI starting block and light years ahead of the pursuing pack, don't eat our lunch again!

Artificial Intelligence (AI) systems with incredible machine-learning capabilities are already available and have revolutionised the advertising market. They are rapidly becoming better and faster at interpreting voice, questions, purchase patterns, images, video, audio and other non-text formats – which will dramatically change the shape of how content is served to readers, with the nimblest and most responsive publishers winning over the next decade.

The opportunity (and race) for publishers, and for the industry as a whole, will be in creating useful AI services for consumers in markets they understand better than the big four digital behemoths without allowing them to own all the data and, along with it, the lion's share of the revenue.

Damian and Laura Santamaria, founders and proprietors of *Sublime* magazine, say the spotlight should be on delivering experiences for the audience and they will be focusing on innovation to meet the challenges of future developments.

After the credit crunch, magazine publishers had to reinvent themselves. The big challenge required a radical shift of mentality to adapt to a new playing field.

A print magazine publisher was concerned with retaining readers and long-term advertising partnerships. It was all about good editorials, conforming within the needs of advertisers and keeping your rival title at bay. Today, the publisher has become a brand manager who is concerned with delivering a wide range of experiences for diverse and dynamic target audiences, while keeping the value proposition relevant for each, and the revenue flowing in.

This situation was not an evolutionary path of innovation or renewal that came from within the industry, but a survival strategy of desperate times, which was accelerated by the surge of digital publishing and the social media revolution. Today, advertisers can arguably make better use of their budget by publishing their own editorials, and readers have become publishers themselves through blogging and social media. In effect, our customers have become our competition, and are claiming a piece of the market share by producing a constant stream of fresh and original content while sipping espresso macchiato at their favourite coffee shop . . .

What is the future then? Of course, the future is omni-channel and surely, we should choose our key partners properly, keep checking on our social media analytics, innovating and polishing our long-tail business model. However, all these tools are accessible to everybody, and are also here today and gone tomorrow. So, the key is not in how but in what publishing is all about . . .

The one and only secret weapon that belongs to the trusted publisher, the bedrock of our industry, is the humble 'endorsement' if you know how to use it, your bank account will be always in positive, now and in 15 years' time.

Jeremy Walters, Editor of the website What's New In Publishing? thinks that the magazine market will be unrecognisable. He says in 10 to 15 years the newsstand, as we know it, will disappear.

The declines of recent times will witness another down leg again very soon. Magazines are no longer the trend and style gatekeepers they once were, and for those titles with general and populist content, the light at the end of the tunnel is indeed a very fast moving train.

In a similar vein, newsstand is finished and I expect that to disappear. If it somehow manages to survive, only a select number of specialist titles will remain.

For those titles with any chance of a sustainable future, the strategy has to be two-fold. First, the magazine must create unique and highly valuable multi-platform content that, in and of itself, people will be willing to pay for.

Second, even these titles will need to leverage their brand and extend it into eCommerce, events and other areas like ring-fenced member communities that add value to readers' lives. Printed magazines will simply be left as just one strand of an overarching strategy, not a central tenet.

The legendary commentator Bo Sacks was heard saying that print is moving from a commodity to a luxury and that there's no room left for bad printing or bad writing. I'd have to agree.

Gregor Rankin, managing director of Green Pea Publishing sees retail newsstands as the biggest threat to mainstream magazine publishing.

> *I think there is a potential 'Curate's Egg' – some sectors will be okay; some will go the way of the men's 'lifestyle' sector and become redundant. However, the biggest threat posed to successful publishing is that the retail sector will become even more challenging. As previously mentioned, publishing is influenced by scale and as the double whammy of the titles dropping out of the market combine with reduced circulations of those that remain, the sector's overall importance to retail landscape diminishes – and supermarkets are very focused on profit per square foot . . .*
>
> *On the advertising sales side I think a lot of clients have realised that digital is just another channel, and not the only route to the customer, and we've seen a number coming back to print, which is refreshing.*
>
> *If magazine publishers think of their readers as members of a club and treat them accordingly with a wide variety of services – albeit in smaller numbers than they may have been used to in the past – then there is still gold to be panned.*

Rob Attar, Editor of *BBC History Magazine* says the way forward is to seek new avenues through which to generate revenue.

> *I think diversification is likely to be key in upcoming years. I'm sure there will be some titles which see growth in UK print circulation and advertising but I can't imagine that will apply to the industry as a whole and so most publishers will need to seek new avenues if they want to increase revenue. This is clearly already happening and I would expect the pace to pick up over the next few years. I would anticipate brands expanding further into international markets (e.g. the growing potential audiences in places like China and India), developing web offerings (both subscription and ad funded), opening eCommerce channels and expanding events programmes, among other things.*
>
> *Obviously, the opportunities available will vary by brand – for some they might be quite limited, in which case we might see more magazines closing over the years. Clearly we don't know what new technological changes might arise over this time that could provide unexpected new threats and opportunities so it is hard to make predictions.*

Steve Newbold, divisional managing director of media and events at Centaur Media sees dramatic changes in the publishing industry in the next 15 years.

> *In all likelihood it will consolidate significantly in most sectors, so we will see more mergers and closures. There will be fewer general interest and lifestyle titles in the consumer space but still room for subscription-driven specialist interest titles.*
>
> *The latter will also have the advantage of attracting niche, target-driven advertisers at higher yields, so these brands will likely fair better than their broad market counterparts.*

> *They will also have a better chance of diversifying revenues by expanding into specialist exhibitions and events, e.g. Homebuilding & Renovating and MCN.*
>
> *There will also be a drive for digital subscriptions. This is already the case in B2B as we see traditional news websites broaden to paid-for information type products.*
>
> *Brands which can't attract paying customers will be wholly dependent on the advertising landscape. This will likely continue to decline, so the future doesn't look bright for standalone B2B print. The brands that continue to thrive will be the ones that have brand extensions (events/awards/reports) and have the ability to drive paid-for-content. These brands can retain print as much for marketing purposes and brand positioning rather than profit in their own right. There will be a place for print but only realistically as part of a multimedia offer.*

Last, but not least … **Steve Hill**, who is joint course leader in MA Multimedia Journalism and a senior lecturer at Westminster University – and the author of Chapter 8. A specialist in online journalism, he says predicting the future beyond the next five years is tricky.

> *So much has changed in the past 15 years. In 2003 we had just experienced the dot-com boom followed by the crash. Neither the iPhone nor Facebook had launched – we had a couple more years to wait for that disruption to occur. So we need to be mindful that by 2033 there will be technology on sale that we can't even imagine today, which is both exciting and, be honest, a bit scary.*
>
> *But let's try to predict the future. First, content reading platforms will become even cheaper than today. I've just bought an Amazon Kindle Fire HD as a gift for my elderly aunt and it cost me just £40. My gym membership is £30 a month. Okay, so the Kindle Fire is being subsidised by adverts for Amazon products that appear on its home screen (you have to pay £10 more if you want a Kindle without adverts). However, the ads are not intrusive and you can live with them. Soon you will buy a tablet for the cost of a paperback.*
>
> *Maybe the exciting growth will be in very thin, cheap or disposable e-paper that will eventually replace printed magazines? Magazine production costs remain high, but AI software could lead to efficiencies in editing and production.*
>
> *People will pay for quality magazine content, but for digital editions Netflix-style 'all-you-can read' models may well become the norm. People talk today about the rise of online video over the printed word, but people will continue to enjoy the pleasure of reading quality long-form journalism on the sofa with a glass of wine.*
>
> *I'm very positive about the future for magazines, as long as they retain their quality and don't chase online hits. I do feel the teen market is sunk – they will remain on social media until they grow out of it.*
>
> *UK magazines will succeed if they think globally and target emerging markets. On this front, I'm finding myself downloading far more American digital editions. I may be very*

late to the party, but I love the beautifully composed long-form journalism in Rolling Stone, *the* New Yorker *and* Fast Company *to name a few. These are becoming true global brands and British publishers need to take note.*

Summary

Magazines have always been my passion. It is a passion I enjoy sharing with others – be it clients or students. Seeing a new launch evolve into a successful magazine is always a privilege and I am fortunate enough to have been involved in some great projects – more recently this has included *Celebrating Poundbury* and *The Mint*.

New launches set the bar for the future; without innovation the industry could not evolve, which is why inspiring our undergraduate and postgraduate journalism students is crucial. Their minds have yet to be prejudiced with pre-conceived ideas of what will and won't work; because of this they are more willing to take risks. This is why I have chosen to give the last word to one of my former students, Alice Freeman.

Back in 2015 Alice and her group (Iga Schlegel nee Kozakiewicz, Josie Tague and Aiden Dalby) were students in my Magazine Business module at Southampton Solent University, who were tasked with developing a media kit and business plan for a new magazine concept. Not easy, given they were only in the second year of their degree.

Passion and dedication are must-have traits for this industry – this group had these attributes in spades. As their project began to evolve I knew this was going to be something very special. By the end of the module their concept, *Tucked* – a magazine aimed at the LBGT community – had exceeded all the expectations of the assessment brief. Once the project had been marked (and second marked) I nominated it for the Magazine Academy Awards in the Best New Concept category. Thus, it was no surprise to me when they won – probably setting the record of being the youngest undergraduates to achieve this accolade.

The moral of the story? Be passionate and take risks, but do your research carefully. As publisher John Jenkins – my former boss and mentor – used to say: "There is a solution to every problem. You just have to think of it in time."

THE LAST WORD WITH ALICE FREEMAN

Alice shares her journey from undergraduate to industry professional and the lessons she learned along the way.

I write this as my first full year as an industry professional draws to a close. So how did I get here?

There are two standout projects that were the making of my university experience. Tucked, *an intimate insight into the UK's drag scene, was the culmination of a group project in my second year in which four of us – Iga Schlegel (nee Kozakiewicz), Josie Tague, Aiden Dalby and I – started as classmates and ended as close allies. Mentored by Mary, we produced an entire magazine package, including a 28-page launch preview issue, media kit and business plan.*

Although it was a student project, we never viewed it as such. Our goal was to create a product that tapped into a relatively unexplored market, so during the process, we surveyed 200 live prospective readers to prove that the concept was viable. Every page was then self-produced with original editorial shoots and interviews, which goes some way to explain how we found ourselves in the dressing room of an 82-year-old drag queen. We treated the launch like a dry run for the real thing and were rewarded with top marks and a Magazine Academy award-win for Best Original Concept.

Building on our experience, I then went on to create a bigger and better solo project in my final year. Guided by lecturer Jayne Toyne and armed with a copy of Mary's book, How to Launch a Magazine in this Digital Age *(2014), I produced* Wunderkammer *magazine – an exploration of all things macabre and curious, such as Victorian mourning traditions and stillbirth photography. The 56-page launch preview issue, media kit and business plan earned me a second Magazine Academy award for Best Original Concept.*

Creating two magazine concepts from scratch was an exciting, exhaustive process. Throughout, I kept a quote from Mary's book in mind: "If no titles exist, there is probably a good reason – the idea could prove unsustainable, in which case you need to proceed with caution." By 'caution', I knew that this meant to conduct careful and thorough prior research. (More on how this statement will continue to influence my career to follow.)

If I were to recommend one area of research that I found crucial, it would be the media kits from existing magazines. Whether you're building a market research portfolio of rival titles for a launch or, more simply, pitching a freelance article, there is no resource quite like it. Be aware that a web search won't always provide the media kit you need, so don't be afraid to direct an email to the advertising team as most magazines are happy to provide it.

Shortly after completing my degree, I interned at a wedding magazine for a few months while applying for various industry positions. I then attended three (yes, three!) interviews for the position of junior writer for IKEA Family Magazine. *I was offered the job and accepted, feeling ready for something new. I always imagined I'd work exclusively on newsstand titles, but it would have been naïve to pigeonhole my career before it had even begun. So I welcomed the challenge.*

IKEA Family Magazine *has been produced by August Media for over a decade. The magazine is one arm of IKEA's free customer loyalty scheme, and reaches across 34 different markets in 32 different languages. The online IDEAS we create for IKEA.com each month receive an estimated 5 million unique visitors. Every piece of content we produce is driven by communication packages (for example, target audience, tone of voice, etc.) to fit with the overall brand message supplied by IKEA. I make up part of the shoot team visiting homes across Europe and write for the print and digital platforms, as well as helping to curate the social media channel.*

As much as I hoped it might, landing my first job in publishing hasn't divulged all the tricks of the trade. As I get to grips with just one, albeit sizeable, example of customer publishing, the industry wheel keeps on turning. My advice is to always keep step, especially as the presence of digital media continues to pick up pace. I do so by picking up a freemium magazine for almost every day of my commute – Time Out, Stylist, ES and NME – and regularly checking in on the status of newsstand titles. (R.I.P. Glamour *magazine as we know it!) A useful way of filling your email inbox is with Stack's weekly newsletter, which showcases a quality independent magazine every week. I also recommend signing up to Gorkana, the journalism jobs site and its daily newsletter. You'll receive job adverts and news of all the movers and shakers in the industry – it's a great way of keeping tabs on those editors leading the change.*

Looking ahead, I plan to work on some start-up titles and eventually launch my own magazine – which is where Mary's valuable and lasting advice will once again guide me through the process. But before that happens, I'm going to spend my time getting to know the industry from the inside out.

A TO Z OF INDUSTRY RESOURCES

A

Advertising Standards Authority (ASA) regulates adverts and promotions across all media platforms. www.asa.org.uk

Adobe is currently the number one software producer of print, digital and online content. In recent years, they have created monthly subscriptions instead of one-off fees and there are student discounts available. www.adobe.com

Alliance for Audited Media, America was founded in 1914 as the Audit Bureau of Circulations. Today it provides cross-media verification across all brand platforms including web, mobile, email and print. https://auditedmedia.com

American Press Association (APA) believes the freedom of the press is the right of all people and thus their website is not just aimed at academic and established press. It is for anyone who feels they have a story, image or video of substance and importance to share with others. http://americanpressassociation.com

Association of Magazine Media, America (MPA) is the primary advocate and voice for the magazine industry. Founded in 1919, it represents 265 domestic, associate and international members. www.magazine.org

Association of Online Publishers, Europe (AOP) was founded in 2003 and is the only pan European Publishers Association focused entirely on digital content strategies, digital business and lobbying. www.opa-europe.org

Association of Online Publishers, UK (AOP) is an industry body representing digital publishing companies that create original, branded, quality content. www.ukaop.org

Audit Bureau of Circulations (ABC) was previously seen as the authority on print circulation figures, delivering industry-agreed standards for media brand measurement across print, digital and events. www.abc.org.uk

Audited Media Association of Australia (AMAA) provides accurate circulation figures across platform coving print, digital and web publications plus eNewsletters, exhibitions, events and conferences. www.auditedmedia.org.au

Australian Human Resources Institute (AHRI) has a range of resources from education and training to events and networking. www.ahri.com.au

B

Barcode1UK supplies barcode images once publishers have obtained their ISSN number. https://barcode1.co.uk/magazine-barcodes

British Press Photographers Association (BPPA) inspires and promotes high standards within the profession and is a great resource for finding freelance photographers. https://thebppa.com

British Rates and Data Directory (BRAD) provides key data on circulation, audience and advertising rates of more than 12,300 UK media titles. https://bradinsight.com

C

Canadian Media Circulation Audit (CMCA) provides accurate circulation figures for more than 650 publications, measuring the combined market penetration of print and digital editions across Canada. www.circulationaudit.ca

Canada Periodical Fund (CPF) provides financial assistance to Canadian print magazines, non-daily newspapers and digital periodicals to enable them to overcome market disadvantages. www.canada.ca/en/canadian-heritage/services/funding/periodical-fund.html

Chartered Institute of Personnel and Development (CIPD) has hubs across UK, Ireland, Middle East and Asia. It sets professional standards for Human Resources including training and development, while driving positive changes in the workplace. www.cipd.co.uk

Chartered Institute of Journalists (CIJ) was founded in 1884; it promotes standards and ethics throughout the profession. http://cioj.org

Chartered Institute of Marketing (CIM) supports, develops and represents marketing professionals including resources such as events and training. www.cim.co.uk

Chartered Professionals in Human Resources (CPHR) is responsible for maintaining national standards in HR, representing some 27,000 members. https://cphr.ca

Companies House will register a limited business and has a directory of every limited company in the UK, which includes accounts and details of directors. https://beta.companieshouse.gov.uk

Confederation of British Industry (CBI) currently represents around 190,000 businesses of all sizes and is focused on helping firms large and small create a more prosperous society. www.cbi.org.uk

Crowdfunder has a community of over 600,000 who are funding start-ups, charities, community groups, sports clubs, political movements and much more. www.crowdfunder.co.uk/about-us

Crowdfunding website Gofundme will help you raise funds for your new concept, brand extension or to invest in developing an existing proposition. www.gofundme.com

D

Department of Labor, America (DOL) has information on health and safety in the workplace with advice for employers and employees. www.dol.gov

Dropbox is a file-sharing and storage facility, which offers a free basic or business account. www.dropbox.com

E

Email marketing – *The Publisher's Guide to Email Marketing* **from Campaign Monitor** is an invaluable resource. www.campaignmonitor.com/resources/guides/publishers-guide-email-marketing

eNewsletters the Opt In guide from Crosscut Public Media addresses all aspects of newsletters from production to design and revenue strategies. https://optin.crosscut.com

F

Federation of International Employers (FedEE) is the global support organisation for multi-national employers focusing on employment law, labour relations and legal/HR compliance. www.fedee.com/fedee-global

FIPP is the network for global media, representing content-rich companies and individuals. Knowledge-sharing and reports on emerging trends are just a few of its resources. www.fipp.com

Folio is a resource for magazine publishers with the latest industry news, best practices and insights as well as award programmes and conferences. www.foliomag.com

G

Google News Lab focuses on four key areas – trust and verification, data journalism, immersive storytelling and inclusive storytelling – to encourage innovation in journalism. All areas are supported with training, research plus a series of programmes. https://newslab.withgoogle.com

GOV.UK guide to setting up a business has a wealth of information on the essentials – from setting up a limited company to employer responsibilities. www.gov.uk/set-up-business

H

HoldTheFrontPage has the latest industry news and is a great resource for magazine publishers, editors and journalists. www.holdthefrontpage.co.uk

Hong Kong Institute of Human Resource Management (HKIHRM) was founded in 1969 and now has around 5,400 members. Resources include events, survey data and its HR Professional Standards Model. www.hkihrm.org

HM Revenue & Customs (HRMC) offers advice on all aspects of tax, National Insurance and PAYE as well as news on the latest legislation. www.gov.uk/government/organisations/hm-revenue-customs

I

Independent Press Standards Organisation (ipso) is the UK's independent regulator for the newspaper and magazine industry. www.ipso.co.uk

InPublishing is the industry's authority on all aspects of magazine and newspaper publishing. Register for your free copy of the printed or digital edition; there is also a wealth of information online. www.inpublishing.co.uk

Internal Revenue Service (IRS) has essential information on tax for business plus a section on starting a business. www.irs.gov

International Center for Journalists (ICFJ) has a range of resources including events, blogs and training. www.icfj.org

International Standard Serial Number (ISSN) is an internationally accepted code which identifies the title of serial publications. It is printed in the form of a barcode on magazine covers. www.bl.uk/bibliographic/issn.html

Internet Advertising Bureau UK (iab) is the trade association for online and mobile advertising, which promotes growth and best practice for advertisers, agencies and media owners. www.iabuk.net

ISSUU is a digital publisher which offers a range of plans for publishing digital editions including a basic free option. https://issuu.com

J

Journalism.co.uk contains a range of resources from jobs and training to its newsrewired events where the latest publishing strategies are shared. www.journalism.co.uk

Journalist's Toolbox has a great range of resources from software to professional advice. www.journaliststoolbox.org

K

Kill fees – details on these **and other freelance payments** can be found at London Freelance, which has an excellent guide on best practice. www.londonfreelance.org/feesguide

L

Libel law and updates on other essential laws for journalists can be found at http://global.oup.com/uk/orc/law/media/mcnaes23e/resources/

Lynda.com is a fantastic learning resource with video tutorials and exercises with more than 6,000 courses in business, technology and creative skills – all taught by industry experts. www.lynda.com

M

Magazines Canada (The Book and Periodical Council) is an industry body representing Canadian consumer content, cultural, specialist, professional and business magazines. www.thebpc.ca

MagCulture is an essential resource for those interested in editorial design, with daily posts reviewing the best magazines and providing industry updates. https://magculture.com

Magazine Networks Inc., Australia was founded in 1995 as The Association of Magazine Publishers of Australia. It represents Australian publishers of consumer, cover-priced and nationally distributed magazines. www.magazines.org.au

Magazine Publishers Association, New Zealand (MPA) is the key source of information and expertise for members, advertisers, agencies, retailers and the community. www.mpa.org.nz

Magazine Publishers Association, South Africa (MPASA) aims to defend members' interests, promote the industry, provide extensive industry information and facilitate a forum for solving circulation and distribution issues. http://mpasa.co.za.dedi2012.nur4.host-h.net/

Media Publishers Association, Singapore (MPAS) represents leading B2B, specialist B2C, customer and digital publishers in Singapore. www.mpas.org.sg

N

National Human Resources Association, America (NHRA) was established in 1951. It has a national focus and range of resources. www.humanresources.org

National Council for Training of Journalists (NCTJ) accredits undergraduate and postgraduate journalism courses in the UK and has its own training programme. www.nctj.com

National Readership Survey (NRS) is the essential UK resource for magazine readership data and metrics for brand reach. www.nrs.co.uk

National Union of Journalists (NUJ) is the voice for journalists and journalism, representing a wide range of media professionals. www.nuj.org.uk

O

Offscreen provides an insight into the lives and careers of creatives including the leading thinkers, makers and founders in technology. www.offscreenmag.com

P

Press Association (PA) is the national news agency for the UK and Ireland supplying words, images, video, graphics, live data and social media content. It also offers editorial services and training courses. www.pressassociation.com

Press Gazette was established in 1965. It has the latest magazine and newspaper industry news and has recently published a free magazine, *How to Be a Journalist*, on ISSUU. www.pressgazette.co.uk

Professional Publishers Association (PPA) is the UK's industry body that also accredits both undergraduate and postgraduate journalism degrees. Whether on the page, through a screen or face-to-face, its members create professional, influential content that resonates with target audiences. www.ppa.co.uk

Q

QuickBooks is a cloud-based accountancy package which enables users to access and update their accounts while on the go. www.quickbooks.co.uk

R

Readly is an online digital newsstand which gives readers access to all digital magazines for a monthly fee, enabling users to access these across up to five devices. https://gb.readly.com

Reporters Committee for Freedom of the Press, America (RCFP) was founded by a group of journalists and media lawyers in 1970. It provides pro bono legal representation and other resources to protect the newsgathering rights of American journalists. www.rcfp.org

S

Seymour is part of the Frontline Group – a joint venture between Bauer, Immediate Media Company and Haymarket Publications. It is one of the largest distributors of UK magazines. www.seymour.co.uk

Subsail is an online subscription platform for selling, managing and overseeing your subscriber database. https://subsail.com

Subscription Genius is a cloud-based software system to facilitate magazine subscription management, enabling publishers to move away from fulfilment houses and spreadsheets. www.subscriptiongenius.com

T

Templates can be found at Lucidpress, which offers a range of free magazine layouts to get you started: a great resource to help shape brand identity for those creating their first magazine. www.lucidpress.com/pages/templates/magazines

The Typographic Hub is part of the Faculty of Art, Design & Media at Birmingham City University, and has a wealth of information on all aspects of typography. www.typographichub.org

U

UK Business Angels Association (UKBAA) is the national trade association and early stage investment representing more than 160 member organisations and around 18,000 investors www.ukbaa.org.uk

UK Copyright Service (UK©CS) has essential information on copyright, trademarks, design rights and patents with details on how to protect your work. www.copyrightservice.co.uk

United Nations Educational, Scientific and Cultural Organisation (UNESCO) includes the UN's code of Professional Journalistic Standards and Code of Ethics. www.unesco.org

Universal Product Code (UPC) aka barcode – see Barcode1UK

US Copyright Office, America offers expert advice and resources on all aspects of copyright. www.copyright.gov

V

Visually offers access to more than 1,000 vetted designers, writers, developers, creative directors and animators who will help you to repurpose editorial in five easy steps. https://visual.ly

W

Warners Group Publications Plc specialises in magazine distribution and marketing into national and international consumer markets. www.warnersgroup.co.uk/publishing-services/magazine-distribution

WordPress is simple to use and offers a range of website site packages from a free basic site to professional packages which include hosting, CSS customisation plus domain name. https://wordpress.com

Writers' Guild of Great Britain (WGGB) is a trade union representing professional writers across platform. It also has a useful Find A Writer directory. https://writersguild.org.uk

X

Xpress Group offers more than just printing; brand web and marketing support is available through its in-house agency. www.xpressgroup.eu

Y

YUDU is a digital publisher and software provider offering a range of publishing packages as well as training apps. www.yudu.com

Z

Zinio is a digital publisher which offers magazine publisher growth services to help increase circulation, ad sales and other audience-building goals. https://gb.zinio.com/publishers

Zuora is a subscription management software platform to help publishers grow their subscription base. Other features include recurring customer and billing management plus collections for recurring revenue. www.zuora.com

INDEX

360-degree content 96, 102, 112; action plan 115–16; advertising 105, 108, 110, 114, 136; brand; extensions 103, 108, 112; branding 102–5, 112; consolidation 103–5, 107; digital media 102, 103, 104–6, 110, 114–15; feature packages 102, 105–7, 112, 114, 115–16; industry perspectives 112–15; maximising content resources 107–12; print media 102, 103, 104–6, 114

ABC system 22–3
Abrams, L. 16
action plans 4, 19, 35, 55, 74, 87, 100, 115–16, 132, 148
ad blocking technology 124, 125
advertising 134–5, 145; 360-degree content 105, 108, 110, 114, 136; action plan 148; advertorial content 135, 137, 140, 141, 143, 144, 147, 148; audience 37, 47, 136, 138, 143, 144–5, 147–8; balance with editorial content 94–5, 96; blurred lines 94–5, 97, 137, 140, 144; caution 144; classified advertising 12, 13, 71, 131, 135–6; content marketing 94, 95, 97, 100, 134, 139–41, 145, 148; creativity and storytelling 136–8; digital media 134, 136, 138, 139; evolution of 135–6; impact on revenue streams 138–41; industry perspectives 145–8; lessons from the past 9–10, 12, 13, 14; market research 24, 25, 32; market sectors 81, 83, 84–5; maximising content resources 110; media kits 144–5; monetising online content 119–20, 121, 123–6, 127, 128–9, 131, 132; native advertising 134, 136–8, 140, 143, 144, 145, 147; print media 134, 136, 138, 139, 140; product endorsements 94–5, 137, 156; return on investment 134, 139, 142, 143; sales teams 58, 72, 111, 135–6, 137, 141, 144, 148; and social media 134, 136, 137–8; strategic partnerships 94, 134, 138, 141–4, 145; and successful business models 58, 59, 63–4, 70–2; supplements 135–6, 142–3; and sustainability 139, 141, 144, 152, 153–4, 155–6, 157, 158; 'takeover advertising' 124; themed issues 135–6
Advertising Sales Pipeline 141, 142
advertorial content 95, 96, 134, 135, 137, 140, 141, 143, 144, 147, 148
AdWords 125
AI (artificial intelligence) 118, 155
Almost Missed You 51
Amazon 117, 127, 146, 155, 158
'ambient news' 120
AOP (Association of Online Publishers) 61, 63
Apple 40, 117–18, 124, 126–7, 131, 155
Apple News 18, 118, 121, 123
apps 18, 36, 126, 127, 129, 130, 131
AR (augmented reality) 118
article theme (feature package model) 106
AskAMum 104
ASME (American Society of Magazines Editors) 144, 145

Index

Attar, Rob 31–2, 52–4, 76, 78, 157
audience: and advertising 136, 138, 143, 144–5, 147–8; creating a community 89–93, 97, 100, 113–14; digital and print media 2–3; engagement *see* audience engagement; keeping up with demand 95–6; learning from history 6–7, 8, 11, 12, 15, 16; loyalty of 13–14, 41–2, 100, 127, 129; market research *see* market research; meeting needs 93–4, 100; monetising online content 123–5; and product endorsements 94–5; reader-centric approach 72, 104, 105, 112, 123–5, 150; as stakeholders 89, 93–4, 97, 100; and successful business models 60–1, 62–3, 65–7, 72–3; and sustainability 153, 154, 155–6; understanding 7–8, 16, 22–3, 46, 51–2, 77, 78, 86–7, 125, 129–30
audience engagement 36, 52; action plan 55; and advertising 138, 147; brand extensions 36, 42, 45, 46–7, 49–51, 52, 54, 55; digital media 39–41, 46–7, 49, 53–4; distribution 36–40, 41, 53; *Good Housekeeping* study 36, 42–6; industry perspectives 52–4; monetising online content 119; overseas distribution 36–9; *Radio Times* study 36, 46–7, 52; return on investment 36, 37, 41; subscription 36, 41–2, 46, 47; and successful business models 59, 68; worldwide 36–41; *Writer's Forum* study 25, 27, 37, 47–51
August Media 161

B2B sector 119, 154, 158; advertising 138, 145; audience engagement 37, 41; health and success of 76, 77–8; maximising content resources 107–12; successful business models 69, 71–2
Bauer 103, 104–5, 107, 142–3
BBC Good Food 69, 85, 86, 130
BBC History Magazine 31–2, 52–4, 76, 78, 157
BBC Holidays 86
Beauty Club (*Glamour* magazine) 94–5
Begley, Ranj 130–2
BFI (British Film Institute) 47
BikeBiz 80
BJTC (Broadcast Journalism Training Council) 107
blogs/blog-style layouts 1, 2, 4, 51, 52, 156
blurred lines 94–5, 97, 100, 137, 140, 144
Booker, Christopher 13
Bostock, David 71–3, 104–5, 112, 155
Bowles, George 8–9

Bowles, Thomas Gibson 8, 9, 13
Bragg, Billy 93
Brand concept and development (Magazine Publishing Strategic Quadrant) 60
brand consolidation 103–5, 107
brand extensions 8, 19, 94; 360-degree content 103, 108, 112; audience engagement 36, 42, 45, 46–7, 49–51, 52, 54, 55; keeping up with demand 95–6; market research 23, 24, 27, 31, 34; market sectors 77–8, 79, 80, 85, 86; monetising online content 132; successful business models 60, 63, 64, 65–8, 69, 70; and sustainability 152, 153, 154, 158
branding 102–5, 107, 112, 122–3, 142–3
Brewer, Robert Lee 51
Brexit 150
Bright Daisy Publishing 29
British Media Awards 47
British Society of Magazine Editors 145
British Vogue 7
Broadcast 79
Budworth, Ben 9–10, 13, 97–100
'Build a Business' courses 65
Business Canvas Model 59–60, 61
business models, successful: action plan 74; advertising 58, 59, 63–4, 70–2; and audience 60–1, 62–3, 65–7, 72–3; balancing cash-flow 57–8, 63, 72–3; brand extensions 60, 63, 64, 65–8, 69, 70; Business Canvas Model 59–60, 61; cost cutting and consolidation 71; digital media 61, 63–4, 65, 69, 71–2; distribution 58–60, 62, 68, 70; industry perspectives 71–3; innovative strategies 61–3; learning from history 6, 13–15; Magazine Publishing Strategic Quadrant model 60–1, 74; market sectors 77; multiple revenue streams 63–5, 68, 73; one-size-fits-all model 6, 18, 58, 64, 72, 73; success of 57, 58–61, 70; sustainability 57, 63–5, 67, 68, 71–2; targeted distribution 68, 70
BuzzFeed 123

Cable, Vince 91
Cameron, Eve 94
Camping & Caravanning Club 126
Capaldi, Peter 47
Carbonara, Peter 64
cash-flow, balancing 57–8, 63, 72–3
Cave, Edward 6
Celebrating Poundbury 26, 29–31, 159
Centaur Media 107, 108, 110–11, 112, 114–15, 157–8

Index

Champcommunal, Elspeth 7
Charles, Prince 29
Cheal, Paul 63
CIE (Chief Income Earner) 22
classified advertising 12, 13, 71, 131, 135–6
Closer 143
Coalition for Better Ads 125
Cocker, Jarvis 93
Code of Conduct (Market Research Society) 28–9
community-issue shares 93
Company 1, 150
Components of a successful brand model 103
Computer Weekly 77
Condé Montrose Nast 7
Condé Nast International 6, 73, 122
Consistency (Components of a successful brand model) 103
content marketing 94, 95, 97, 100, 134, 139–41, 145, 148
content resources, maximising 107–12
control over platform 119
Cosmopolitan 121, 143, 154
Country Living 65–8, 69
covers 34, 67, 80, 96, 131, 147; pictorial 17, 30, 33, 43, 48, 53, 66, 82, 86, 92, 98, 113, 146
creating a community 89–93, 97, 100, 113–14
creativity and storytelling 136–8
cultural analysis 34–5
Curtis, Amy 103
cycling magazines 2, 76, 78, 80–1, 85

Daily Mirror 154
Dalby, Aiden 159, 160
Darkin, Stewart 139–41
data protection codes 28–9
'demand fulfilment' 125
demand, keeping up with 95–7
Dennis Publishing Ltd 79
Dennis, Felix 6
digital downloads 125
digital media: 360-degree content 102, 103, 104–6, 110, 114–15; and advertising 134, 136, 138, 139; audience engagement 39–41, 46–7, 49, 53–4; comparison with print media 2–3, 7, 14, 17–18, 39–40, 72, 77, 99–100; creating a community 89–93; learning from history 5, 6, 7, 9, 14–15, 17–18; market corrections 5; market sectors 77, 80; monetising online content *see* monetising online content; and successful business models 61, 63–4, 65, 69, 71–2; and sustainability 151–3, 155–8

The Digital News Report 121
digital newsstands 39–40, 91
Dinning, Mark 145
'direct consumption' 121
disposable income 22–3
distribution 89, 91, 93, 100, 152; 360-degree content 105, 108; and advertising 137–8; audience engagement 36–40, 41, 53; digital media 39–40; learning from history 5, 12, 14; market sectors 80–1, 83; monetising online content 118, 119, 120–1, 122, 129; overseas markets 36–9; and successful business models 58–60, 62, 68, 70; targeted distribution 68, 70, 81
Distribution: strategies and channels (Magazine Publishing Strategic Quadrant) 60
Downton Abbey 78
Drapers 69
Dukes, Angela 85
Dunton, John 5, 16

early adopters 104, 130
Easy Living 150
economics theory 120
The Economist 2, 40, 90, 91, 107, 108, 111, 119, 121, 126–7
education level 22–3
Elle 143
Empire 145–8
Enlightenment 16
Evelegh, James 153–4
Excellence (Components of a successful brand model) 103
exchange rates 38

Facebook 28, 69, 72, 104, 117–20, 121–2, 123–6, 128–9, 155, 158; Live Streaming 119, 123
'fake news' 44, 122
family history titles 79
Fast Company 159
feature package model 106, 112
feature packages 102, 105–7, 112, 114, 115–16
FHM 40
Fifty Shades of Grey 131
Finance and revenue streams (Magazine Publishing Strategic Quadrant) 60
focus groups 24, 25, 26, 29, 31, 32, 35
Food and Travel 38, 85–7
Foot, Paul 13
Ford, Henry 34
franchise model 81–4

free content 15, 18, 67, 71, 85, 111, 120
Freeman, Alice 159, 160–1
freemium model 1, 128, 161
future scenarios 33

gatekeeping 119
gender 2, 5–6, 7, 8, 11, 16, 76, 78, 80–1, 121, 130, 131
Genealogy & History News 79
The Gentleman's Magazine 6
Glamour 73, 94–5, 122, 150, 154, 161
Good Housekeeping 2, 36, 42–6, 94
Good Housekeeping Institute 44, 94
Google 69, 72, 117, 120, 121, 124–6, 127, 128, 141, 155
Grazia 142–3, 154
The Great Game of Business 64
Green Pea Publishing 38, 85, 157
Greenberg, Julia 118
The Grocer 77–8
Grocer Price Index 77
The Guardian 10, 122, 124, 125, 127

Hargreaves, Ian 120
Harper's Bazaar 7
Hather, Michelle 46
Head, Alice Maud 44
Healy, Hazel 93
Hearst Corporation 42, 45–6, 65
Hearst, William Randolf 42, 44
Heat 143
Hellberg, Per 128
heritage 11–12, 13, 122
Hill, Steve 158–9
Hilton, Phil 147
Hislop, Ian 14, 15
history, learning from 5, 15–16; digital media 5, 6, 7, 9, 14–15, 17–18; early pioneers 5–6; fashion and culture titles 6–13; gender 5–6, 7, 8, 11, 16; monetising online content 119–20; political satire 13–15
Hogarth, Mary 160–1
'Hollaback Girl' 125
Holland & Barratt 68
Home Handbook 76, 81–4, 85, 89
House & Garden 7
How to Launch a Magazine in this Digital Age 90, 160
How to Start a Magazine 2
Huffington, Arianna 6
The Huffington Post 6

IKEA Family Magazine 161
Immediate Media 46, 47

In Style 154
industry perspectives 3–4, 16–19, 32–5, 52–4, 71–3, 85–7, 97–100, 112–15, 130–2, 145–8
Ingrams, Richard 13, 14
Innovation Lab 57, 61–3
InPublishing 7–8, 61, 94–5, 153–4
Inside History 79–80, 85
Instagram 3, 18, 69, 120, 121, 122, 123, 124, 154
Instant Articles technology 124
InStyle UK 5
iNTERGAMINGi magazine 139–41
Interscope Records 125
iPads 18, 47, 49, 100, 104, 121; *see also* tablets
iPhone 117, 127, 158

Jarvis, Jeff 123
Jefferies, Keiron 37–8, 70
Jenkins, John 159
Johnson, Rachel 8, 9, 10, 11
Jones, Felicity 131
Jouning, Jamie 122

Kaldas, Lydia 121
Kelsey Publishing Ltd 103
KISS (keep it simple stupid) principle 6
Kitchen Table Talent 65
Klems, Brian A. 51
Kobak, J. 2

The Lab 57, 61–3
The Ladies Mercury 5, 16
The Lady 2, 8–13, 16, 97–100
The Lady and The Revamp 11
The Lawyer 107–15
Leveson-Gower, Henry 90–3
Levithan, David 51
life cycles 2, 5
lifestyle sector 16, 64, 76, 78, 94, 119; audience engagement 37, 41, 44, 46–7; market research 32–4; number and sustainability of titles 1–2, 5, 6, 67, 150, 157
List for Life 57, 61–3
local sector 26, 29–31, 76, 81–5, 89, 90
Look 62–3
loyalty 13–14, 41–2, 67, 100, 127, 129, 139

MacGregor, Sue 14
Magazine Academy Awards 159, 160
Magazine Publishing Strategic Quadrant model 60–1, 74

Magzter 40, 128
Marie Claire 143
market corrections 5
market research 21, 31–2, 62, 111, 161; ABC system 22–3; action plan 35; aims and objectives 21, 23–5, 31, 34; audience engagement 54; brand extensions 23, 24, 27, 31, 34; case study 29–31; data protection codes 28–9; focus groups 24, 25, 26, 29, 31, 32, 35; industry perspectives 32–5; questions and responses 26–8; and return on investment 21, 24, and social media 23, 28; surveys 23–4, 25–8, 29, 31, 32; target groups 21, 22–3; *who, what, where, why* and *how* 21, 24
Markle, Meghan 46
Matalan 142–3
McGinn, Caroline 122–3
McPeake, James 44
media kits 144–5, 160, 161
meeting needs 93–4, 100
membership model 90–3
membership packages 41–2, 77, 90–3, 108, 110, 111, 113–14
Mercer, Cassie 79
millennials 61
The Mint 90–3, 97, 159
Mitford sisters 8, 9
Modern Rustic 66
Mole Valley Farmers 70
Molnar, Sheila 14–15
monetising online content 117–18, 129–30; action plan 132; advertising 119–20, 121, 123–6, 127, 128–9, 131, 132; apps and digital editions 126–8; brand investment 122–3; economic challenge 118–19; future revenue streams 128–9; industry perspectives 130–2; learning from digital-only rivals 123; and print media 119–20; revenue generation 120–9; social media 117, 118, 119, 121–2, 123–4, 125–7, 128–9; subscription models 126–8, 129, 130–1; unique content 120
Moss, Tyler 51
Mother & Baby 104–5
MRS (Market Research Society) 28–9
Mumsnet 104

National Geographic 121
native advertising 134, 136–8, 140, 143, 144, 145, 147
Native Advertising Institute 134
native advertising model 137–8

Naughton, John 125
NCTJ (National Council for the Training of Journalists) 107
NEKS (NewEconomic Knowledge Services) 91
Netflix 128, 131, 146
New Internationalist 93–4
New Yorker 159
Newbold, Steve 110–15, 157–8
Newsweek 131
Newton, Thandie 47
Nicholson, Lindsay 44–6
NME 1
Nuts 150

OC&C Strategy Consultants 118
off-platform publishing 118
Ogilvy, David 137
Oh Boy, You're Having a Girl 51
The Oldie 2
one-size-fits-all model 6, 18, 58, 64, 72, 73
online approach (feature package model) 106
online tools 4
Osmond, Andrew 14
Osterwalder, A. 59
Outdoor Fitness! 103
outsourcing 71

parenting market 103, 104–5, 107
partnered-themed features 95, 96
PEP (Promoting Economic Pluralism) 91
perceived value 41
Pettifor, Ann 91
Phillips, Miriam 29, 31
Pigner, Y. 59
podcasts 53, 54, 78, 120, 154
Poetic Asides blog 51
political satire 13–15
Ponsford, Dominic 93, 120
PPA (Professional Publisher's Association) 107
Pregnancy & Birth 104
Press Gazette 11, 93, 120, 126
print media: 360-degree content 102, 103, 104–6, 114; and advertising 134, 136, 138, 139, 140; audience engagement 39–40, 46; comparison with digital media 2–3, 7, 14, 16, 17–18, 39–40, 72, 77, 99–100; creating a community 89–90; market sectors 77, 80; monetising online content 119–20; sustainability of 151–3, 155–7, 158
print quality focus 96
print/digital angle (feature package model) 106

Private Eye 2, 13–15, 16, 94
product endorsements 94, 137, 156
product testing 42, 44–5, 62, 94
promotional opportunity (feature package model) 106
Psychologies 131
Punch 14

Radio Times 36, 46–7, 52
Radio Times Festival 47
Rankin, Gregor 38, 85–7, 157
Read, Watch, Listen strategy 121
reader-centric approach 72, 104, 105, 112, 123–5, 150
Readly 117, 128, 130–2
Reed Business Information 77
reputation 8, 12–13, 29, 34, 37, 39, 43–4, 122, 124, 129–30, 144
Reuters Institute 121, 122, 127
Roderick, Leonie 143
Rohumaa, Liisa 155
ROI (return on investment) 21, 24, 70, 112, 132, 150; and advertising 134, 139, 142, 143; audience engagement 36, 37, 41; market sectors 77, 81
Rolling Stone 159
Running 103
Rushton, Willie 13
Russo, Richard 51

Sacks, Bo 156
sale or return model 37
sales teams 58, 72, 111, 135–6, 137, 141, 144, 148
Santa Barbara Writers Conference 37
Santamaria, Damian 155–6
Santamaria, Laura 32–5, 155–6
scarcity of content 119
Schlegel, Iga 159, 160
Scottoline, Lisa 51
Settle, Alison 7
She Kicks 2
Shell, Rita 8
Shop Direct 143
Shulman, Alexandra 7–8, 16–19
smartphones 104, 117, 121, 128, 154
Smash Hits! 119
Smith, Susy 65–8
Snapchat 118, 121, 122, 123, 124, 154
social media 3, 18; 360-degree content 103, 104, 116; and advertising 134, 136, 137–8; audience engagement 47, 50, 54; keeping up with demand 95–6, 97; and market research 23, 28; monetising online content 117, 118, 119, 121–2, 123–4, 125–7, 128–9; and sustainability 151, 153, 154–5, 156
specialist sector 23, 26, 37, 41, 52, 68–70, 105; health and success of 76, 78–81; sustainability of titles 153, 156, 157–8
Sprite 124
SRC Holdings Corporation 64
Stack, Jack 64
stagnation 9, 59, 61, 70, 96
A Stake in the Outcome 64
stakeholders 89, 93–4, 97, 100
Stefani, Gwen 125
strategic partnerships 8, 42, 64, 68, 81, 94, 134, 138, 141–4, 145
Strawser, Jessica 51, 57
Strong concept (Components of a successful brand model) 103
Sublime 32–4, 155–6
subscriptions 13–14, 27–8, 58, 77, 98–100; 360-degree content 108, 111, 113, 115; and advertising 139, 142; audience engagement 36–7, 41–2, 46, 47; monetising online content 117, 126–8, 129, 130–1; and sustainability 152, 155, 157–8
supplements 8, 17, 135–6, 142–3
surveys 23–4, 25–8, 29, 31, 32, 35, 54, 59, 160
sustainability 1–2, 90, 91, 97, 120, 150–1, 159; 360-degree content 103, 10, 107, 112; and advertising 139, 141, 144, 152, 153–4, 155–6, 157, 158; audience engagement 36, 42, 44, 46; business models 57, 63–5, 67, 68, 71–2; and digital media 151–3, 155–8; lessons from the past 6, 9, 15, 16, 18; looking to the future 153–9; and market research 24, 29, 31, 32–3; market sectors 77, 79, 86, 87; print media 151–3, 155–7, 158; and social media 151, 153, 154–5, 156
Sutcliffe, Sonia 15
Swarm at South format 123

tablets 18, 39–40, 91–2, 96, 100, 104, 117, 121, 130, 158; *see also* iPads
Tague, Josie 159, 160
'takeover advertising' 124
Target audience and potential reach (Magazine Publishing Strategic Quadrant) 60
target groups (market research) 21, 22–3
targeted distribution 68, 70, 81
TechTarget 77

themed issues 114, 135–6
Thompson, Emma 93
Tilberis, Liz 7
Time Inc 5, 57, 61–3
TimeOut 40, 122
The Times 117, 127
timing 2, 6, 15–16, 42, 80, 105, 112
Todd Dorothy 7
Top Gear 131
Toyne, Jayne 160
trends 1, 2, 4, 72–3, 96, 105, 150, 156; and advertising 134, 136–7, 139, 143; market research 25, 26, 32–4; market sectors 76, 78, 85, 87
Trust (Components of a successful brand model) 103
Tucked 159, 160
Turnure, Arthur Baldwin 6
Twitter 28, 69, 80, 120, 121, 122, 134, 154

unique content 120
Usborne, Peter 13, 14
USP (unique selling point) 5, 18, 67, 103, 152
UX (user experience) 123, 124

value proposition 34, 59, 72, 112, 136, 156
Vanity Fair 8
Vegetarian Living 26, 142
Vegetarian Society 142
Very 143
Victorian Farm 78
Viner, Katharine 124
Vogue 2, 6–8, 16–19, 123
VR (virtual reality) 118

Walker, Keith 61–2
Walker, Patrick 129

'walled garden' 121
Walters, Jeremy 156
Ward, Peter 81–4, 89
Warners Group Publications Plc 37, 70
Warren, Matt 10–12
Watson, Carole 154–5
wealth status 22–3
Website for Writers guide 135
Weddings Today 135
What's New In Publishing? 156
WhatsApp 129
White, Terri 145–8
Who Do You Think You Are? 79
who, what, where, why and how 21, 24
Wiggins, Bradley 2, 76
Wild Bunch Media 2, 80
William Reed Business Media 77
Wintour, Anna 7
Wired 118
Withers, Audrey 7
Woman 154
Women's Cycling 2, 76, 78, 80–1, 85
Women's Football 2
Women's Running 2
Writer's Digest Conference 47, 51
Writer's Forum 25, 27, 37, 47–51, 59, 68, 96, 135, 136
Writer's Web directory 135, 136
Writers' Digest 36, 47–52, 57, 78
Writing Magazine 48–51
Wunderkammer 160

Yell 83
Yellow Pages 81
Your Family History 79
YouTube 69, 121, 123, 129

Zuckerberg, Mark 124